PRENTICE HALL INTERNATIONAL

Language Teaching Methodology Series

Applied Linguistics
General Editor: Christopher N. Candlin

Learner Strategies
in Language Learning

Other titles in this series include

Learner Strategies in Language Learning

Edited by

ANITA WENDEN

York College, City University of New York, NY.

and

JOAN RUBIN

Joan Rubin Associates, Berkeley, CA.

ENGLISH LANGUAGE TEACHING

Prentice Hall

New York   London   Toronto   Sydney   Tokyo   Singapore

First published 1987 by
Prentice Hall International (UK) Ltd,
66 Wood Lane End, Hemel Hempstead,
Hertfordshire, HP2 4RG
A division of
Simon & Schuster International Group

Printed and bound in Great Britain at the
University Press, Cambridge

Library of Congress Cataloging-in-Publication Data

Learner strategies.
(Language teaching methodology series)
1. Language and languages – Study and teaching.
2. Language acquisition. 3. English language – Study and
teaching – Foreign speakers.
I. Wenden, Anita, 1933—
II. Rubin, Joan, 1932–   .   III. Series.
P53.L39 1987   418'.007   86–12264

ISBN 0-13-527110-X

British Library Cataloguing in Publication Data

Learner strategies. – (Language teaching methodology
series)
1. Languages, Modern – Study and teaching
I. Wenden, Anita   II. Rubin, Joan
II. Series
418'.007   PB35

ISBN 0-13-527110-X

4 5 6   93 92

To our Students,
from whom we have much to learn.

Contents

Foreword by John F. Fanselow

I'm sure you have had the same experiences in learning a foreign language that I have had. You have observed that, both inside and outside of the class, as students we all do our exercises differently. When we use the target language we use it in different ways, and we all have definite ideas about how we learn.

The most vivid memory I have of the unique way each of us goes about language learning occurred in Somalia. Two friends and I had somehow driven off the normal route — there was no road — and so we were unsure in which direction we should be proceeding. We were not only lost but more than two-hundred miles from a village of any size and in an area where often no vehicles were seen for days on end. After some time, we saw some nomads not too far off, so we walked towards them. After greetings, we waited for the most fluent speaker of Somali in our group to ask directions. When he didn't, we asked what he was waiting for. "I'm not sure of the right pronunciation of *lost* in the right tense" he replied. "If I say it wrong now, I won't be able to say it right later" he continued. The less fluent ones took over, feeling like murdering the most fluent. Instead, however, they murdered not only *lost* in the right tense but also all other aspects of the Somali language imaginable. The less fluent ones made extensive use of a twig, drawing and redrawing all manner of lines in the sand we were standing on. We finally found our way because we were more than one learner, each with his own strategies. I often wonder what the most fluent would have done if he had been alone!

In class, we have all seen students who never speak and others who cannot keep quiet, those who ask for rule after rule and those who abhor listening to rules being given much less studying them. And outside of class from all of these different types, we have heard lengthy explanations which contain a rationale for each person's own behavior.

Curious indeed that what we have all seen and experienced — distinct ways we think we and others learn — has been systematically explored so little and ignored so long! Perhaps like my friend lost in Somalia, we all rely on what we know and are used to doing rather than on what others may know and do, thus ironically ignoring knowledge that could help us find our way.

In 1978, Anita Wenden decided to write her dissertation in the relatively unexplored area of learner strategies, having been excited by Joan Rubin's 1975 article in the TESOL Quarterly and *The Good Language Learner* by Naiman, Fröhlich and Stern. I was delighted at the time. I am even more delighted now that Anita has not only continued her work beyond her dissertation in a number of articles but also collaborated in this collection with Joan Rubin, one of the first to take the area seriously.

As important as this collection is both for its contributions that reveal ways learners say they learn and that reveal the wide range of research methodologies used to discover learners' ways, I think the collection is even more important as a symbol. In medical practice, ways are being sought to get medical personnel to listen to what patients say. In business, workers are seen as sources of ideas to improve both working conditions, production or services. This collection shows that in our field we realize that we need to listen to our clients too. Some of what they say about how they learn and how they want to learn may sound to us like cliches — I need more grammar — or be seemingly uninformed — I need repeating, repeating, repeating — or out of tune with current theory — I want to speak and write not just listen — but it is what learners seem to believe. This collection, by virtue of its publication, is not only saying we can learn from our students but that we must. It also says students have a lot to offer and share with each other and with teachers. The learned helplessness teaching can sometimes engender in students is less likely if we see our students as active partners. When students share strategies, they may start to learn to empower each other. When we serve as soundingboards for their explanations we have the opportunity to foster independence rather than dependence and learned helplessness. By not offering just one way to explore the learning strategies of our students, this collection also has the potential to empower us. The collection shows that we can explore in a systematic way through counting *or* describing, through the use of technical terms *or* the use of ordinary language.

Because the collection is so broad, both in approaches to the exploration of learning strategies and descriptions of the results of such explorations, it would be easy to see this the way I saw the directions from the nomads in the opening incident, as *the* way back to a well-travelled route. I think this collection, like others that explore new territory, should be seen as the classic tales of journeys: Chaucer's *Canterbury Tales*, Cervantes' *Don Quixote*, Fielding's *Tom Jones*, Twain's *Huck Finn*. In all of these, and in this collection too, the journey itself is more important than the destination. Consequently, I think that this collection will be successful to the degree that it leads more of us to seriously explore what our students have to say about their learning and to take what they say seriously rather than as a series of findings to apply to students we teach.

John F. Fanselow

Teachers College,
Columbia University,
New York

Foreword by H. H. Stern

It has always seemed to me that in language acquisition research too little attention has been paid to the conscious efforts learners themselves make in mastering a foreign language. This deficiency is now made good by this book. Its central theme, learner strategies, is the concept that refers to this neglected field of enquiry. The idea of investigating learner strategies was first thought of over fifteen years ago by Joan Rubin, one of the editors of this splendid collection of studies, in an attempt to capture the purposeful activities learners engage in when they are face to face with the tremendous task of language learning.

However, the mainstream of language learning research (wrongly, in my view) has always mistrusted this concept. Partly because it is elusive and hard to define; but chiefly, because researchers felt it was too subjective and could not be investigated "scientifically," and they looked askance at the only research techniques it seemed to be amenable to: diaries, protocols of introspection, or interviewing learners about their own learning experiences. As a result, a whole area of possible insight into the mystery of second language learning and its problems was given the cold shoulder and was thoroughly undervalued.

Fortunately, a few researchers persevered and were not deterred by the arguments of the hardliners. They have steadfastly continued to explore by the best means at their disposal the language learners' conscious efforts. As this book shows, the perseverance of these researchers has paid off. In the last few years, research approaches have become more flexible, and the interest in learner strategies has greatly increased and has indeed gained a new momentum.

The papers in this rich collection have yielded an enormous amount of information and fruitful insights on the strategies, beliefs, and views of adult language learners and the influence of these strategies on their ways of learning.

The broad spectrum in the two introductory chapters by the two editors provides the necessary background and sets the stage, first, for one paper on research methodology, followed by six empirical in-depth studies on different approaches to language learning, and, finally, three chapters on experiments in learner training. The different sections of the book are introduced by helpful editorial notes, and each chapter is followed by challenging questions and excellent bibliographies.

The entire volume should be of great value to all thoughtful language teachers and students of language education. It will also be a stimulating source of information and questions for researchers on second language acquisition.

In the vast literature that now exists on second language learning and teaching this pioneering work on learner strategies deserves a special place. Quite apart from the fact that a monograph treatment of the concept of learner strategies was badly needed, one of the main values of this work, for me, lies in the fact that it counteracts two tendencies which are implicit in much language learning research and language pedagogy. One is the tendency in pedagogy to infantilize learners and to maintain them in a state of intellectual and emotional dependency on teachers, course materials, tightly organized "methods," and gadgetry. The other is the tendency in research to overemphasize unconscious acquisition processes which are largely beyond the learner's or the teacher's control. The importance of these processes is not in question. But that is no reason to think in disparaging terms about the many conscious efforts learners make and must make to come to grips with a new language.

This book shows that adult learners are active, task-oriented, and approach their language learning with certain assumptions and beliefs which have bearing on the way they tackle the new language. The pedagogic direction of this volume is to try to understand the learner's strategies, to build on them, and to cultivate self-reliance and ultimately to attempt to develop learner autonomy. The book is therefore very much in line with modern thought on adult education.

The bulk of the experience of the writers in this collection lies in the area of English as a second language and, as was pointed out already, with adults as learners. But let me hasten to add that its message is not confined to either adults or ESL learners. The arguments and findings of this work are relevant to learning any language, and they have significance also for language learners at the school level. Currently, efforts are being made, for example, in Britain and Canada to encourage among second language learners in schools greater language awareness and a more informed knowledge about learning how to learn in order to foster intelligent participation and, thus, develop greater self-reliance as language learners. Therefore those who are interested in these new and constructive directions in language education at the school level would also find ample food for thought in this volume.

The reader who takes the trouble to study these papers and to answer some of the thoughtful questions that accompany each chapter will come away with a deeper understanding of language learners and how they attempt to learn.

H. H. Stern

Ontario Institute for Studies in Education,
Toronto

Contributors

ROBERTA G. ABRAHAM is Assistant Professor of English at Iowa State University, where she coordinates ESL instruction and teaches in the MA/TESL program. Her research interests include the relationships between cognitive styles and learner strategies, and the evaluation of computer-assisted language learning. She is also working on a program to evaluate the speaking and teaching proficiency of prospective non-native teaching assistants. Her publications have appeared in *Studies in Second Language Acquisition* and the *TESOL Quarterly*.

ANNA UHL CHAMOT investigates learning strategies in second language education at InterAmerica Research Associates. She was the ESL specialist for the *Study of Learning Strategies with Students of English as a Second Language*, and project director for the study *Review, Summary, and Synthesis of Literature on English as a Second Language*. Her publications include articles in professional journals and ESL textbooks. She is currently working in the area of the application of learning strategies to content-based ESL instruction. Previously Dr. Chamot was assistant professor at the Foreign Language Education Center at the University of Texas at Austin.

ANDREW D. COHEN is Associate Professor of Applied Linguistics in the School of Education, at the Hebrew University of Jerusalem. He is currently Coordinator of Scientific Commissions for AILA and Foreign Secretary for the Israel Association for Applied Linguistics. His current research interests are in cognitive strategies in learning a second language and in language testing. His publications include *A Sociolinguistic Approach to Bilingual Education* (Newbury House, 1975) and *Testing Language Ability in the Classroom* (Newbury House, 1980).

HENRI HOLEC is Professor in Applied Linguistics and chair of the Department of Applied Linguistics at the University of Nancy II (France). He is also director of the Centre de Recherches et d'Applications Pédagogiques en Langues (C.R.A.P.E.L.) at the same university. He has been involved in developing and testing a variety of autonomous language learning schemes since the early seventies. Many of these projects have been reported on in *Mélanges Pédagogiques*. He is also author of the monograph *Autonomy and Foreign Language Learning* (Pergamon Press, 1981).

ELAINE K. HORWITZ is Assistant Professor of Curriculum and Instruction at the University of Texas at Austin where she teaches graduate and undergraduate courses in second language acquisition and second language methodology. She is also coordinator of foreign language student teaching. She has published in the areas of individual differences and communicative approaches to language teaching. Her current research interests include foreign language anxiety and student beliefs about language learning.

J. MICHAEL O'MALLEY is presently Senior Associate for the InterAmerica Research Associates in Rosslyn, Virginia where he has directed research projects on learning strategies, second language acquisition, Hispanic achievement in high school, and teacher qualifications. His publications on these projects have appeared in *Language Learning* and the *TESOL Quarterly*. Dr. O'Malley is also Director of the Georgetown University Bilingual Evaluation Assistance Center.

JOAN RUBIN received her doctorate in anthropology from Yale University and her Masters in Linguistics from the University of Michigan. She is a specialist in second language learning and cross-cultural communication. Over the past ten years, she has conducted research on the strategies which good language learners use. Two major products of this research are the publication, *How To Be A More Successful Language Learner* (co-authored with Irene Thompson), and the interactive videodisc, *The Language Learning Disc* (produced by Joan Rubin Associates). Dr. Rubin taught ESL for several years at Georgetown University, in Brazil at the Academia Brasileiro Americano, and in California to the pre-literate Mien. She was the coordinator of technical training in ESL for Peace Corps programs in Turkey and Afghanistan. Dr. Rubin has been professor of anthropology and linguistics at the University of North Carolina, Georgetown University, University of Hawaii, and Tulane University. She has also undertaken innovative research on sources of miscommunication across languages and cultures. She is currently President of Joan Rubin Associates.

IRENE THOMPSON is presently at the George Washington University, where she teaches Russian linguistics, language teaching methodology, proficiency testing and its application to language teaching. She has also directed the Russian language program and the State Department's Foreign Service Institute. Dr. Thompson is the author of a number of articles on aspects of learning Russian as a foreign language and has recently co-authored *How To Be A More Successful Language Learner* with Rubin. Her special research and professional interests include learner strategies, teacher training, and curriculum design.

ROBERTA J. VANN is Associate Professor of English at Iowa State University where she directs the Intensive English and Orientation Program and teaches in the MA/TESL program. In addition to learner strategies, she is interested in the relationships between the oral and written language of ESL learners and co-edited a book on that topic entitled *Exploring Speaking–Writing Relationships: Connections and Contrasts*.

ANITA WENDEN received her doctorate from Teachers College (Columbia University) with a specialization in adult and second language learning. She holds masters degrees in applied linguistics and TESL from the same institution. Her research interests are in metacognition, specifically adult L2 learners' beliefs about how to approach language learning. She is also involved in the development and testing of methods and materials for learner training. Her publications on this research and its educational applications appear in *Language Learning, Canadian Modern Language Journal, TESOL Newsletter, System, English Language Teach-*

ing Journal, Applied Linguistics. She is presently Assistant Professor of ESL at York College (City University of New York). She also teaches a course in the Masters' Program in TESOL at Teachers' College (Columbia University). The course, which she has designed and developed, introduces graduate teachers to the concepts and skills necessary for implementing learner training in the second language classroom. She has taught ESL at the National Taiwan University and at Columbia University.

Overview of the Contents

This is a book about language learning. It is intended to provide some new perspectives on two basic questions that are of concern to both teachers and researchers — What do learners do to acquire second language competence? What can be done to facilitate this process?

The research described in the volume brings into focus the fact that learners are actively and deliberately involved in their language learning process. In other words, they bring to the task of language learning a varied repertoire of learning skills. Preliminary evidence as to whether and how these learning skills may be nurtured and refined is also presented. Thus, the book adds to our knowledge of the cognitive abilities of language learners and suggests, yet, another dimension to be taken into account in the development of learner-centered methods and materials.

Part One, *An Introduction to Learner Strategies*, provides a conceptual orientation to the papers in Parts Two and Three. The ideas, early research and methodological procedures that are fundamental to learner strategy research and its educational applications are explained, and the educational and theoretical purposes of the research made explicit.

The papers in Part Two, *Studying Learner Strategies*, report on the exploratory and descriptive stages of research. They analyze what learners *do* to learn a second language, how they *manage* these enterprises, and what they *know* about this process in general and their own in particular.

Part Three, *Promoting Learner Autonomy*, takes up the implications of the research presented in Part Two. It is suggested that teachers of second languages not only help L2 learners acquire linguistic competence but that these endeavors be complemented by an equally systematic approach to helping them develop their competence as learners. The papers in this section demonstrate different ways of doing this.

Each chapter includes a set of *follow-up activities*. In some cases readers will be expected to *discuss the issues* in order to clarify their understanding of views presented in the readings and to evaluate them. Or, they may be asked to *make links*, i.e. to compare and contrast these views with ideas discussed elsewhere in the book, in the literature on second language learning and teaching, and with their own experience as learners and teachers. Sometimes readers will *interpret data* to come up with their own conclusions. Finally, they will be given suggestions for *applying the ideas*. They will use concepts presented in the readings to gain insights into their own and their students' learning experiences; they will adapt procedures (e.g. interviews, surveys) to collect data on how their students learn; they will use this information to test generalizations about language learning and to plan activities that will help learners improve their learning skills.

ANITA L. WENDEN
JOAN RUBIN

Part One

AN INTRODUCTION TO LEARNER STRATEGIES

What are learner strategies? How is information on learner strategies obtained? What assumptions about language learning underlie its research objectives, procedures and analytical concepts? What are the educational implications of this research? The papers in this section address these questions.

Wenden refers to developments in the field of cognitive science that have provided the impetus for the study of learner strategies and draws on the literature in adult learning for insights into the main educational goal of the research — an autonomous language learner. She also explains what is intended by the term "learner strategies", as it is used in this volume. Rubin's description of some of the earlier research and her typology of three main kinds of strategies that have been identified in these studies provide the empirical basis for the concept "learner strategies". She also makes explicit the assumptions underlying the research and so further specifies its educational and theoretical concerns. Cohen's paper deals with the methodology for collecting information on learner strategies, i.e. verbal reports. It provides a descriptive overview of the kinds of verbal report data that can be obtained and of the different procedures for obtaining the data. He also addresses the criticisms aimed at verbal report data. Can mental processes be studied? Is verbal report data valid, accurate, and comprehensive?

Chapter 1

Conceptual Background and Utility

ANITA L. WENDEN

Since the early seventies research concerns in the field of second language learning and teaching have shifted from the methods of teaching to learner characteristics and their possible influence on the process of acquiring a second language. Gardner and Lambert's (1972) seminal research on attitude and motivation pointed to the importance of affective factors.[1] Other writers, notably Schumann (1976b, 1978), have pointed to the influence of social factors which determine the extent to which a non-native speaker group may remain "socially distant" from the culture of the target language group.[2] The importance of the learners' cognitive abilities has also been stressed (cf the papers of Kennedy, Macnamara and Richards in Oller and Richards, 1973). The following are some of the questions that research on this learner characteristic has examined:

— What are the abilities that constitute foreign language aptitude? (Carroll, 1973, 1981)
— Does intelligence facilitate second language learning? (Genesee, 1976)
— How is intelligence related to foreign language aptitude? (Wesche, Edwards and Wells, 1982)
— How do field dependent and field independent cognitive styles influence foreign language achievement? (Hansen and Stanfield, 1981; Stanfield and Hansen, 1983; Hansen, 1984)
— What are the perceptual learning style preferences of non-native speakers of English? Do they prefer visual, auditory, kinesthetic, tactile modalities? Do they feel they learn better alone or in groups? (Reid, 1985)

As regards learner strategies, it has been acknowledged that language processing strategies exist and influence second language acquisition (cf for example, the papers of McLaughlin, Kinbourne, Cole, Bates and MacWhinney, Wode, Winitz in Winitz (ed) 1981). Some interlanguage studies, which examine and analyze learner language, have referred to universal language processing strategies, such as overgeneralization, transfer, and simplification. The operation of these strategies, it is maintained, should be considered as one cause of learner errors and the changing nature of the learner's interlanguage system (cf Taylor, 1975; Richards, 1975). Analysis of learner language has also yielded information on communication strategies learners use when faced with a gap between communicative need and linguistic repertoire (e.g. Faerch and Kasper, 1983; in Chapter 2, Rubin reviews some of the earlier studies).

These studies on universal language processing strategies and communication strategies focus on the cognitive processes involved in second language acquisition (cf page 6 for the distinction between processes and strategies). However, they do not examine the learners' perception of what they do to learn or manage their learning. They do not seek to present the process of L2 learning from the learners' viewpoint. Nor have they looked at the conscious strategies learners utilize as they attempt to complete a learning or communication task. It is this, heretofore, unexamined learner characteristic that the learner strategy research presented in

3

this volume will bring to light. In this introductory chapter, the conceptual background of the research will be made explicit. What is intended by the term "learner strategies," as it is used in this volume, will also be explained.

Learner Strategies and Cognitive Science

The theoretical impetus for examining how learners approach the task of learning a second language can be attributed to a changing view on the nature of mind put forward by the theory and research in the field of cognitive science. Hunt (1982) describes this relatively new psychological discipline as "a systematic inquiry into our thinking selves (15) . . . a discipline devoted to exploring how our minds work . . ." (17) For some cognitive scientists this means a study of problem solving and formal logical reasoning. For others, it includes everything that goes on in the mind between input and ouput, i.e. perception, memory, learning, inference, concept formation . . .

Interest in understanding human behavior (including how people learn) by studying mental processes and the contents of human consciousness dates back to the late 19th century. At that time Wilhelm Wundt, often identified as founder of scientific psychology, trained introspectionists to "think aloud" as they performed mental tasks. That is, as they carried out perceptual and associative tasks, these observers examined the contents of their consciousness and reported on what they did and noted. Eventually, however, Wundt discontinued these initial attempts at studying the workings of the mind because he felt this methodology conflicted with his views on what should constitute a rigorous approach to empirical science and experimental study. "All accurate observation implies (he stated) that the observed subject is independent of the observer." (Wundt, 1874). Moreover, he felt that higher mental processes were of "too variable a character to be subjects of objective observation." (Wundt, 1896).

Nonetheless, the study of human mental processes through introspection was continued into the early part of the 20th century by psychologists at the University of Würzburg. Their work brought to light new aspects about the nature of human thinking, i.e. that elements of thought change as they are combined; that thought is directed and guided by some human motive; that experience is not copied in the mind; and that some thinking is imageless. However, criticisms were directed at their methodology. It was also felt their results were negative. They could not agree on what exactly subjects became aware of — were their thoughts imageless or were they, somehow, portrayed visually? They were also criticized for not developing a theory. Therefore, their findings were not taken up and built upon.

Moreover, in the 1930s, with the publication of Skinner's experimental analysis, *The Behavior of Organisms*, a new paradigm was presented for viewing behavior (including learning). Actions (responses) could be attributed to a stimulus. Behavior was the outcome of a conditioning process. Skinner also argued for an independent science of behavior based on observable and quantifiable data. He made it clear that in such an approach, "the traditional description and organization of behavior represented by the concepts of "will", "cognition", "intellect", and so on, cannot be accepted so long as it pretends to be dealing with a mental world. . . ." (1938:441). It is true that he did not directly apply the results of his analysis to human behavior. Moreover, as a scientist he would "neither assert nor deny discontinuity between human and subhuman fields" since so little was known about either. However, it was his personal opinion that "the only differences . . . between the behavior of a rat and a man (aside from enormous differences of complexity) lie in the field of verbal behavior". (442) Skinner's views influenced psychological theory and research for several decades, especially in North America. It was not only considered methodologically impossible to study mental processes but also irrelevant.

It was not until the sixties that an interest in the study of thinking re-emerged and cognitive science, as a new and valid field of study, was born. According to Johnson-Laird and Wason (1977) this was due to the confluence of theoretical concerns in several disciplines. Cultural anthropologists raised questions about the apparent difference in the reasoning ability of people without formal schooling in less industrialized countries and the literate populations of the more industrially advanced nations. In linguistics, Chomsky's explanation of language behavior in terms of the structures underlying the comprehension and production of language rejected the behaviorist paradigm of learning. The notion that linguistics could offer a description of language from the standpoint of the ideal speaker-hearer led psychologists to explore the possibility of using formal logic to provide a prescriptive analysis of human reasoning. Studies of child development, spearheaded by Jean Piaget, focused on the cognitive structures and processes that underlie human development and growth. Finally, with the invention of the computer, psychologists were given a new metaphor with which to study the mind. For computers could do many of the same things that humans do — store, manipulate, and remember information as well as solve problems, reason and use language. Moreover, computer programs also made it possible to test more precisely and systematically hypotheses about the workings of mental processes.

This renewed interest in understanding the workings of the mind is expressed in a great variety of questions — all of them pertaining to the learning of a second language, either directly or indirectly. Hunt (1982:29,30) lists the following:

> "Do we learn what we learn primarily as a result of mere repetition — or of comprehension — or of the linkage of new material to previously known material? . . . By what methods do we locate, in our memories, whatever we want to remember? Has what is forgotten merely faded out, or been erased, or merely misfiled? Does the human mind spontaneously come to reason along the lines of formal logic or does it, instead, have a quite different natural logic of its own? What do we do that enables us to see, at some point, that certain things can be grouped into a coherent category, or that a general rule can be extracted from a series of experiences? Do we learn to imitate grammatical speech as we grow up or are grammatical structures genetically prewired in the brain's language area? What are the processes we use consciously and unconsciously when solving problems both great and small, and can the individual's problem solving ability be improved by training? What do highly creative people do that ordinary people don't do? What kinds of thinking go on unconsciously, as contrasted to those kinds that are conscious? How is our thinking affected or skewed by our sex, age, personality, and background?"

Underlying these questions are cognitive science's assumptions about human cognition (thinking in the broadest sense). The most basic of these assumptions is that humans are processors of information. In very general terms, this means that information comes in through our sense receptors. At this time selected items of information are attended to, identified, and, then, moved into the short-term or working memory. In short-term memory a series of mental operations are applied to this information. Then the changed or modified product is stored in long-term memory to be retrieved when it is needed. The mental operations that encoded incoming information are referred to as processes. The changes brought about by these processes are referred to as organizations of knowledge or knowledge structures. The techniques actually used to manipulate the incoming information and, later, to retrieve what has been stored are referred to as cognitive strategies.

With the resurgence of interest in studying human thinking, there has been a return to the use of verbal reports as a source of data about learning processes. Learners are asked to report what they are doing and take note of either *while* they are completing a learning task, *just after* they have completed it, or *sometime after* they have completed it. Cohen (Chapter 3) describes how these procedures differ and the kind of data they yield (also cf Cohen and Hosenfeld, 1981). Criticisms, somewhat similar to those voiced by Wundt and his colleagues earlier, have been directed at this methodology once again (cf Nisbett and Wilson, 1977). It is asked whether mental processes can be accessible to learners and if verbal report data can be considered accurate and comprehensive. These criticisms have been addressed by proponents of the methodology (e.g. Ericsson and Simon, 1980). As will be noted by Cohen (Chapter 3), they have indicated (1) what kind of information about mental processing can be collected using this method and (2) the conditions to be taken into account in collecting and interpreting verbal report data.

Clarifying Terms

Research on learner strategies in the domain of second language learning may be viewed as a part of the general area of research on mental processes and structures that constitute the field of cognitive science. To date the research has been guided, primarily, by the following general questions:

1. What do L2 learners *do* to learn a second language?
2. How do they *manage* or *self-direct* these efforts?
3. What do they *know* about *which* aspects of their L2 learning process?
4. How can their learning skills be refined and developed?

The term *learner strategies*, as it is used in this volume, refers to the distinct but closely related phenomenon referred to in the first three of the above questions.

First of all, the term *learner strategies* refers to language learning behaviors learners actually engage in to learn and regulate the learning of a second language. These language learning behaviors have been called strategies. Information about them has been collected by observing language learners or by having them describe what they are doing while performing a learning or communication task, e.g. while reading, completing a cloze exercise.

Secondly, the term *learner strategies* refers to what learners know about the strategies they use, i.e. their strategic knowledge. This knowledge is revealed in statements learners make when they are asked to think back or retrospect on specific or general aspects of their language learning, e.g. when they are interviewed, complete a questionnaire, or write in a diary. In such cases, learners' reports may point to strategies they have actually used in a particular category of situations, strategies they assume they have used, or strategies they think they should use.

Finally, the term *learner strategies* also refers to what learners know about aspects of their language learning other than the strategies they use, e.g. what personal factors facilitate L2 learning; general principles to follow to learn a second language successfully; what is easy or difficult about learning a specific language; how well or poorly they can use the language. It is assumed that this knowledge may influence a learner's choice of strategy.

A few words also need to be added about the term "strategy". In the literature, strategies have been referred to as "techniques", "tactics", "potentially conscious plans", "consciously employed operations", "learning skills, basic skills, functional skills", "cognitive abilities", "language processing strategies", "problem solving procedures". These multiple designations point to the elusive nature of the term. In their discussion of five different views on strategies, Naiman, Fröhlich and Stern (1975) acknowledged "a consensus on a definition of the term is lacking". Eight years later, Bialystok (1983:100) makes an almost identical statement, "There is little consensus in the literature concerning either the definition or the identification of language learning strategies".

Some of the questions underlying the differing views are:
1. Are they general characteristics that determine behavior or specific techniques or actions?
2. Are strategies conscious? unconscious? sometimes conscious and sometimes not?
3. Are they learned behaviors? or part of our mental hardware?
4. And if they are learned, must they always come under conscious control? or can they become automatized?
5. What might prompt language learners to use strategies?
6. Are strategies tied to specific learning content and tasks? or are they more general in their use?

It is not the purpose of this introductory chapter to argue the merits of a theoretical view that would provide answers to these questions. Instead a more inductive approach will be taken, and six criteria that, generally, appear to characterize the language learning behaviors that have been referred to as strategies in this book will be briefly described.

(1) First of all, strategies refer to *specific actions or techniques* (e.g. comparing TL rules with NL rules; repeating a phrase to remember it; listening to a TV program). They are not characteristics that describe a learner's general approach, as when language learners are said to be reflective, or risk takers.

(2) Some of these actions will be *observable* (asking a question) *and* others will *not* be *observable* (making a mental comparison).

(3) Strategies are *problem oriented*. Learners utilize them to respond to a learning need, or to use a more technical definition from cognitive psychology, "to facilitate the acquisition, storage, retrieval or use of information."

(4) However, as Rubin's paper (Chapter 2) will illustrate, this definition has been broadly interpreted. Thus, strategies will be used to refer to language learning behaviors that *contribute directly to learning* — what learners do to control and/or transform incoming knowledge about the language (e.g. guessing from context, outlining a reading); to retrieve and use this knowledge (e.g. practice strategies); *and* to regulate learning (noting if one understands, deciding to pay attention to one's pronunciation). It will also refer to language learning behaviors that *contribute indirectly to learning* — how learners use their limited linguistic repertoire to communicate (e.g. describing or circumlocuting when they do not know a word; using gestures) and what they do to create opportunities to learn and use the language (going to movies, making friends).

(5) Sometimes strategies *may be consciously deployed*. The following examples taken from the cognitive developmental literature (e.g. Lefebvre-Pinard, 1983; Flavell, 1979) suggest that this may happen when something new is being learned; when accuracy and/or appropriateness are considered important; when there is a need to correct or relearn familiar material; when there is an unexpected breakdown in understanding. However, it is also possible for learners to develop facility in the use of a strategy. For certain learning problems, strategies *can become automatized* and remain below consciousness or potentially conscious (cf Ericsson and Simon, 1980; Brown *et al.*, 1983; Faerch and Kasper, 1983; Mclaughlin *et al.*, 1983).

(6) Strategies are behaviors that are *amenable to change*. They can be modified, rejected, and unfamiliar ones can be learned. In other words, they are a part of our mental software. This is a view that underlies an increasing number of intervention studies and strategy training programs in the cognitive literature (cf for example O'Neill, 1978; Pressley and Levin, 1983).

Learner Strategies and Learner Autonomy

One of the leading educational goals of the research on learner strategies is an autonomous language learner. It is intended that insights derived from the research guide the development of learner training activities so that learners become not only more efficient at learning and using their second language but also more capable of self-directing these endeavors.[3] Few second language teachers will deny the importance of this educational goal. However, although methodological trends in second language teaching and learning in the seventies have highlighted the central role of the learner, an explicit commitment to autonomous or self-directed learning is relatively new to the field of second language teaching and learning, especially in North America. (cf Holec, 1981 for a description of experiments in France, Great Britain and Sweden.) Therefore, it is to the literature on self-directed learning in adult education that one must turn for an appreciation of its educational purposes.

Research on self-directed learning in adult education began with Houle's exploratory study of the self-educating person (1961) and the more encompassing survey of adult participation in educational activities by Johnstone and Rivera (1965), which also included a section on self-directed learning. These first studies established the fact that adult learners do initiate and organize their own learning. However, it was not till the early seventies with Allen Tough's study, *Adult Learning Projects* (1971), that systematic investigation of the efforts of self-directed adult learners began. He demonstrated that efforts of self-directed learners are organized around a "learning project" and documented learners' planning tasks, motivation and the content of their learning projects. In his critical review of the research initiated by Tough's work, Brookfield (1985) states that it has been replicated in some form or other in more than fifty follow-up studies, primarily with white, middle-class, educationally advantaged populations. In 1978, another national survey by Penland established the popularity of self-directed learning — 80% of adults in the United States are involved in some kind of learning each year and 75% of them plan their own learning.

The research served to demonstrate the existence and popularity of self-directed learning. However, it was the writings of practitioners, such as Knowles, that made self-directed learning the "distinctive paradigm of thought and action" of the seventies (Brookfield, 1985). According to Knowles, because of the complexity and rapidity of change in our highly technological societies, "one mission of the adult educator . . . can be stated positively as helping individuals to develop the attitude that learning is a lifelong process and to acquire the skills of self-directed learning". (1976:23) In the context of such a society, the traditional purpose of education, namely, the transmission of knowledge is no longer adequate. For knowledge acquired at an earlier stage in life can become obsolescent and new knowledge can bring about changes that will affect adults in both their personal and professional lives. Therefore, Knowles concludes, it is imperative that adults be equipped with the skills necessary to continue learning on their own when they leave a formal educational experience so that thay may be able to adapt and respond to these changes. In fact (he adds) successful adult educators can be measured in terms of the extent to which participants leave their educational activities "with increased ability to carry on their learning".

These social considerations are also applicable to second language classrooms. Of course, it is not the case that knowledge about the language learned in the classroom at an earlier stage in life will become obsolete. However, social and personal changes, such as those alluded to by Knowles, can render an adult's acquired language skills inadequate. Moreover, in many cases the time and place constraints of institutionally bound programs make it impossible for some adults to attend classes. In other cases, adult needs may be so specified that there may be no course sufficiently specialized to meet them. As for adults who are able to enroll in formal classes, they may find it difficult to achieve their linguistic objectives in a group class where student needs are so often varied. Developing curricula that respond to the needs of a particular group of learners for more specialized language skills is not enough. To paraphrase Knowles, attention should also be given to helping learners gain an awareness of the need that they will have to continue learning the language on their own once they leave the classroom *together with* the skills they will need to do so.

A set of assumptions about the psychological characteristics of adult learners. developed by theorists in adult education in both Europe and North America, further underlines the importance of developing self-directed language learners.[4]

The first of these assumptions states that the self-concept of the adult is that of a self-directing personality: ". . . the point at which a person becomes an adult psychologically, is that point at which he perceives himself to be wholly self-directing . . . as being able to make his own decisions and face their consequences, to manage his own life . . ." (Knowles 1976:40). Secondly, according to Knowles, an adult has accumulated a vast and varied reservoir of experience which "defines who he is, establishes his self-identity" (1976:44). In learning situations which do not utilize this experience or which minimize it, adults may experience personal rejection. Thirdly, in making a decision to learn, adults are usually prompted by the developmental tasks of their social roles. For example, a young adult who has entered the world of work needs to find a job and, therefore, will want to learn what is required to find one. Finally, adults expect their educational experiences to provide immediate solutions to the needs which led them to return to school. Their approach to learning is problem-centered. Their time perspective has changed from one of postponed application of knowledge to immediacy of application.

These psychological characteristics of the adult learner are also acknowledged in the literature on the methodology of second language learning and teaching. The view of the learner as capable of self direction is central to the work of Charles Curran (1976). A counseling psychologist, Curran has used the concepts and techniques of his discipline to develop a "counseling-learning approach" to foreign language learning. His investigations of language learners who learn a second language in this way has revealed how they progress from dependence on the counselor/language facilitator to self-sufficiency and, in so doing, assert in their role as language learners the autonomy they exercise in other aspects of their lives.

Stevick (1976) approaches the question of the learner's experience and needs from the perspective of memory and learning. In his discussion of "depth" in foreign language use, he distinguishes two levels of meaning that a communication may have. When teachers are admonished to have their students "use the language to communicate," he says, it is not sufficient to take into account the more surface level facts or pseudo facts language learners be asked to talk about. They should also remember the "depth" level, which connects what is communicated "with our plans, our inmost memories and our needs" (1976:36). He, then, cites experiments that have shown the positive influence on learning and recall of items that are of personal significance to the learner. In other words, it is implied that learning will be enhanced when the experience of adult learners and the needs for which they seek an educational solution are taken into account in our language learning curricula and methology.

Therefore, an adequate response to the educational needs of adult learners, including language learners, requires that this capability and desire for autonomy which is at the heart of much adult striving, be nurtured and developed. In this way language learners, themselves, may be enabled to better utilize the experience they bring to their language learning. They can become more intimately involved in providing solutions to their linguistic needs as they arise.

Recent literature on self-directed learning (Brookfield, 1985) contrasts two main approaches to providing adults with the educational experiences that nurture and refine their capacity and need for autonomy. The first is concerned with the technological implications of the psychological facts. It is exemplified in Knowles' definition of self-direction (1975):

> "In its broadest meaning, self-directed learning describes a process in which individuals take the initiative, with or without the help of others, in diagnosing their learning needs, formulating learning goals, identifying human and material resources for learning, choosing and implementing appropriate learning strategies, and evaluating learning outcomes." (p. 18)

Holec's (1981) analysis of what self-direction entails for *second language learners* is quite similar. He writes:

> Let us remind ourselves that with total self-direction, action by the learner is concerned with:
> — fixing objectives
> — defining the contents and progression
> — selecting the methods and techniques to be used
> — monitoring the acquisition procedure
> — evaluating what has been acquired (p. 9)

This is an approach that focuses on the self-instructional techniques necessary to organize and conduct learning events. Brookfield has labelled it as external and technicist.[5]

In contrast, Brookfield (1985) emphasizes the need for a reflective approach — for an internal change in consciousness together with technical expertise in the use of instructional techniques. Self-directed autonomous learning in the fullest sense of the word, it is stated, requires that adults become aware of the structure of cultural and psychological assumptions that form the meaning context of behavior. The network of ideals, values, and beliefs, the abstract social, political and educational concepts that are constituent elements of their cultural assumptions need to be critically examined and re-interpreted or recreated. Similarly, "dependency producing psychological assumptions" adults have acquired about themselves earlier in life also need to be brought to light (Mezirow, 1985:20). This process of critical reflection is to be directed not only at *how* one approaches learning but also at *what* and *why* one decides to learn. It is further stated that for learning to be autonomous, learners need a critical awareness and understanding of a range of alternative action paths and the limits of these possible choices (Chené, 1983). Finally, at the heart of this internal change there needs to be a growing appreciation on the part of adults of their personal power. They need to become aware of their ability to make choices, initiate action, to become responsible for and influence the course of their lives.

In his description of how autonomy can be fostered in *second language* learners, Holec (1980) also stresses the importance of critical reflection. If learners are to be weaned away from their state of dependence to one of independence or autonomy (he says) they must not only acquire a number of relevant learning techniques but also experience a change of psychological attitude towards what learning is. They must go through a gradual "deconditioning" process. For when a learner begins a learning program ". . . he has very clear ideas of what a language is, of what learning a language means, of the respective roles of teacher and learner, of the materials which are necessary and so on . . ." (41). Therefore it is necessary that (s)he re-examine these prejudices and preconceptions (i.e. ". . . that you can only learn a language in the presence of an expert teacher, that you must never make use of the mother tongue, that learning objectives cannot be defined by someone who does not know the language . . ." 41) as well as the advantages and disadvantages of autonomous learning and what learning in this way entails.

As I already mentioned, to date, explicit and systematic attempts to promote learner autonomy in the second language classroom have been rare. The field of learner training is relatively uncharted. Researchers of learner strategies who have advocated that learners be taught to use strategies appear to be emphasizing the importance of techniques. The projects described in Holec (1981) are also mainly technical in their orientation. However, as we continue to move forward in this area, it is important that both dimensions of autonomy be kept in mind. Facility in the use of self-instructional techniques or strategies must be accompanied by an internal change of consciousness. Otherwise, attempts at strategy training will meet resistance and may be doomed to failure. In the case where learners do cooperate, these attempts will be limited in their effectiveness. Therefore, together with the training in the use of strategies, the fostering of learner autonomy will require that learners become critically reflective of the conceptual context of their learning. They must be led to clarify, refine and expand their views of what language means and of what language learning entails. They should also understand the purpose for which they need to learn a second language. To add a more active meaning to Holec's term, such critical reflection will lead to "self-deconditioning". However, even this will be insufficient, if critical reflection does not take into account the fact that learners will also need to learn to believe in their potential to learn and to manage their learning *and* to be willing to assume a more responsible role in the process.

Conclusion

How is a second language acquired? How can we best use our classroom time to prepare our students to meet their communication needs in their second language? Learner strategy research is a merging together of these theoretical and practical concerns. It presents researchers with another learner characteristic to take into account in the equation of factors they may consider in determining how and with what degree of efficiency a second language is acquired. To practitioners, it presents the challenge of applying the insights gained from a systematic examination of learners' perceptions of their learning. Thus, it is an enterprise whose ultimate goal — an autonomous and effective language learner — depends upon the collaboration of researchers, curriculum experts, materials developers, classroom teachers, and learners.

Notes

1.   For other studies on attitude and motivation see Teitlebaum, Edwards and Hudson, 1975; Oller, Baca and Vigil, 1977; Gardner, Smythe and Clement, 1979; Gardner, Lalonde and Marcroft, 1985. For studies on other affective factors, such as personality, cf Guiora *et al.*, 1972b; 1975; Brodkey and Shore, 1976; Strong, 1983.

2.   Schumann's case studies of adult immigrant workers have highlighted factors such as the importance of economic dominance relationships between the target language group and the non-native speaker group; the cohesiveness and relative size of the groups; degree of assimilation desired; intended length of residence in the TL area.
3.   The term "learner training" refers to activities that help learners expand their repertoire of strategies and refine their knowledge of the learning process.
4.   Knowles refers to the work of Dusan Savicevic (1968) with adult educationists in Yugoslavia.
5.   In fact, although Knowles' definition of self-direction refers exclusively to the technical aspects, his methodology (cf *Self-Directed Learning: A Guide for Learners and Teachers*, 1975) does take into account the need for adults to reflect critically on the assumptions underlying their approach to learning and on their self-concept.

Follow-up Activities

Discussing the Issues

1. Chené (1983) defines autonomy as ". . . independence from all exterior regulations and constraints. Autonomy means that one can and does set one's own rules, and can choose for oneself the norms one will respect."
    (a) Referring to this definition, discuss to what extent language learners can achieve autonomy.
    (b) How does Chené's view of autonomy compare with the views put forth by Holec and Knowles? Brookfield and Mezirow?
2. Knowles uses the terms self-directed learner and autonomous learner inter-changeably. Holec sees self-direction in a means–end relationship with autonomy.
    (a) What is your view of the relationship between the two terms?
    (b) What is your operational definition of a self-directed language learner, i.e. what are they able to do? of an autonomous language learner?
3. What reasons does Wenden put forth to support the notion that language learners should become autonomous learners? Can you think of others?

Making Links

4. The questions which Hunt has listed as part of the research agenda of cognitive scientists point to issues that pertain to second language learning.
    (a) Identify those which you consider to pertain directly to second language learning.
    (b) Tell why and/or how they relate to second language learning.
5. Wenden lists four questions that have guided learner strategy research, i.e. what do learners do to help themselves learn? How do they regulate their efforts? What do they know about various aspects of their language learning process? Can their learning competence be developed and refined?
— What would you expect the answers to these questions to be? Refer to your own informal observation of language learners and to the literature in second language learning and acquisition.
6. The methodological principles set forth by Charles Curran and Earl Stevick both take into account the psychological profile of the adult learner.
— Refer to other literature on the teaching of second languages (e.g. methodology and/or curriculum) to determine whether an appreciation of the psychology of the adult learner is implicit or explicit in the approach that is advocated.

Chapter 2

Learner Strategies: Theoretical Assumptions, Research History and Typology[1]

JOAN RUBIN

Parallel with the explosion of methodologies in the late 70s and early 80s in which language teachers faced increased options in the selection of methods and materials, there has been a steadily growing interest in considering the task from the learner's point of view and in changing the focus of classrooms from a teacher-centered one to a learner-centered one. In particular, there is growing interest in defining how learners can take charge of their own learning and in clarifying how teachers can help students become more autonomous.

There is by now a substantial body of research outlining the behaviors learners use and describing the thought processes they engender while learning a foreign or second language. In particular, the focus of research has been on identifying the behaviors and thought processes used by language students to learn a foreign or second language.[2]

In this chapter, we will describe some of the theoretical underpinnings and assumptions on which this research rests, outline the research history of language learner strategies[3], provide a typology of learner strategies, and consider the research describing the effect of teaching these strategies to novice learners.

Theoretical Underpinnings and Assumptions

1. Some language learners are more successful than others

Teachers and researchers have all observed that *some* students approach the language learning task in more successful ways than others. That is, all other things being equal, some students will be more successful than others in learning a second or foreign language. The learning strategy literature assumes that some of this success can be attributed to particular sets of cognitive and metacognitive behaviors which learners engage in. Further, it is assumed that successful learners will differ to some extent in the particular sets of cognitive processes and behaviors which they use to enable them to be successful. For example, given the same learning environment, the same target language, the same native language, and the same language level, some learners will be more analytic in their approach to the learning task while others will be more intuitive; some learners will prefer to use written materials to access a foreign language while others will prefer to hear the language. It is assumed that there will be several paths to success depending on the individual's learning style. However, it is assumed that some approaches will not promote success for any learner.[4]

15

2. The learning process includes both explicit and implicit knowledge

Research into learner strategies rests on the assumption that both explicit and implicit knowledge can contribute to learning (the process of obtaining/getting, storing, retrieving and using information). A number of researchers support a model of learning in which the process of learning is not limited to information gotten in an unconscious manner (Bialystok, 1978; Smith, 1981; and McLaughlin, 1978). Cohen (1981) said: "I believe that information gotten consciously can subsequently be put into the subconscious or made automatic." For some learners and for some tasks, it is assumed that conscious attention to the learning process is the first step to making language automatic.

3. Consciousness-raising is not incidental to learning

It is assumed that making learning decisions conscious can lead both poorer and better learners to improve the obtaining, storing, retrieving and using of information, that is, can lead them to learn better. Smith (1981) affirms that "consciousness raising is not a time-wasting procedure" (p. 165). Further, students of learner strategies assume that making strategies conscious may enable learners to use their strategies more effectively and efficiently. In the Rubin–Henze study (1981), Henze reported that conscious attention to her learning strategies "helped her focus her learning" and that the writing of a diary helped her "evaluate her own learning strategies, enabling her in some cases to manipulate strategies so that she received the most benefit" (p. 24).

Not all learners do their best by approaching the learning task through an intuitive, sub-conscious, "natural" process. For example, although cognates may be deliberately used in language texts, if they are not explained many students never see the relationship of these cognates to words in their own language. Once the student's attention is drawn to the relationship, the same student may learn several hundred words in a very short time. Hence, some kinds of conscious intervention are assumed to be helpful in the process of learning.

4. Successful strategies can be used to good effect by less effective learners

It is assumed that once the strategies of good language learners are identified, they can be made available and, where useful, used by less successful learners to enable them to learn a foreign/second language more effectively (Hosenfeld, 1979).

5. Teachers can promote strategy use

It is assumed that once the range of possible learner strategies is identified, one important role of the teacher would be to provide an environment which facilitates the identification by students of those strategies which work best for them. Another role of the teacher would be to suggest alternative strategies for organizing and storing information and to encourage students to consider which strategies work best for them. It is assumed that this task would be an important part of the teacher's role.

6. Once trained, students become the best judge of how to approach the learning task

It is assumed that once students develop an ability to evaluate their own learning process, they become the best judge of how to approach the learning task. The fact is that teachers cannot follow the learning path of each of their students because much of it is not readily accessible to the teacher. Hence, teachers are of necessity limited in their efforts to track such cognitive paths. So, since teachers may find it difficult to determine how each student learns best, students must be taught to help themselves. Researchers of learner strategies feel it is essential for language students to begin to take control of their learning.

7. Self-direction promotes learning both inside and outside the classroom

Students who use effective strategies are better able to work outside the classroom by themselves, once the teacher is not around to direct them or provide them with input. It is assumed that it is essential for students to be able to control their own learning process so that they can learn outside the classroom once they are on their own. If students are dependent on teachers to shape language to suit them and to provide them with proper input, they can't begin to take charge of their own learning when the teacher is not there.

8. Language learning is like other kinds of learning

Learning theory would suggest that it is best to build on what the student knows or better still, to help students build on what they know. Since each student's knowledge differs, it is essential for students to be able to assess their own knowledge. This knowledge includes what they know about their own learning process, what they know about language (their own and any second or foreign language), and what they know about the communication process. Second or foreign language learners do not come to the learning process as a *tabula rasa* — rather they come to the situation as speaking human beings who know a great deal about language and communication. It is essential to start by making this knowledge explicit and building on it.

In spite of wide differences between existing theoretical approaches to learning (Skinnerian, Piagetian, human information processing), most learning theorists would agree that learning is best achieved when the students play an active role in the process. Being active means that students cannot just be given information; rather they must have opportunities to internalize information in ways which are meaningful to them. Internalization — working through the information — is an active process. Hence, students need to work with new ideas and new experiences to make them their own. The learning environment must provide ideas and experiences as well as opportunities to work through them. Being active is related to another assumption of learning theorists — namely, that problem-solving is the approach which best aids learning. If students are involved in problem-solving, then they are required to find ways to internalize material for themselves. Problem-solving includes activities like making inferences — both inductive and deductive.

Language learning like other kinds of learning involves problem-solving, which requires that learners be active in order to internalize information. For example, often the meaning of a word or phrase ("a problem") is only clarified by its use in a specific sentence or social situation. The only real way to understand a speaker's message or intention is to properly infer the meaning. By making inferences (a form of problem-solving) students are able to confirm their understanding of a conversation. Inferencing requires active involvement on the part of the student so that he/she may ascertain appropriate relationships among the words, phrases and social interactions, and thereby determine the meaning of a social event.

9. The success of learner training in other subjects is applicable to language learning

Recent research in learner training has demonstrated some effective modes of learner training (Brown and Palinscar, 1982; and Dansereau et al., 1975).[5] Brown and Palinscar's work indicated that "evidence is accumulating to suggest that an ideal training package would consist of both practice in the use of task-appropriate strategies, instruction concerning the significance of those activities and instruction concerning the monitoring and control of strategy use" (p. 7). Since similar kinds of strategies are being isolated for language learning, it is assumed that similar kinds of learning training would be effective in this task. However, the focus of training, whether on cognitive or metacognitive strategies (for a definition see section ahead "Typology of Strategies"), may depend on the learning preferences of a particular student.

10. The "critical" faculty used by all humans in communicating is important in language learning

Morrison and Low (1983) argue that human language use depends on both creative and critical faculties. "The creative faculty, dipping down into the internal reservoir of stored rules and patterns, assembles strings of language for private consumption or for articulation as utterances" (Morrison and Low, 1983, p. 228). "At the same time, a critical faculty, . . . gives awareness of what has been created, making it possible to check, either before or after articulation, for the frequent slips of the tongue, grammatical errors, social infelicities and other deviations from intention that characterize normal speech" (p. 228). Further, they argue that the creative faculty operates beyond the back edge of consciousness and is therefore essentially unruly. The critical faculty, which is essentially our awareness of language, gives lease to the creative faculty, keeps it in check and possibly learns from it, according to Morrison and Low. Then, when errors or other discrepancies from intention are detected, repairs may be made. The critical faculty (called monitoring by Morrison and Low) is linked to planning and repair.

Whereas this critical faculty operates in both first and second language communication to edit text and ensure that intention is clarified, Morrison and Low suggest that it may also be linked to learning. In the process of monitoring, learners will (1) identify a problem (2) make some sort of decision about the nature and seriousness of the problem (3) decide whether to correct the problem and if they decide to do so (4) correct the error and (5) notice any feedback on whether their correction was acceptable, permitting learning to take place. It is assumed, then, that in order to be able to learn in the sense defined (see note 2), students must be able to monitor (in the sense described above, steps 1–5) their output and take actions to correct them when appropriate. Hence, monitoring is essential to learning.

Research History

In this section, we will review the research which has identified and described learner strategies. Although many variables can contribute to the success of learners, our focus here is on the behaviors and thought processes that learners use in the *process* of learning, not those variables which may provide a background to learning success (called a filter by some researchers). In this latter category we include: psychological characteristics (such as risk-taking, tolerance for ambiguity, field dependence, and empathy among others), affective variables (such as liking or disliking the teacher, the culture, the natives, one's classmates or one's state of mind at the time of the learning activity), or social style (such as degree of sociability and outgoingness or social competence) and those social strategies which follow from social style. All of these variables may make important contributions to learning success but they are not the focus of what we here call learner strategies.

As used in this chapter, learner strategies includes any set of operations, steps, plans, routines used by the learner to facilitate the obtaining, storage, retrieval and use of information (after O'Malley *et al.*, 1983; and Brown *et al.*, 1983), that is, what learners *do* to learn and *do to regulate* their learning. In addition, to better understand how learner strategies come to be used, it is essential that we account for a learner's knowledge about language and his/her beliefs about the language learning process (that is, what he/she knows) because this knowledge can form the basis for selecting and activating one strategy over another.

Much of the research on learner strategies has concentrated on identifying what (self-defined) good language learners report they do to learn a second or foreign language or, in some cases, are observed doing while learning a second or foreign language.

Research on learner strategies dates back to 1966 when Aaron Carton first published his study *The Method of Inference in Foreign Language Study*. In this study he noted that learners vary in their propensity to make inferences and in their ability to make valid, rational, and reasonable inferences. Carton also recognized that tolerance of risk (which we have called a background variable) would vary with ability to make good inferences. In a second article (1971), Carton provides a detailed discussion of inferencing as a strategy used by second language learners. He divides inferencing into three kinds of cues:

1. intra-lingual cues in which the cues are supplied by the target language — used when a student already has some knowledge of the target language
2. inter-lingual cues which are brought to bear on loans between languages, cognates and regularities of phonological transformations from one language to another
3. extra-lingual cues — in which the learner uses what he/she knows about the real world to predict what is said in a foreign communication.

Carton argues for the importance of student perception of "probabilistic contingent relations" since he suggests that it provides for improved selection of appropriate linguistic units in production and for improved interpretation of these units in comprehension (p. 57). For Carton, language learning is a kind of problem-solving in which the student can bring to bear his/her prior experience and knowledge in the processing of language.

Following leads from Carton and learning theory, in 1971, Rubin initiated research which focused on the strategies of successful learners. Her assumption was that, once identified, such strategies could be made available to less successful learners. The research results described in her (1975) paper included the following variables: learner psychological characteristics (risk-taking, tolerance for ambiguity and vagueness, willingness to appear foolish), learner communication strategies (use of circumlocution and gestures), learner social strategies (seeking out opportunities to use language) and learner cognitive strategies (guessing/inferencing; practicing; attending to form by analyzing, categorizing and synthesizing; and monitoring) exhibited by and used by self-defined good language learners. Rubin's 1981 report of subsequent research classifies strategies in terms of *processes that may contribute directly to learning* (i.e. clarification/verification, monitoring, memorization, guessing/inductive inferencing, deductive reasoning, and practice) and *those that may contribute indirectly to learning* (i.e. creating opportunity to practice and use of production tricks).

Research conducted by Naiman *et al.* (1978) also focused on personality traits, cognitive styles and strategies that were critical to successful language learning. The initial frame of reference for their analysis of the strategies was Stern's (1975) list of ten strategies necessary to attain second language competence. This list was modified by the statements and views of the interviewees in the Naiman *et al.* study to form a list of five general strategies and related techniques. According to the list, good language learners

(1) actively involve themselves in the language learning process by identifying and seeking preferred learning environments and exploring them,
(2) develop an awareness of language as a system,
(3) develop an awareness of language as a means of communication and interaction,
(4) accept and cope with the affective demands of L2,
(5) extend and revise L2 system by inferencing and monitoring.

At about the same time, Wesche (1975) completed her dissertation on the learning behaviors of successful adult language students in the Canadian Civil Service. Wesche found these students used many of the same strategies listed by

Rubin and Stern. Her findings, summarized in a 1979 article, brought to light the following: (1) there was a greater variety and quantity of learning behaviors pursued by those who improved most rapidly, and (2) many of the observed learning behaviors occurred together. Wesche's hypothesis that "it may be complexes of them (i.e. behaviors) rather than specific ones which characterize different kinds of learners" (p. 419) is worthy of further research.

In her study of five Chicano students who were learning English, Wong-Fillmore (1976) identified social strategies used by successful language learners. Further, Wong-Fillmore found that by using a few well chosen formulas, learners could continue to participate in activities which provided contexts for the learning of new material. Wong-Fillmore notes that staying in the conversation had an important connection to learning because the new material became learnable and memorable by virtue of being embedded in current, interest-holding activities (p. 670). The author provides strong evidence of the link between strategies which contribute indirectly to learning (social strategies and communication strategies) and learning strategies (inferencing through what is known and storage through associations and context).

Bialystok (1979) reports on research which showed the effects of the use of two functional strategies — inferencing and functional practicing — and two formal strategies — monitoring and formal practicing. According to Bialystok, the focus of functional practicing strategies is language use. On the other hand, formal practicing strategies focus on language form. Bialystok uses the term "monitoring" in the more narrow sense where the focus is on the form (but not upon the intention of the communication). Results indicated that the use of all four strategies had positive effects on achievement in certain kinds of tests, and that only the functional strategies significantly modified performance for all tasks.

Tarone studied the communication strategies of second language learners. In her 1977 and 1981 papers, she identified several communication strategies which learners use to remain in a conversation (e.g. word coinage, mime, circumlocution, appeal for assistance, approximation, silence or hesitation, questioning repeat, approximating the speaker's message, and explicit indication of comprehension).

Hosenfeld (1977) reports on the reading strategies of successful and unsuccessful second language learners obtained by using the "think aloud" type of introspection. Hosenfeld found that successful readers use some form of contextual guessing — based on the process of inductive reasoning. In addition, Hosenfeld reported on a metacognitive strategy in which the student evaluates thinking by assessing the appropriateness of the logic of a guess. In her 1979 article, Hosenfeld reports on one of the first attempts to train learners in the use of strategies, in this case, efficient reading strategies.

Hosenfeld (1978) hints at what has become an important part of meta-cognition, namely, a student's "mini-theory of second-language" (see Wenden, this volume, for an elaboration of beliefs about language learning). Hosenfeld calls for research about student assumptions, how they develop, how they are influenced by teachers and textbooks, and how they operate.

In their studies Cohen and Aphek focused primarily on the strategies students used in the learning of vocabulary (1981) and the role of mnemonic associations in the retention of vocabulary over time (1980). They found that in most instances students tried to memorize words. However, Cohen and Aphek also identified eleven categories of associations utilized by students. They concluded tentatively that the use of such strategies facilitated the retention of vocabulary over time. The authors also pointed toward some strategies which prevented learning: (1) poor memory techniques (2) poor inductive inferencing strategies, and (3) poor deductive reasoning.

The work of the seventies contributed to our understanding of language learning by identifying strategies which contribute directly to learning (identifying a range of cognitive strategies), by identifying strategies which contribute indirectly to language learning (identifying communication and social strategies).

The work of Wenden (1982, 1986) has added an important new dimension to our understanding of learner strategies — namely, the importance of metacognitive knowledge in second language learning. Wenden identified 5 areas of metacognitive knowledge: (1) the language (2) student proficiency (3) outcome of student's learning endeavors (4) the student's role in the language learning process, and (5) how best to approach the task of language learning. Wenden's research has contributed important insights on metacognition in second language learning, namely, what learners know about their L2 learning (metacognitive knowledge) and how they plan it (a regulatory process).

Chamot and O'Malley (this volume) provide the first clear contrast between cognitive and metacognitive strategies. Metacognitive strategies include the regulatory processes by which learners plan, monitor (considered in a broad sense), and evaluate their learning.

Building on existing inventories of learner strategies, a recent study by Politzer and McGroarty (1985) compared self-report of strategy use to the development of linguistic and communicative competence. Their findings indicated some areas that merit future research: (1) Adding to Wesche's (1979) observation, they suggest that "good behaviors may be differentially appropriate for various types of skills. . ." (p. 118). They further suggest that appropriate complexes of strategies may be differentially related to linguistic and communicative competence (2) they query the universal validity of good strategies and suggest that behaviors may be culturally specific[6] and (3) they recommend caution in defining a behavior as absolutely helpful. Rather, it may be good or bad depending on the level of proficiency or frequency of use. In fact, they urge research on whether frequency of use makes a given behavior more or less effective for language learners. Their research provides important leads for future research in learner strategies.

In the future, we will need more work on clarifying the nature of the interaction between metacognitive beliefs and knowledge, metacognitive strategies, cognitive strategies and student achievement. We need to determine the conditions under which complexes of strategies are helpful for particular levels and particular skills and for particular learners (taking into account learning style, cultural background, etc.). Further, we need to determine the effect of learner training on language learning achievement.

Typology of Strategies

Most of the research to date has enabled us to identify many of the major strategies (for a definition of strategies, see p. 21 this article) used by language learners. Following Rubin, 1981, we suggest that there are three kinds of strategies which have been identified which contribute directly or indirectly to language learning: learning strategies, communication strategies, and social strategies.

Learning strategies are strategies which contribute to the development of the language system which the learner constructs and affect learning directly. Very recently, students of learning strategies have come to recognize two major kinds of learning strategies: metacognitive and cognitive strategies. While it is difficult to separate these two kinds of strategies, some attempts to do so have been made by Brown and Palinscar (1982) and O'Malley *et al.* (1983). In the latter's view, metacognitive refers to: (1) knowledge about cognitive processes, and (2) regulation of cognition or executive control or self-management through such processes as planning, monitoring, and evaluating. Cognitive strategies refer to the steps or operations used in learning or problem-solving that require direct analysis, transformation, or synthesis of learning materials. Cognition consists of those processes or strategies through which an individual obtains knowledge or conceptual understanding. It is important to note that cognitive learning theorists have found mounting evidence to suggest that "an ideal training package would consist of both practice in the use of task-appropriate strategies, instruction concerning the significance of those activities, and instruction concerning the monitoring and control of strategy use" (Brown and Palinscar, 1982, p. 7). As O'Malley *et al.* (1983) conclude: "Students without metacognitive approaches are essentially learners without direction and ability to review their progress, accomplishments, and future learning directions" (p. 6).

Cognitive Learning Strategies

Rubin (1981) identified six general strategies which may contribute directly to language learning:

1. *Clarification/verification* refers to those strategies which learners use to verify or clarify their understanding of the new language. In the process of creating or confirming rules in a new language, they may seek confirmation of their understanding of the language, they may ask for validation that their production of words, phrases, or sentences is consistent with the new language. Finally, they may seek to clarify the communication rules of the specific language variety they are attempting to learn. Verification allows the students to store information for further use.

2. *Guessing/inductive inferencing* refers to strategies which use previously obtained linguistic or conceptual knowledge to derive explicit hypotheses about the linguistic form, semantic meaning or speaker's intention. It involves using hunches from a wide range of possible sources to determine the speaker's intention. Thus, learners can use what they know about their own or a second language to infer meaning. They may also use what they know about the communication process to infer the meaning by considering such information as: Who the participants are, where the communication is taking place, what the history of the communication process between the speakers

is, what the topic is, what the register or genre is, and other kinds of social and discourse information.

To narrow their inferencing learners may attend to the relation of words to action, and the relation of the syntactic frame to the item in question. Learners use a top–down approach looking at the overall picture (or larger meaning) from which to infer the meaning of individual items. In forming hypotheses, learners have to define what is important in a sentence, phrase or utterance and ignore irrelevant items. Students use their knowledge of the world in decoding unfamiliar items. They may use their first language as a basis for understanding and/or producing the second language but they must also recognize the limits of using this knowledge as a source of inferencing.[7]

Hosenfeld (1977) identified a number of inferencing strategies used by successful second language readers: "(1) Keep the meaning of a passage in mind while reading, and use it to predict meaning; (2) Keep unfamiliar words and guess the meaning from remaining words in a sentence or later sentences; (3) Circle back in the text to bring to mind previous context to decode an unfamiliar word; . . . (4) Identify the grammatical function of an unfamiliar word before guessing its meaning; . . . (6) Examine the illustration and use information contained in it in decoding; (7) Read the title and draw inferences from it; (8) Refer to the side gloss; . . . (12) Recognize cognates; (13) Use knowledge of the world to decode an unfamiliar word; . . . (14) Skip words that may add relatively little to total meaning . . ." (p. 59).

3. *Deductive reasoning* is a problem-solving strategy in which the learner looks for and uses general rules in approaching the foreign or second language. Here the learner uses previously acquired linguistic or conceptual knowledge to derive specific hypotheses about the linguistic form, semantic meaning or speaker's intention. The difference between inductive and deductive reasoning is that in inductive reasoning the learner is looking for a *specific* meaning or *specific* rule whereas in deductive reasoning the learner is looking for and using more general rules. The process is used to find organization and patterns that make sense to the learner in order to obtain and store information about a language in an organized and retrievable (to the specific learner) fashion. Logical procedures include: analogy, analysis, and synthesis. At the same time, learners are always on the lookout for exceptions, limitations, restrictions to whatever rules or patterns they have identified. As Stern (1975) points out "the good language learner constantly probes the language and forms hypotheses about it in order to discover rules and relationships and to organize the discrete elements into an ordered whole or system" (p. 313).

4. *Practice* refers to strategies which contribute to the storage and retrieval of language while focusing on *accuracy of usage*. Practice involves strategies such as: repetition, rehearsal, experimentation, application of rules, imitation, and attention to detail.

5. *Memorization* also refers to strategies which focus on the storage and retrieval of language; therefore some of the strategies, such as drill and repetition, used for practice are the same as memorization strategies. However, in the case of memorization, attention is paid to *the storage and retrieval process*. The goal of these strategies is organization. Some mnemonic strategies

learners listed were: finding some sort of association or grouping (phonetic, semantic, visual, auditory, kinesic, even olfactory or sensory), using one item to recall a number of others (called key word), using some sort of mechanical means to store the information (taking notes, writing out items with or without context, etc.), or selective attention in which students focus on certain details to aid in recall, or directed physical response in which students aid retention by associating the item with their own physical movement. For a further discussion of memory strategies, see Thompson, this volume and Cohen (1984).

6. *Monitoring*[8] refers to strategies in which the learner notices errors (both linguistic and communicative), observes how a message is received and interpreted by the addressee, and then decides what to do about it.

The monitoring process appears to be a combination of cognitive and metacognitive strategies. For example, identifying a problem, determining a solution, or making a correction (steps 1, 2 and 4) are cognitive since they involve direct analysis, transformation or synthesis of learning materials. However, deciding on the action to be taken or evaluating the action (steps 3 and 5) are metacognitive since they involve self-management, that is, deciding on what action is to be taken or evaluating the effect of an action taken.

Metacognitive Learning Strategies

Metacognitive strategies are used to oversee, regulate or self-direct language learning. Wenden (1982, 1986) examined how learners regulate their learning by planning, monitoring and evaluating their learning activities. In particular, Wenden focused on what learners know about various aspects of their language learning and how this influences their choice of strategies.

Wenden (1982) identified several planning strategies which students use. Students may assess their needs and preferences and *choose* what they want to learn and how they should learn a language. This choice may be dependent upon the student's beliefs of how language is to be learned (Hosenfeld, 1978, and Wenden, 1986). They can choose how to use resources. They may then *prioritize* the aspects of language that they want to learn. By choosing and prioritizing, students set their own learning goals. Finally, students may *plan* what their learning strategies should be and change them if they are not successful.

O'Malley *et al.* (1983) provide an extended list of planning strategies: self-management, advance preparation, advance organizers, directed attention, selective attention, and delayed production.

Learning Strategies and Communication Strategies

Both cognitive and metacognitive strategies can contribute directly to language learning. Communication strategies are less directly related to language learning since their main focus is on the process of participating in a conversation (i.e. functional practicing) and getting meaning across or clarifying what the speaker intended. Communication strategies are used by speakers when faced with some difficulty due to the fact that their communication ends outrun their communication means or when confronted with misunderstanding by a co-speaker (Corder, 1983; Tarone, 1983). The relationship of communication strategies to learning strategies is not always so clear since in the process of clarifying meaning, learners may uncover new information which they then store in their language system. Thus, although use of communication strategies may lead to learning, the purpose for their use is better communication.

Communication Strategies

From the point of view of the learning process, communication strategies are very important because they allow the learner to remain in the conversation. By continual exposure to natural conversation, learners may also learn (1) through opportunities to hear more of the target language, and (2) through opportunities to produce new utterances and test their knowledge. Further, with successful communication, motivation for more learning can be enhanced. It is felt that communication strategies are used when there is a difference between the learner's knowledge and the learner's communicative intent.

In order to remain in the conversation, learners must (1) find ways to continue producing the target language despite limitations, (2) recognize when their production has not been properly interpreted, and (3) indicate their reception of the speaker's intentions (cf. Tarone, 1981; and Faerch and Kasper, 1983, for discussions of the interactive nature of communication strategies).

A common communication strategy is to use one's linguistic or communicative knowledge to remain in the conversation. Examples include: use of synonyms, use of cognates (whether equivalent in meaning or not), use of simple sentences, use of semantic contiguity (for example use of the word "chair" for "stool"), use of gestures or mime, and use of circumlocution or paraphrase (Tarone, 1977; Rubin, 1981).

Learners may contribute to or remain in the conversation if they give the impression they know the target language by using a few well chosen conversational formulas (called prefabricated conversational patterns by Wong-Fillmore, 1976). By using such formulas, learners can continue to participate in activities which provide contexts for the learning of new material. Hence they can remain in conversation even though they are not as proficient as their use of these prefabricated patterns might indicate. Further, the new material is learnable and memorable by virtue of being embedded in current, interest-holding activities (Wong-Fillmore, 1976). Some of these prefabricated patterns include: opening and closing a conversation, pausing, getting and giving and keeping turns, and requesting assistance. Such formulae can encourage native speakers to continue to speak to the learner despite deficiencies.

As Tarone (1977) has noted, many learners may use an avoidance strategy in production: avoiding words, phrases or topics with which they may be uncomfortable and using others instead to remain in a conversation. Such strategies promote communication but are not directly related to learning since learners are using what they know and not directly addressing areas of confusion.

Learners who recognize that the addressee has not understood their production can also use strategies to clarify their intention. Rubin (1981) listed the following clarification strategies: write a word out, spell the word out, repeat utterances or use gestures. Learners also may provide a larger context for the addressee by putting the word into a larger linguistic context in order to clarify their meaning [e.g. sing (a song)].

Another communication strategy is one where learners indicate to their interlocutor the extent to which they have followed the speaker's utterances, for example: appeal for assistance, questioning repeat, silence/hesitation, approximate the speaker's message, mime, and explicit indication of comprehension.

Although it is clear that these strategies play an important role in providing the learner with an opportunity to participate in conversations with native speakers and hence attain more exposure to the target language, there is no evidence to date that communication strategies contribute *directly* to language learning, i.e. to the obtaining, storing, retrieving and using of language. Nonetheless, as I have already stated, since they allow the learner to remain in the conversation and gain essential opportunities to practice what they have learned and test new hypotheses, they are essential to, but may not contribute directly to, learning.

Social Strategies

Social strategies are those activities learners engage in which afford them opportunities to be exposed to and practice their knowledge. In themselves they do not contribute to learning since they merely put the student in an environment where practice is possible.

Wong-Fillmore (1976) identified two social strategies: join a group and act as if you understand what is going on, even if you don't, and count on your friends for help. Although these strategies provide exposure to the target language, they contribute only indirectly to learning since they don't lead directly to the obtaining, storing, retrieving and using of language.

Rubin (1981) also listed other activities which may contribute indirectly to learning, all of them under the rubric: "creates opportunity for practice." The list includes: creates situation with natives in order to verify/test/practice; initiates conversation with fellow student/teacher/native speaker; answers to self, questions to other students; spends extra time in language lab; listens to television/radio, attends movies or parties or uses advertisements, reads extra books often first in native language, then in target language; and (from Naiman, Fröhlich and Stern, 1978) identifies learning preferences and selects learning situations accordingly.

Productivity of these Strategies

The major task which researchers have pursued to date has been to identify a conceptual framework for learner strategies, based largely on an information processing model of learning. The task has included identifying what the specific strategies are and constructing a typology which organizes these strategies. The strategies have been obtained largely from learner introspection and retrospection and observation of more successful language learners. Another major task for which considerable research is needed is the determination of how these strategies work together to ensure success for particular kinds of learners' levels of language skill (beginner, intermediate or advanced in a specific foreign/second language) and particular environments. Further, we need to determine whether these strategies can be taught to less experienced (novice) learners to enhance their learning experience. In this section, we will review the few experiments which attempt to verify the effectiveness of promoting the use of some of the strategies outlined above.

A 1977 study by Bialystok and Fröhlich found that by providing the appropriate information to second language readers, their comprehension was enhanced. Working with high school students of French as a second language, the authors found that when they provided a picture representing the main point of the passage or an English summary sentence representing the main point that comprehension was significantly improved. In other words, the authors provided the basis for correct inferencing, although they did not train the learners in inferencing strategies. Bialystok, in press, repeated the reading experiment but this time included training as part of the experiment. She provided four conditions: providing a picture which summarized the gist of the passage; providing a dictionary with all lexical items in the passage; and providing training in inferencing (using information they have about prefixes, suffixes, cognates or through the context of the passage) and no cue. She concluded that the study suggests that "deliberate provision of different kinds of contextual information and instruction in inferencing techniques are pedagogically expedient in second language reading comprehension" (p. 31). Of interest is the finding that students were able to follow the instructions on inferencing and apply them to similar material on their own. Further research is needed to determine: the most effective way to teach inferencing, the long-term effect of such instruction, and the generalizability to various tasks of teaching inferencing in reading.

Cohen and Aphek (1980) trained 26 learners of Hebrew as a second language to generate associations of their own choosing for new vocabulary items. They found a generally high success rate for recall of words that were learned through association. However, since a subgroup of students who learned some words without association were able to recall these words as well as words for which they did find associations, the question is raised as to the type of learner who benefits from learning vocabulary through association. Cohen and Aphek suggest that some questions which this research suggest are: (1) need for more precise information about the process of choosing an association, (2) need for more precise information about why students were unable to generate associations for certain words, and (3) need to find ways to encourage students to tap their own potential for generating associations that would improve their learning of second language vocabulary. There is a need for more research to enable us to understand how association promotes memory in second language.

O'Malley (this volume) reports on an experiment in which students received training on the use of learning strategies with three language tasks; vocabulary, listening skills, and speaking. His major conclusion was that strategy training was effective for listening and speaking but not for vocabulary. The implication of these findings is that important language skills can be learned in classrooms.

We observe that, thus far, there has been only a limited amount of work done in assessing the effects of learner training, though some of the research is extremely suggestive of its potential. Now that we have identified the strategies and a typology for understanding these strategies, there is an urgent need for such research to be carried out in order to validate the extent to which and the conditions under which these strategies can help less efficient and more novice learners.

In conclusion, there have been tremendous strides forward made in defining the strategies which good language learners use and in placing these within a typology. We have a good scheme for studying these strategies though many of the details remain to be filled in. What is needed now is experimentation with the complex array of strategies that will work best for different kinds of learners and a determination of the best approach for teachers to use in facilitating such strategy use.

Notes

1. My thanks to Anita Wenden and Michael O'Malley for their comments; the paper was considerably improved by their kind attention.
2. By learning, we mean the process by which information is obtained, stored, retrieved, and used.
3. For a definition of learner strategies, see page 21.
4. Stern, 1975, notes that "the poor learner's language does not develop into a well-ordered system or network. It remains an untidy assemblage of separate items. He makes no attempt to relate items to each other. Because his approach is passive, unsystematic, and fragmented, he will complain that he has no memory for language" (p. 314). Similarly, it has been my experience that students who insist on always doing word for word translation rarely make much progress in language learning.
5. My thanks to Michael O'Malley for calling my attention to this literature.
6. Some evidence suggests they may not be culturally specific. A recent thesis by Huang (1984) found that successful Chinese students of English used many of the learner strategies listed in the Rubin and Stern–Naiman inventories. The issue calls for more research.
7. Laufer and Sim (1985) suggest that not all students are successful in their use of textual and extra-textual knowledge to infer the meaning of a sentence. In a small experiment they conducted they found that students who have an insecure language base (vocabulary) may generate incorrect hypotheses. Their recommendation is that making inferences with too small a vocabulary can be deleterious. We suggest that good inferencing requires considering the logic of such interpretations to see if they really are tenable.
8. This definition differs from that of Krashen, 1976. Krashen's definition refers only to linguistic knowledge consciously obtained. Our definition not only includes conscious but sub-conscious monitoring. It includes learner attention to sociolinguistic knowledge as well as linguistic knowledge. It should be noted that as used here, the term monitoring includes what Brown and Palinscar (1982) call both monitoring and evaluating.

Follow-up Activities

Discussing the Issues

1. Rubin lists ten assumptions about second language learning that underly the research on learner strategies.
    (a) Use the assumptions to construct a survey questionnaire.
    (b) Administer the questionnaire to yourself and to another teacher. Next to each assumption indicate whether you agree, disagree or are unsure. Star those views about which you are most convinced.
    (c) Discuss with your co-teacher the reasons for your answers.
    (d) When you have completed the readings and follow-up activities in the book, re-administer the survey to yourself. Determine why your views did or did not change.

Applying the Ideas

2. Rubin describes a typology of three kinds of strategies — learning, communication and social strategies. Learning strategies are further categorized as cognitive and metacognitive.

(a) Distinguish the strategies from one another in terms of purpose.

(b) Choose a context where a learner has to use the language, e.g. watching TV, speaking to an instructor, and indicate how all four strategies might come into play in such an instance.

3. Ask your students to keep a learning journal.

(a) Have them describe problems they encounter in learning or using the language in particular instances (e.g. making a telephone call, writing a letter, reading the paper). The instances you suggest should be based on the special linguistic goals of your learners.

(b) Use the typology described by Rubin to analyze the diaries.

(c) What does the analysis indicate about your students' learning competence? How do they describe their language learning process? How much do they know about it? How varied is their repertoire of strategies?

(d) Evaluate Rubin's typology in terms of its comprehensiveness and pedagogical utility.

Chapter 3

Studying Learner Strategies: How We Get the Information[1]

ANDREW D. COHEN

As educators have become more interested in the strategies[2] used in learning a second or foreign language, they have come to see the value of complementing the results of classroom observation by a trained observer with reports of the learners' own intuitions and insights. In this paper I will consider the potential of such verbal reports and the ways they can be obtained.

First, let me describe some of the limitations of restricting our study to observation of the learner's behavior in the classroom. These approaches assume that observable behavior will reveal the learning process; they rely in part on detailed observation schedules (see, for example, Fanselow, 1977, 1983; Rubin, 1981). However, it has become apparent that it is difficult to obtain accurate insights about learners' conscious thought processes through conventional observations of teacher-centered classroom sessions. By "conscious thought processes" what is meant are all thoughts that are within the realm of awareness of the learner, whether they are attended to fully or not.[3]

Classroom observations can record the physical movements of students — nods of the head, smiles, eye movements, and what they say, but cannot easily capture what they are thinking about, how they are thinking, or how they feel. Hence, observations regarding language learning behavior are generally limited to students who speak out loud. Such observations tell us nothing about those who remain quiet, and not a great deal about those who do not. Rubin (1981) suggests that it is possible to make observations of student learning strategies, but that the approach is tedious and not so productive in most classrooms because teachers tend to focus on product rather than on process and because opportunities have to be created to verify the observers' interpretations of these strategies.

Consider what a strategy might be like. A student learning to conjugate a new verb might go through a thought process something like this one that I went through in dealing with a new Hebrew verb:

> Now, how am I going to learn how to conjugate the verb *rigel* 'to spy' in Hebrew? Oh, I see. It is conjugated just like *diber* 'to speak.' So now I know its forms — no problem.

In this case, I used the strategy of analogy to learn the appropriate forms of the verb. Sometimes the strategies seem obvious. Sometimes they are quite surprising. Thus, the outside observer has little chance of guessing accurately either the likelihood that a certain strategy is being used or the frequency with which it is used. Verbal reports from learners about the kinds of strategies that work well for them can be most helpful in learner training — in training learners to make more efficient use of their time spent learning a second language.

After a number of hours of classroom observation, Naiman *et al.* (1975) concluded that very few learning techniques were overtly displayed in the

31

classroom. For example, although the researchers had hoped to investigate the extent to which learners used circumlocution in their utterances, they found very rare cases of its use. It was not that it did not occur, but rather that it was difficult for an outside observer to determine when the learner was, in fact, using circumlocution. Naiman and his colleagues did not feel that more time in the classroom would help. They suggested that students be interviewed directly regarding what were largely covert forms of learning behavior in the daily classroom routine. They felt that only through interviews, could one have access to techniques that were invisible to any observers — such as "attempting to answer to themselves every question asked by the teacher" (Naiman *et al.*, 1975:68).

Because of these limitations on observational techniques, there has therefore developed a new focus in research on strategies: the collection of learners' reports of their own insights about the strategies they use.

Types of Verbal Report Data

What kinds of data can be obtained from learners' reports of the processes they use? At the outset it is important to point out that these reports are limited to that subset of *learning* strategies that the learner is conscious of. In other words, we can only learn about the conscious strategies that learners utilize in their efforts to master a language. We are not talking about what have been posited as separate second-language *acquisition* processes (Krashen, 1982) — namely, unconscious processes that lead to mastery. (There is still debate as to whether such a separation exists). The learning strategies that interest us span a wide range of activities. They include: how learners attend to language input, how learners arrive at spoken utterances, how readers process a text, how writers generate text, and how vocabulary is learned initially and retrieved subsequently. These strategies may be effective or they may not work for the given learner. In other words, they may result in enhanced learning or they may not.

In order to tap the conscious mental processes involved in language learning, researchers have utilized three basic categories of learner report data: They will be referred to as "self-report," "self-observation," and "self-revelation" (see Table 1). The first refers to learners' descriptions of what they do, characterized by generalized statements about learning behavior (e.g., "When I have a word I really want to learn, I say it over to myself several times and try to associate it with some other word I already know.") or labels they apply to themselves (e.g., "I'm a 'speed listener' in another language. I make a quick search for the key words, and if I don't know them, I try to figure out their meaning from context.") Such statements are usually based on beliefs or concepts that the learners have about the way that they learn languages, and are often not based on the observation of any specific event.

"Self-observation," on the other hand, refers to the inspection of specific language behavior, either while the information is still in short-term memory, i.e., introspectively, or after the event, i.e., retrospectively (usually after 20 seconds or so).[4] Retrospection can be immediate (e.g., within, say, an hour of the event) or delayed (a few hours, days, or even weeks after the event). It appears that the bulk of the forgetting occurs right after the mental event. Thus, data from immediate retrospection may only be somewhat more complete than data from delayed retrospection.[5]

The term "self-revelation" is introduced here to refer to learner's report that is neither a description of general behaviors, nor based on inspection of specific ones. Rather it consists of "think-aloud" stream-of-consciousness disclosure of thought processes while the information is being attended to.[6] The data are basically unedited and unanalyzed.

Any given report may have different types of data in it. For example, data from self-report studies may include learners' retrospections about specific language learning behaviors, just as data from retrospective studies can include generalized pronouncements, extending beyond the observation of a given event. Furthermore, it is sometimes difficult to establish whether students are actually *thinking aloud* — without analysis — or whether they are instead *observing* that behavior, whether introspectively or retrospectively. For example, a student wants to learn a new word in Spanish, *sacar* "to take out," and is asked to think aloud while doing it. The report data may look like these data that I collected on myself:

> Let me see. It sounds like a "sack," like in "a sack of garbage." Is that the best I can do? Will I remember it? Let me picture myself actually taking out the garbage. O.K. Did that work? Yeah, I think so. I think I managed to learn that word by its similarity in sound to a word in English that can be linked to it by meaning.

Most of this report contains think-aloud data, but at the end I was self-observing retrospectively — when analyzing the process of finding a mnemonic aid for remembering the word *sacar*. When learners are left to their own devices, the choice of a particular mnemonic device for a given word will vary according to their language repertoire and learning preferences.

Descriptors of Data Types

There are at least six major factors which characterize the data obtained from the three categories of verbal report described above. These include: the number of participants, the research context, the recency of the event, the mode of elicitation response, the formality of elicitation, and the degree of external intervention (see Table 1). "The number of participants" refers to how many investigators and respondents take part in the data collection process. Informants may collect data by themselves, as in the case of diary studies when there are no directions provided by outside investigators (Schumann and Schumann, 1977, Bailey and Ochsner, 1983). Alternatively, one or more investigators can work with individual informants or with groups of informants at a time. The classroom teachers may be involved as investigators in this form of research, as long as their participation does not interfere with their teaching duties. Teachers, in fact, may be in a special position to encourage and train learners to report accurately on their learning.

"The research context" refers to the "when," "where," and to some extent the "how" of data collection. The data may be collected in the classroom — either during a class session, at a break, or after class. Similarly the data can be collected elsewhere in an institutional setting — as in a language laboratory or a video studio. The data could also be collected in a variety of other places — as is customary of diary studies. More formal settings allow for data collection procedures not possible elsewhere. For example, it is possible to seat informants at booths in a

TABLE 1. *Types of Data and Their Descriptors*

Type of data	Descriptors										
	# Participants			Context		Recency	Mode			Formality	Degree of External Interven.
	Gp.	Indiv. +Invest.	Indiv. Alone	Dur. Class	Other		Elic. O W	Resp. O W			
Self-Report	X	X	X		X	LO-HI	X X	X X		LO-HI	LO-HI
Self-Observation:											
introspection	X	X	X	X	X	HI	X X	X X		LO	LO-MED
retrospection	X	X	X	X	X	LO-MED	X X	X X		LO-MED	LO-MED
Self-Revealment:											
think-aloud		X			X	HI	X	X		LO	LO

Key:

 # Participants: group, individual + investigator, individual alone
Context: during class, other
Mode: elicitation — oral, written; response — oral, written

language laboratory and have each one tape-record think-aloud data at given intervals during a discussion or while reading a passage.[7]

"The recency of the event" relates to the proximity of the verbal report to the actual learning event. Whereas think-aloud data is obtained at the time of the learning event, self-observational and self-report data can vary with respect to how soon after the learning event they take place. Researchers may wish to increase the recency by methodological procedures. For example, the teacher could stop a class session to find out how a student's thinking led to a certain utterance (Cohen and Aphek, 1981). In a like manner, students could note inferences made during class sessions at the moment that these inferences occur — by jotting them down in their notebooks along with their other notes (Rubin and Henze, 1981).

"The mode of elicitation and response" concerns whether the investigator elicits the verbal report data orally or by means of written instructions (if there is an external investigator), and whether the informants respond orally or in writing. Both oral and written responses can be videotaped, providing a visual record of the event. Such a record may help in subsequent analysis of think-aloud — i.e., in checking the relationship between what learners were saying and what they were actually writing down on paper (see Jones, 1982; Tetroe and Jones, 1982).

"The formality of elicitation" has to do with the degree of formal structure imposed on the elicitation by an outside investigator. For example, self-report data could reflect a questionnaire with high formal structure, through a set of fixed questions (whether general or specific to a given learner) or with less structure through the use of a flexible questionning format, allowing for the respondents to provide information along the lines that they themselves determine. Oral interviews — more than written questionnaires — may cater to this flexible approach. In this case, the researcher later provides the structure to the responses through content analysis.[8]

The final factor, "the degree of external intervention," is the extent to which the investigator shapes the respondent's reporting process. Self-observational studies, for example, can be shaped through the types of instructions given the informants. For example, informants could write a diary on language learning reflecting any behaviors that they wish to describe, or they could be requested to limit their insights to one or more areas of interest to the investigator. Even think-aloud data can be directed along certain lines according to the investigator's instructions.

Table 1 has been filled out to show which descriptor variables tend to apply to particular types of data, or the extent to which the descriptors apply. These ratings are meant to be suggestive. For example, think-aloud data are usually collected orally from an individual by an investigator, out of class, at the moment the thoughts are taking place, with a low degree of formality of elicitation, and with little external intervention by the investigator. It would be possible to find exceptions to this pattern, and such variations might provide useful research insights.

Issues of Controversy Regarding Verbal Report

For many years, psychologists have been debating the merits of verbal report data as a research tool. It appears that at present, mentalistic approaches enjoy the modified support of a respectable group of cognitive psychologists (Bakan, 1954; Radford, 1974; Lieberman, 1979; White, 1980; Ericsson and Simon, 1980). As such approaches have become more prevalent in second-language research, reservations have begun to appear concerning the merits of applying verbal report data to this field (Seliger, 1983a). Whether such data can really be used as evidence regarding the inner workings of the learner's mind has been called into question.

An objection to using verbal reports as data rests on the assumption that much of language learning takes place at an unconscious level and is therefore inaccessible to mental probes. Seliger (1983a) sees verbal reports as at best a source of information on how learners *use* what they have learned, and not as a means of describing internalized systems responsible for interlanguage performance.[9] The issue is raised as to how much of verbal report is a description of the actual processes used in learning to understand and produce second language utterances and how much is *post hoc* guessing or inferencing based on production.

It is true that much of the verbal report data in second-language research to date has concerned language *using*, rather than language *learning*. But this is not to say that data on the processing of language in language learning is necessarily inaccessible. It is also true that after the particular learning event, it need not be clear to an outside investigator whether the bit of information has, in fact, been learned, and if it has been learned, whether it really has been learned the way that the learner says that it has. However, as we begin to accumulate descriptions of second-language learning events, patterns emerge which begin to take on a certain reality as they are corroborated by more learners.

Taking a somewhat historical perspective on this methodological approach, we note that at the same time that learners' errors were being analyzed to determine the nature of interlanguage, studies also began to appear which used learners as informants to better understand the process of rule learning (e.g., Cohen and Robbins, 1976). Although such studies generally focused on *what* had been learned or not learned, rather than on *how* it had or had not been learned, it was possible to use the learner's explanations of how they learned to reconstruct the way the particular forms came into the learner's interlanguage.

In eliciting data on the language learning process, we are both asking someone to use language to do certain tasks and also to use language to describe how they did these tasks. We are, in effect, asking for a description of language processing at the level of performing one's language competence. If there were some language learning involved, we would also be asking for a verbalization of the learning process as well. Thus, we are taxing the learner's capacity to remember a stage of performance once that stage is passed, and even to hold on to information within a single stage. Memory of mental events is problematic for the learner, and could lead to faulty reporting, but it then is the challenge for the researcher to tap this information while it is still available.

While it is true that much of what we process is done unconsciously, White (1980) would suggest that we underestimate the extent of conscious processing. The reason he gives is that we simply do not pay attention to all conscious processes. It has also been pointed out that the nature of the verbal report task itself will dictate the degree of attention we pay to our mental processing.

Evidence from self-observational studies calling for introspection shows that depending on the task, subjects may be successful at consulting their memory of cognitive processes and describing them. That is, subjects may have accessible memory for such processes and awareness of the information while the process is going on (Ericsson and Simon, 1980:245–246). This conclusion is based on an extensive review of the literature, involving a variety of cognitive tasks — e.g., learning lists of paired associates (A-B, B-C, then A-C), solving anagrams, verbalizing rules for sorting illustrated cards or other stimuli, discovering geometrical proofs, and solving a puzzle with disks and pegs or numbered tiles. We note that this series of tasks includes those requiring both linguistic and visual processes. In fact, it is not so unnatural to ask subjects to verbalize their reasoning dealing with nonverbal tasks since such tasks may well be accomplished with the assistance of linguistic processing.

For example, subjects may talk to themselves about why they are putting a disk in one place and not in another, or about why an illustrated card is being sorted into one pile and not into another. Such categorization tasks are an integral part of second-language learning, as in the learning of agreement between subject and verb in person, number, and gender. Just as cognitive psychologists may have subjects indulge in consciousness raising to try to determine how they accomplish tasks such as those listed above, so applied linguists can apply these methodological techniques to investigate the accomplishment of language learning tasks. As we will discuss in the next section, however, verbal report data must be collected with care.

Care in Collecting Verbal Report Data

In a recent study of the process of writing, Hayes and Flower (1983) corroborate a finding by Ericsson and Simon that introspective verbal reporting does not change or slow down the reporting of memory traces that are verbal.[10] They did find that if the respondents are asked to report information usually *not* attended to (i.e., within their realm of conscious awareness but receiving little or no attention), introspection does modify the normal sequence of mental processes. They also found in retrospective reporting that subjects forgot some information about processes that was available during the task performance: e.g., the writer would struggle with the choice of words and word order in a difficult sentence and then later deny having had a problem. As they put it, ". . . the delicate structure of goals and subgoals erected to construct the sentence was destroyed when the goal was accomplished" (Hayes and Flower, 1983).

Poor verbal report data are often the result of poor methods of reporting. Ericsson and Simon give three instances where this might happen. First, they claim that faulty reporting can result if the information is not attended to, since for information to be available from short-term memory,[11] it must be attended to (1980:224). Thus, in the case of probes requesting subjects to produce verbal reports about information not attended to, it is possible that the subjects will infer missing information and generalize incomplete memories. Secondly, they suggest that faulty reporting can result if not all the information which is in short-term memory at the time of the reporting, is actually reported. For this reason, it is important to utilize elicitation procedures that obtain reports that are as complete as possible. Finally, faulty reporting can result when not all information previously available in short-term memory has been retained in long-term memory, or is retrievable from long-term memory.

White (1980) adds that the reporting tasks should be easy — not requiring excessive concentration or effort. He also points out the need for the subjects and the researcher to conceptualize the situation the same way. In fact, faulty data may result from an inadequate understanding on the part of the respondents as to how they are supposed to report. Hosenfeld found, for example, that her respondents sometimes needed prodding in order for them to produce think-aloud data rather than retrospective data (Cohen and Hosenfeld, 1981). The fact is that respondents may need training in how to provide the desired form of data. It would appear that some pretraining and specific instructions may be necessary in order to have respondents reveal their learning processes.[12] For example, one researcher (Cavalcanti, 1982) found that left to their own devices, subjects asked to think aloud while reading would actually read large chunks and then retrospect. To avoid this pattern, she trained them to give think-aloud data each time they noticed that they had paused in the course of reading.

From all these considerations, it emerges that verbal report data can be a useful research tool under certain conditions and with certain limitations. Ericsson and Simon put it as follows:

> For more than half a century . . . the verbal reports of human subjects have been thought suspect as a source of evidence about cognitive processes . . . verbal reports, elicited with care and interpreted with full understanding of the circumstances under which they were obtained, are a valuable and thoroughly reliable source of information about cognitive processes . . . They describe human behavior that is as readily interpreted as any other human behavior. (1980:247)

Hayes and Flower (1983) point out that whereas verbal report protocols are incomplete because many important psychological processes are completely unconscious, the collecting of verbal report data is still beneficial in that it provides direct evidence about processes that are otherwise invisible, yields rich data and thus promotes exploration of cognitive processes.

The potential value of verbal report data to the study of language learning is similarly great. It may well provide further important insights for enhancing learners' attention to language input, facilitating their efforts to speak fluently, assisting them in reading more efficiently, and guiding them in successful vocabulary learning. As we find out more about the processes that learners use, we will be better equipped to test hypotheses about strategies that we would predict are likely to produce the greatest success for given types of learners. For example, as we learn more about the mnemonic devices that learners actually use to try to remember L2 vocabulary, we could perhaps design an experiment in which the learners would receive mnemonic aids which we hypothesize as most beneficial to them, given the vocabulary learning preferences we find them to exhibit (e.g., hearing a word vs. seeing it in print, seeing a picture of a word vs. hearing a description of the word). As the field of second language acquisition emerges, we will surely find more and more possible applications for verbal report data.

Notes

1. A more expanded version of this paper appeared in *Applied Linguistics*, 1984, **5**(2). I would like to thank both Herb Seliger and an anonymous reviewer for their helpful comments and encouragement.

2. "Strategy" is used here to refer to the mental operations that learners choose to utilize in accomplishing learning tasks. Some researchers prefer to reserve the term "strategy" for general categories of behavior (e.g., "viewing language as a system," "monitoring L2 performance"). They refer to more lower-level activities within a given category (e.g., "classifying the verbs into groups that are conjugated similarly," "checking to make sure that nouns and adjectives agree in gender and number") as "techniques" (Naiman *et al.*, 1975) or "tactics" (Seliger, 1983b). For our purposes, we will refer to all such operations as strategies.

3. One set of models about how attention works, referred to as the "capacity" models, would suggest that all simultaneous inputs can be processed to one degree or another in parallel. If the number of stimuli requiring analysis exceeds a certain capacity, the learner sets priorities in processing. Consequently, some stimuli will be analyzed fairly completely, while others will receive only superficial analysis. Some of the latter stimuli may still be available to conscious memory or awareness (Wingfield and Byrnes, 1981: 214–215). Thus, it is possible for one to be conscious of information but not attend to it.

4. Ericsson and Simon (1980) proposed a model for verbalization processes that is very similar to the one developed by Cohen and Hosenfeld (1981), with slight variations in terminology. They refer to "think-aloud probing," and to "concurrent" and "retrospective verbalizations," rather than to "introspective" and "retrospective self-observation," as in this paper.

5. One study had two groups of students retrospect about test items that they had taken — one group (n = 18) within six hours of having taken the test and one group (n = 23) three days later. In the first group, the first student started being interviewed thirty minutes after taking the test, the last student about five hours afterwards. The investigator noted few observable differences in the report data, other than a few more memory lapses among students in the group doing more delayed retrospection (Larson, 1981).

6. Mann (1982) describes think-aloud data as that produced when the subject "externalizes the contents of the mind while doing something." Accordingly, an alternative to "self-revelation" could be "self-externalization."

7. I am aware of only two studies that have utilized the language laboratory for purposes of obtaining simultaneous verbal report about language learning from each individual in a group. One was an investigation of college-level reading in Spanish and English (Serrano, 1984), and the other an exploration of second-language composing aloud in a remedial ESL college writing class (Raimes 1985).

8. Several research efforts on L2 learning strategies have utilized the semi-structured interview format, fashioning categories on the basis of content analysis of informants' responses. They include, for example, the interviewing of 34 learners by Naiman *et al.* (1975), four learners by Stevick (1981), and 25 learners by Wenden (1982).

9. Selinger's reference to verbal report as a source of information on how learners *use* what is learned can be interpreted as referring (1) to learners' application of L2 rules (cf Cohen and Robbins, 1976) and (2) to their communication strategies.

10. This study investigated native-language writing processes. It is possible that introspective verbal reporting in *second-language* writing may change or slow down reporting in that it would require switching back and forth between languages if the reporting were in L1, and could cause difficulties in self-expression if the reporting were in L2.

11. Short-term memory is defined by Ericsson and Simon as "information that is heeded or attended to. The amount of information that can reside in short-term memory at one time is limited to a small number (four?) of familiar patterns (chunks)" (1980:224).

12. There may sometimes be a fine line between providing enough external structure so as to produce the desired types of data and providing so much that the respondents feel inhibited. There is the further danger that the researcher may inadvertently plant ideas in the respondents mind.

Follow-up Activities

Discussing the Issues

1. Cohen has put forth some of the arguments made for and against the use of verbal report data — his

information is, in part, based on the work of cognitive scientists, such as Ericsson and Simon, who support this approach to data collection. A less optimistic view of the utility of verbal reports has been presented by Nisbett and Wilson (*Psychological Review*, **84**(3), 1977).

(a) Read both these articles.

(b) Summarize and evaluate both views on the utility of various types of verbal report data and the conditions under which such data should be collected.

Applying the Ideas

2. Cohen defines three types of verbal report — self revelation, self observation and self report. Use these categories to identify the kind of verbal reporting used in the studies in part 2.

3. Cohen also distinguishes verbal reports on the basis of six descriptors. Compare the studies in Part Two using these descriptors.

4. In "Learning about learning: discovering our students' strategies", Hosenfeld (*Foreign Language Annals*, 1976/9) illustrates how students may be trained to think aloud.

(a) Read the article. Then think aloud and tape record your thought processes as you perform one of the following tasks: (i) prepare your next class, (ii) read a newspaper, (iii) write a letter in your second language.

(b) Analysis the difficulties you had thinking aloud.

5. In her research Hosenfeld discovered that there was a discrepancy between what students actually learned from teacher-prepared exercises and what teachers expected them to learn.

(a) List some of the assumptions you may have about the utility of a typical language test you administer. Have a student complete the test and think aloud as (s)he does so.

(b) Examine the data to determine how the learner completed the tasks that constitute the test. Referring to the taxonomies provided in Chapter 2 (or 6) look at the strategies that were used. Also list the views the learner may have expressed about the nature of the tasks, his/her ability, feelings.

(c) Compare your assumptions about the utility of the test with what you learned by analyzing the student account.

6. Cohen has noted that researchers have found classroom observations of limited utility as a means of collecting data on students' learning processes.

(a) Go into a second language classroom and observe two students (cf Chamot Chapter 6 for a guide for classroom observations).

(b) Interview the same student. Ask about some of the tasks you observed him/her completing, i.e. how they were completed, difficulties they had and how they dealt with them.

(c) Compare and evaluate the data obtained through observation and self-report. Does your observational data vary with the kind of exercise your students are engaged in? Are your conclusions about observation data similar to those of Cohen and Chamot?

7. In question 1 you considered the utility of verbal report data on the basis of arguments put forth by researchers in the field. Complete the following activities to evaluate the data on the basis of your own experience, i.e. Would you use verbal report data? If so when? Which type? If not, why not? What factors would you take into account in collecting it?

(a) Observe yourself doing something you have learned to do well and something you're just learning to do. Describe the two instances in terms of extent and specificity of awareness.

(b) Before watching a favorite TV news program, determine for yourself what you intend to listen for. At another time listen without a particular purpose or focus. Again, compare the two instances in terms of extent and specificity of awareness.

(c) Interview a student about his/her past attempts to develop facility in some aspect of language learning, e.g. reading, learning vocabulary. Refer to Chamot's or Wenden's chapters for suggestions regarding questions to ask. At a different point it time, interview the same student while (s)he is trying to accomplish the same task, i.e. as he is learning vocabulary, reading in his second language. Compare the type of data collected in each instance.

Part Two

STUDYING LEARNER STRATEGIES

The earlier research reviewed by Rubin (Chapter 2) shows that L2 learners use three main kinds of strategies — learning, communication and social strategies. Papers in this section begin to look at the interactive nature of strategies, i.e. at strategies-in-context. The metacognitive literature (e.g. Brown *et al.*, 1983) describes three factors that interact dynamically with the strategies learners may actually use in a learning situation. These are (1) the task, (2) the characteristics of the learner and (3) the nature of the materials. In fact, according to Brown, these factors have been shown to be of interest not only to teachers and researchers but also to expert learners, who consider them when they plan their learning.

What is the relationship between a learning or communication task and strategy use in L2 learning? Papers by Thompson and Abraham/Vann suggest that some strategies may be more appropriate to the efficient performance of specific language learning tasks than others. Thompson's review of the literature on memory describes mnemonics that have had varying success in the learning and recall of vocabulary. The secret of the successful language learner studied by Abraham and Vann was his ability to choose strategies that were appropriate to the acquisition of the language skills necessary to function in college. The less successful learner was not as flexible in his use of strategies.

It also appears that the nature of the language learning task may determine the number and kind of strategies used. Chamot's high school learners, for example, used more strategies to perform discrete language learning tasks (e.g. vocabulary learning) than they did to perform integrative language learning tasks (e.g. listening). Abraham and Vann's analysis showed that the particular strategies used most frequently by both learners to complete three different kinds of formal learning tasks (i.e. fill-in the blanks, a cloze test, and a composition) varied for each task.

The learner characteristics Brown refers to are primarily cognitive kinds of knowledge and skills, including strategies. Cohen's survey indicates the somewhat limited repertoire of strategies high school and college language learners bring to the task of processing teacher feedback on their compositions. On the other hand, the studies of Chamot and Abraham/Vann confirm what was suggested by the earlier research. Good language learners are characterized by a varied repertoire of learning and communication strategies — two of the main types described in Rubin's typology. Chamot's study outlines a variety of cognitive and metacognitive strategies used by good language learners of high school age to perform learning and communicative tasks in both formal and informal settings. She notes a third type of learning strategy not documented in the earlier research, i.e. social affective. Her analysis also points to the fact that language proficiency of learners influences their choice of learning strategy. Abraham and Vann's case study of two college language learners describes a successful language learner who is distinguished by his varied repertoire of cognitive and communication strategies.

In Chapters 8 and 9, Wenden and Horwitz build on Wenden's earlier findings on language learners' metacognitive knowledge and beliefs (cf Chapter 2). These two studies show that learners have *explicit* views on matters such as (1) the role of foreign language aptitude, (2) the difficulty of language learning, (3) the role of culture in language learning, (4) personal factors that influence language learning and (5) principles that should guide one's approach to the task of language learning. Wenden's paper also illustrates how this knowledge was reflected in what her interviewees' did to learn and manage their learning. The relationship between learners' *implicit* beliefs and learner strategies is also referred to by Abraham and Vann. They suggest that implicit beliefs about language may influence the variety of strategies learners use and their ability to use them flexibly.

Thompson's review on the role of memory in language learning also includes literature on how learner characteristics and the nature of materials are brought to bear on the task of comprehension and recall of written discourse. Specifically, she summarizes what research in this area has shown about (1) the effect of learners' background knowledge, (2) the rhetorical structure of the text and (3) the trainability of reading strategies that would take advantage of the two preceding factors.

Chapter 4

Memory in Language Learning

IRENE THOMPSON

"The stream of thought flows on; but most of its segments fall into the bottomless abyss of oblivion. Of some, no memory survives the instant of their passage. Of others, it is confined to a few moments, hours, or days. Others, again, leave vestiges that are indestructible, and by means of which they may be recalled as long as life endures. Can we explain the differences?" William James. *The Principles of Psychology*. vol. 1. New York: Henry Holt and Co., 1890, p. 643.

Introduction

It is difficult to think of any educational goal for which the ability to retain information is unimportant. Human memory is crucial to the concept of learning. Since language learning is another instance of learning in general, memory is also central to the acquisition of linguistic skills. The ability to understand spoken and written language, and to produce it in speaking and writing depends on the ability to recognize and retrieve information stored in memory, and the difficulty in carrying out such tasks is often contingent upon the weight of memory demands that they require.

Given the importance of memory in second language learning, it is surprising to find that relatively little research is devoted to it. Most memory studies deal with material in the first language, while research on the role of memory in L2 learning is still in its infancy.

This chapter deals with memory as it applies to two aspects of second language learning: (1) vocabulary learning through various mnemonic techniques, and (2) comprehension of written discourse as measured by recall.

Learning Vocabulary Through Mnemonic Techniques

"Mnemonic" means "aiding memory" (Higbee, 1979) and since so much of language learning depends on being able to memorize and retrieve all kinds of language routines, it is somewhat surprising that foreign language learners, who should be prime customers for mnemonic devices, tend to know little about them. Often referred to as "memory tricks," mnemonics work by utilizing some well-known principles of psychology: a retrieval plan is developed during encoding, and mental imagery, both visual and verbal, is used. They help individuals learn faster and recall better because they aid the integration of new material into existing cognitive units and because they provide retrieval cues. Mnemonics can be adopted voluntarily, and once learned are difficult to forget. They are adaptable to individual learning differences, and most users report that they enjoy using them (Levin, 1981).

Linguistic Mnemonics

The Peg Method. This method allows unrelated items, such as words in a word list, to be recalled by linking these items with a set of memorized "pegs" or "hooks" which can vary from rhyming words to digits.

One well-known set of pegs is contained in the rhyme "one is a bun, two is a shoe, three is a tree, four is a door, five is a hive, six are sticks, seven is heaven, eight is a gate, nine is a line, ten is a hen." When a list of words is to be memorized, the first word is learned by forming a composite picture of it and a bun (e.g., if the first word is "cat" the image would consist of a cat eating a bun), the second word is learned by forming a composite picture of it and a shoe, and so on down the list. In learning L2 vocabulary, pegwords can be chosen from L2 making the pairing entirely in the second language. English-speaking subjects who studied French vocabulary using French pegwords remembered twice as many words as when they studied the same number of words by rote memorization (Paivio and Desrochers, 1979).

The peg method can also be used to learn grammatical categories. It led to better recall when it was used to teach French gender to English-speaking subjects who were instructed to form an interactive image consisting of the French word, the pegword and the image of a male or female to represent the gender of the noun than a traditional method (Desrochers, 1980).

The Keyword Method. This is perhaps the best known and most researched mnemonic technique. Developed by Atkinson (Atkinson, 1975; Atkinson and Raugh, 1975), it calls for establishment of an acoustic and imaginal link between an L2 word to be learned and a word in L1 which sounds similar. For instance, the German word *Ei* "egg" can be learned by first establishing an acoustic link with the English word *eye* and then conjuring up an interactive image of an egg with an eye in the middle of it. Similarly the Spanish word *pan* "bread" can be learned by imagining a loaf of bread in a pan.

The Keyword method has been shown to be effective in improving both immediate and delayed recall of vocabulary in several foreign languages (Atkinson and Raugh, 1975; Raugh, Schupbach and Atkinson 1977) as well as unfamiliar L1 words (Pressley, Levin, and Miller 1981). It helps adults remember words more easily (Pressley, 1977) and in a more lasting fashion (Atkinson and Raugh, 1975). It was found to be more effective for memorizing vocabulary in both first and second language than other methods, such as finding roots, learning synonyms, or using a meaningful context (Pressley, Levin and Delaney 1982). It has a comparably facilitating effect on foreign vocabulary recall for both high and low language ability individuals (Pressley *et al.*, 1980). It also appears to aid both recognition where subjects are asked to give an L1 equivalent to an L2 word, and production where subjects are instructed to provide an L2 equivalent to an L1 word (Pressley *et al.*, 1980). The method appears to work better if the keywords are generated by the subjects themselves (Delaney, 1978; Dickel and Slack, 1983), especially for learners with richer vocabularies (Pressley, Levin and Delaney, 1982).

Spatial Mnemonics

The Loci Method. To use this ancient technique, which dates back to the Romans who used it to memorize speeches (Yates, 1966), one imagines a familiar location, such as a room, a house or a street. Then one mentally places the first item to be remembered in the first location, the second item in the second location, and so forth. To recall the items, one takes an imaginary walk along the landmarks, mentally examines each one and retrieves the item one has "put" there. Subjects who used this method to learn lists of L2 nouns recalled almost three times as many words as those who learned the list by rote (Bower, 1973). In another study, subjects who used the spatial mnemonic recalled twice as many words in L1 after five weeks as those who studied the words by rote (Groninger, 1971).

Spatial Grouping. Rearranging words on a page to form patterns, such as a triangle, appears to improve recall. For instance, arranging L1 words in distinctive patterns on a page as opposed to just listing them in a column enhanced both immediate and delayed recall (Belleza, 1983). Arranging words in several columns on a page as opposed to listing them all in only one column was also helpful (Decker and Wheatley, 1982).

The Finger Method. Another variation of the spatial method is to associate the item to be learned with a finger (first item=left pinky, second item=left ring finger, etc). This method doubled the digit span after some practice when numbers were associated with fingers (Reisberg, Rappaport and O'Shaughnessy, 1984).

Visual Methods

Pictures. Pairing pictures with words in L2 results in better recall than pairing them with their L1 equivalents. This has been shown to be effective with such diverse languages as Russian (Kopstein and Roshal, 1954) and Indonesian (Webber, 1978).

Visualization. Instead of using real pictures, a word or the contents of a passage may be visualized. This is more effective than mere repetition (Steingart and Glock, 1973; Satz and Dunnenworth-Nolan, 1981). Since individuals with low verbal ability benefit more from visual than from verbal elaboration (Delaney, 1978), the visualization method may be particularly helpful for these learners.

The Physical Response Method

Physically enacting the information in a sentence results in better recall than simple repetition. Subjects who were instructed to pretend that they were doing something (e.g., "Pretend you are a chef flipping a pancake") remembered the sentence better than those who merely repeated the sentence "The chef is flipping a pancake" (Satz and Dunnenworth-Nolan, 1981). Some recent innovative classroom methods involve a certain amount of physical activity. The best known among them is the method of the Total Physical Response developed by James Asher (Asher, 1965, 1966, 1969, 1972; Asher and Price, 1967; Asher, Kusudo and de la Torre, 1974). There is also a significant element of physical action in the work of Rassias (1968, 1972) who uses melodrama in the classroom. The *Silent Way* of Caleb Gattegno (1972) also utilizes physical activity, requiring that students manipulate rods of different sizes and colors in response to certain commands. It has also been reported that individuals use the physical response strategy spontaneously in learning ESL (O'Malley *et al.*, 1983).

Verbal Elaboration Methods

Grouping. It is well known in psychology that if the material to be memorized is organized in some fashion, people can use this organization to their benefit. This happens because organized material is easier to store in and retrieve from long-term memory. Organization can be imposed by making the items to be learned fit into a pre-existing framework, or by creating some new cognitive framework that would bind the items to be learned into a unit which is structured in some fashion.

A great deal of empirical work dealing with organization has been done using a free-recall paradigm. In these studies, subjects are given a list of words to study and are later asked to recall as many of these as they can in any order. In one such study, subjects had to memorize a 60-word list containing 15 words from each of the following categories: animals, names, professions, and vegetables (Bousfield, 1953). Although the words were presented in random order, when the subjects attempted to recall the list, they recalled words belonging to the same category contiguously. For instance, they would attempt to recall animals before attempting to recall names. Another study showed that if a list of words is organized in some fashion before memorization, recall is improved (Cofer, Bruce and Reicher, 1966). In this study, subjects had to memorize the same number of words in the same amount of time but under two experimental conditions. In one condition, words representing different categories were presented in random order. In the other condition, the same words were listed contiguously under the different categories. As predicted, contiguous listing not only produced more clustering but also improved recall. In another study, subjects who were instructed to classify words into categories before learning them had better recall than subjects who simply memorized the list (Craik and Tulving, 1975).

Since grouping words in L1 enhances recall, it stands to reason that it would also facilitate vocabulary learning in L2. The question is, do L2 learners spontaneously use grouping strategies? O'Malley *et al.* (1983) reported that all strategies which require active manipulation of the material to be learned, including grouping, were among the lower frequency strategies cited by high-school ESL students. In addition, Chamot (1984) found that grouping strategies were more favored by students with greater ESL proficiency than by beginners. Finally, there is some indication that low-proficiency ESL learners rely more on sound similarities in recognizing vocabulary while high-proficiency learners rely more on semantic factors (Henning, 1974).

The Word Chain. Instead of associating each item with a cue, such as a pegword or a familiar location, each item in a list is associated with the preceding and following one. To remember "car," "house," "flower," etc., one forms an image of a car in front of a house, a house surrounded by flowers, etc., with each word cuing the recall of the following one. This method was successful when L1 words had to be recalled in the same order as the one in which they were presented (Delin,

1969). We do not know, however, if it would be helpful if words had to be retrieved out of the particular sequence in which they are presented.

The Narrative Chain. The story mnemonic is known to many classroom teachers but there is no research on its effectiveness in L2 learning. To use it, one links the words in a list together by a story. Used with children, the method proved to be highly effective in L1: subjects who learned 12 lists each consisting of 10 unrelated words by weaving the words into a story remembered seven times as many words as those who studied the words by rote (Bower and Clark, 1969). Since it has been shown that individuals with high verbal ability profit more from verbal elaboration than from mnemonics relying on imagery (Delaney, 1978), this method could be especially well-suited for high-verbal L2 learners.

Other Memory-Enhancing Techniques

Self-Testing. Practicing retrieval has been shown to improve long-term recall. For instance, subjects who were tested during the learning session involving the memorization of words in L1 demonstrated better long-term recall than those subjects who studied the material without being tested. This happens because of the increasing organization of the list since with each attempt at recall subjects organize words in the list into groups and more and more words are added to the groupings with each successive recall. During recall, subjects first retrieve the groupings and then report the words in the groupings (Mandler, 1967; Tulving, 1968).

Spaced Practice. It is a well-known fact in psychology that spaced practice leads to better long-term recall. It is also well known from practice that long periods of study are less helpful to L2 learners than shorter but more frequent study periods. Bloom and Schuell (1981) had subjects learn French vocabulary either in distributed (three units on three successive days) or in massed practice (all three units in one day). While the two groups performed almost identically during immediate recall, after four days, the distributed practice group remembered a third more words than the massed practice one.

Real-Life Practice. There are many studies which show that when material learned in one context is retrieved in another, memory performance tends to suffer (Tulving and Thompson, 1973; Godden and Baddeley, 1975). The military have long known, for instance, that memory for skills learned under safe conditions tends to disintegrate under stressful or dangerous conditions on the battleground (Jones, 1979). Military training, therefore, always includes practice under conditions which simulate the ones likely to occur in the field. This is not too dissimilar from language learning which usually takes place in the relative safety and calm of the classroom in a highly familiar environment. However, language skills learned under these conditions often have to be used under considerably more stressful real-life communication conditions. When this happens, as many a language learner has, no doubt, discovered, linguistic breakdown can occur. If language is to be eventually used in real-life situations, then the fidelity of simulation during training should be emphasized. This suggests that participation in real-life communicative situations during language training should be attempted at all levels of proficiency to ensure a greater match between encoding and retrieval conditions. Familiarity with stress, resulting from such training, will usually produce a diminished stress response in real life communication situations. The training would also allow the speakers to learn how to deal with their own stress responses and other unpredictable extraneous events surrounding communication without reducing their ability to retrieve the necessary linguistic information. Thus, language learners should be encouraged to engage in functional language practice, since as Bialystok (1979) noted, it consistently and significantly contributed to L2 achievement.

Summary and Conclusions

Although mnemonic devices have been around for many centuries, little empirical work has been done on their application to learning meaningful material, including material in L2 (Higbee, 1979; Belleza, 1981; Paivio and Desrochers, 1981). Most studies conducted in the last two decades involve the learning of words in L1 with relatively few studies devoted to L2 so that little is known to date about the underlying mechanisms of mnemonics and about the optimal conditions for their use in L2 learning. It seems clear, however, that what is known so far seems to generally support the notion that mnemonics, particularly the imagery keyword technique, enable learners to memorize vocabulary more efficiently.

Although the focus in L2 teaching in recent years has been on the acquisition of grammar, it cannot be overlooked that learners must also remember a great deal of vocabulary. While active manipulation of structure is usually heavily emphasized in the classroom, vocabulary memorization is often left to the individual learner. Moreover, although there are some suggestions to the teacher as to how to teach vocabulary, there is little guidance to the learner who asks: "How do I memorize vocabulary better?" It is in this area that mnemonic devices seem to hold the most promise, particularly where long lists of words are involved (Levin, 1981). An additional benefit of mnemonics may be that for less experienced language learners, learning how to construct and use various mnemonic devices may provide an opportunity to discover how their own minds work and how creativity with language pays off. At the same time, experimenting with mnemonics can teach beginning language learners that language learning is not all grim and that having fun may also be beneficial.

No discussion of mnemonics would be complete, however, without mentioning some of the questions which arise with regard to their potential use in L2 learning.

(1) Learning a mnemonic for a small amount of material may take more time than rote learning or some alternative method particularly if learners have to generate the mnemonic cues themselves (Belleza, 1981; Levin, 1981). If time is limited, mnemonic methods can lose their advantage over other methods (Bugelsky, Kidd and Segmen, 1968).

(2) The learner who automatically relies on a mnemonic may fail to perceive the inherent meaningfulness of the material to be remembered. Thus mnemonics are probably most useful for language materials which lack inherent structure, such as word lists (Belleza, 1981). At the same time, some researchers worry that forming

associations may force attention away from the meaning and contextual use of words, particularly polysemantic ones (Cohen, 1984).

(3) It is not known if continual use of the same keywords, pegwords, or locations may produce interference from words previously learned with the same mnemonic (Belleza, 1981).

(4) It is unclear if keywords can interfere with L2 pronunciation.

(5) People vary in their ability to form imagery (DiVesta and Sunshine, 1974) so it may well be that visual imagery may not be helpful to some individuals. For instance, children below grade 5 do not benefit from instructions to use visual images, and need to be provided with a keyword and an interactive image in the form of a picture (Pressley, 1977; Pressley and Levin, 1983).

(6) It may be difficult to generate mnemonic associations for L2 words representing abstract concepts (Pressley, Levin and Delaney, 1982; Cohen, 1984) and easier to do so for concrete high-imagery words because the latter may have richer association networks (Day and Belleza, 1980). Words with roots that are not easily identifiable can also make the forming of associations more difficult (Cohen and Aphek, 1980). Some classes of words are easier to learn through mnemonic devices than others: for instance, nouns are easier to learn than adjectives or verbs (Atkinson, 1975; Raugh, Schupbach and Atkinson, 1977).

(7) Strategies favored for a particular language learning task may be determined by learner proficiency level (Cohen and Aphek, 1981; Chamot, 1984).

(8) Efficacy of mnemonic devices may depend on individual learning differences. For instance, it has been shown that high verbal ability individuals profit more from verbal than from visual elaboration, while for low verbal ability learner the reverse holds true (Delaney, 1978).

(9) Subjective awareness of the workings of one's own memory (metamemory) is related to the adoption of memorization strategies. Research on the relationship between metamemory and memory behavior is still in its infancy but what is known so far seems to indicate that learners need explicit feedback on their own performance using different methods of memorization before they show awareness of the superiority of one of them and become willing to extend the method to other memorization tasks (Pressley, Levin and Ghatala, 1984). This means that learners have to personally experience that one method of memorization works more effectively for them than some other method before they will direct their subsequent strategy choices. In other words, instruction in the use of a mnemonic alone is not enough.

(10) There may be a cultural element in the utilization of mnemonic strategies. For instance, speakers of languages whose cultures emphasize rote learning, may be more reluctant to engage in visual and verbal elaboration on which various mnemonic devices are based.

(11) Most empirical evidence on mnemonics has been based on research in which subjects after having used a mnemonic device to memorize a list of words were tested by being presented with a L2 vocabulary item for which they had to supply the L1 equivalent. The question remains, however, as to how well they would be able to retrieve the L2 word in natural language use situations in which speed of retrieval is essential, particularly since there is evidence that speed of retrieval in L1 is slower when mnemonics are used (Corbett, 1977).

Reading Comprehension

Memory plays an important role in reading comprehension since, as Carroll (1972) pointed out, there is little use in comprehending a message unless the outcome of that comprehension is remembered. In addition, most tests of reading comprehension involve memory since in most studies of reading comprehension, subjects first read a passage, then the passage is removed and they have to answer questions about its contents. Evidence from such studies indicates that comprehensibility and recallability are highly correlated in memory for prose in L1 (Bransford and Johnson, 1973). Therefore, to the extent to which we can explain how texts are comprehended, we can also explain how the information contained in them is recalled (Rumelhart, 1977; Bernhardt, 1984).

Research on the comprehension of written discourse conducted in the seventies has also demonstrated that it is the result of an interaction between the reader and the text. The reader brings background knowledge and a certain set of reading strategies to the reading task at hand, while the text, on the other hand, provides the reader with a certain kind of rhetorical organization. Thus three major factors are involved in comprehending and storing the information contained in a text: (1) ability to use background knowledge about the content area of the text; (2) ability to recognize and use the rhetorical structure of the text; and (3) ability to use efficient reading strategies.

Effects of Background Knowledge

To a large extent, reading comprehension is a process whereby a message intended by the writer is recognized by the reader against the background of information already stored in the reader's memory (Bransford and Johnson, 1973; Rumelhart, 1975, 1977, 1980; Thorndyke, 1977; Bower, 1978; Kintsch and van Dijk, 1978). Research shows that the greater the familiarity with the content area of a text, the greater the comprehension and recall of that text (Stevens, 1982). For instance, people remember culturally familiar events and passages better than unfamiliar ones. Identical passages in L1 that had only a few words changed to redefine topic as familiar (e.g., game of horse-shoes) or unfamiliar (Indian game of huta) were recalled differently: the familiar version was recalled more accurately than the unfamiliar one (Freebody and Anderson, 1983). Americans and Indians who read letters about an American and an Indian wedding recalled more information from the native passage than from the foreign one (Steffenson, Joag-dev and Anderson, 1979). In addition, information recalled from the non-native culture was often distorted to make it conform to native norms.

There is also some evidence that background and cultural knowledge have an effect on reading comprehension and recall in L2. For instance, the cultural origin of a story (Iranian vs. English) had more effect on reading comprehension and recall of ESL readers than the level of syntactic and semantic complexity (Johnson, 1981). Similarly, familiarity with Halloween enabled ESL readers to recall a passage about Halloween and recognize sentences from it, while providing key vocabulary items before reading did not have a significant effect on comprehension and recall (Johnson, 1982).

Carrell (1983) studied the effects of three components of background knowledge on reading in L1 versus reading in L2. These were: (1) context-no context: presence or absence of title and picture page which informs reader in advance of reading what the content area of the text is; (2) transparent-opaque: presence or absence of specific words which provide cues to the content of the text; (3) familiar-novel: presence or absence of prior knowledge or experience of the content of the text. All three factors significantly affected the recall of L1 readers with no interactions among the factors. The results were quite different for L2 readers. Recall of advanced L2 readers was significantly affected only by familiarity with the topic. For intermediate L2 readers, none of the factors had any significant effect on recall. Carrell concluded that native readers read, understand and recall passages using context and familiarity with the topic to make predictions of what will follow using lexical cues to confirm or disconfirm their predictions. L2 readers, on the other hand, do not read like native readers. Being unable to make use of these cues they tend to be bound to the text, processing it linearly — one word at a time.

Effects of Rhetorical Structure of the Text

Each type of text (stories, expository prose, dialogs, newspaper and scientific articles) has its own structure, or text grammar, which is called "schema" after Bartlett (1932) and which can vary from language to language (Burtoff, 1983). Knowledge of how certain types of texts are organized helps readers to comprehend and recall the text (Meyer, 1975; Thorndyke, 1977; Kintsch and van Dijk, 1978). Even first-graders are aware of the schematic structure of stories, and use it to organize comprehension and recall (Mandler and Johnson, 1977; Mandler, 1978; Johnson and Mandler, 1980). Failure to activate an appropriate schema during reading may result in inability to comprehend the author's message. This may happen because readers either do not possess the schema intended by the author at all, or have failed for some reason to activate a schema that they possess.

Effects of Different Types of Textual Organization. Meyer and Freedle (1984) described five distinct varieties of organization in English prose which affect the reading comprehension of native English readers. These are collection (list), description (attribution), causation (cause and effect), response (problem and solution) and comparison (contrast). They concluded that the more tightly organized the passage, the better reading comprehension tended to be. For instance, recall of texts that had an overall organization based on causation, response and comparison was better than for collections and descriptions.

Carrell (1984) investigated the effects of different types of rhetorical organization of English prose on immediate and delayed recall of intermediate ESL readers of different language backgrounds. She found that they were similar to native English readers inasmuch as they, too, were affected by the overall structure of the texts. In a manner similar to native English readers, they recalled texts which were organized by causation, response and comparison better than texts which merely listed ideas and facts, or which consisted of descriptions. In other words, the more highly organized texts were easier to recall than the more loosely organized ones both for L1 and L2 readers with some variation in the effect of text structure related to the linguistic background of the L2 readers.

There is some evidence that readers of different language backgrounds react to the structure of texts in a culturally specific way. For instance, English and Japanese readers responded to stories organized in a typically English or a typically Japanese way differently (Hinds, 1982, 1983).

Effects of Hierarchical Structure of Texts. Several studies in L1 showed that the main ideas are recalled better than supporting details (Wilhite, 1983; Luftig, 1983; Kintsch and Young, 1984). Connor (1984) reported that L1 and L2 readers recalled the same number of main ideas from a newspaper text, but L2 readers were able to recall significantly fewer details from the text than native readers because of the need to allocate more memory resources to linguistic processing. Walker and Yekovich (1984) pointed out that increased processing may be necessary to improve recall of peripheral information.

Effects of Genre. There is evidence that the same content is recalled better if presented as a drama than as a narrative (Dubitsky and Harris, 1983).

Effects of Chronological Sequencing of Events in the Text. There is some evidence that recall is facilitated if statements in the text appear in the same order as the events they describe (Haberlandt and Bingham, 1984).

Reading Strategies

Studies of Good Readers. Several studies in L1 attempted to describe the characteristics of good readers. For instance, it was reported that good comprehenders among ninth-graders used the same overall structure of a text in organizing their recall as the author of the passage, but low comprehenders did not (Meyer, Brandt and Bluth, 1980). Another study showed that good readers activate a schema before reading a story (i.e. approach the story with an idea of how it is going to be structured) while poor readers do it significantly less (Whaley, 1981). Good readers recalled more topical than non-topical information from a paragraph by evaluating the information with respect to its relevance to the overall structure of the paragraph while poor readers did not make such a distinction (Eamon, 1978–79).

There is one study of effective reading strategies in L2. On the basis of self-reports, Hosenfeld (1977) noted that successful L2 readers kept the meaning of a passage in mind while reading and used the accumulated information to predict further meaning.

We do not know whether good L1 readers are also good L2 readers although there is some evidence that L2 learners fail to transfer their good L1 reading strategies when it comes to reading in L2. Clark (1979) referred to this non-transfer of good reading strategies from L1 to L2 as the "short circuit" and ascribed it to limited command of the language.

Teaching Good Reading Strategies. There are several studies which demonstrate that efficient reading strategies can be taught to improve comprehension in L1. We do not know whether the same strategies could be effectively taught in L2.

(1) Flow-charts and hierarchical summaries. School children were instructed to

flow-chart a scientific text in order to teach them how to search for text structure and to recognize its various components (Geva, 1983). This significantly improved their recall of the text since the memory load was lessened when the text was broken up into structural units. In another study, children who were taught to construct a hierarchical summary after reading a science text recalled more material than those who answered questions and discussed the text after reading it, or those who simply read the text (Taylor and Beach, 1984).

(2) *Titles*. L1 readers who were given a title to a vague passage before reading it had better recall than those readers who were given the title after reading or those readers who were not given the title at all because the heading helped make the processing of the text more meaningful by activating appropriate background knowledge (Bransford and Johnson, 1973). When the topic is provided before-hand, the reader (or listener) has available a schema that can serve as a source for generating appropriate predictions of meaning, that can assist in clarifying ambiguous points in the text, that can provide a framework for storing textual information in retrievable form, and that can help in developing a retrieval plan.

(3) *Embedded headings*. A simple technique of using embedded headings as advance organizers reliably improved delayed recall in L1 when subjects were instructed in the use of these headings as mnemonic aids (Brooks *et al.*, 1983).

(4) *Pre-reading questions*. Pre-reading questions which directed attention to the main ideas in the text facilitated recall not only of these ideas but also of other information and pre-reading questions about details also facilitated recall as compared to absence of pre-reading questions (Wilhite, 1983).

Hudson (1982) examined the role of schema in L2 reading comprehension by beginning, intermediate and advanced ESL students who were proficient readers in L1. Each group was given three graded reading passages. There were three conditions. (1) *Pre-reading condition*. Subjects were given a set of pictures about the general topic of the passage and then were asked a set of questions about each of the pictures. After that each subject wrote self-generated predictions of what s/he expected to find in the reading passage. Then the subjects read the passage and took a reading comprehension test. (2) *Vocabulary condition*. Subjects were given a list of vocabulary items which would appear in the reading passage. First they read the list silently, then the instructor went over the list aloud item by item giving definitions for all items. After that, subjects read the passage and took the same reading comprehension test. (3) *Read-reread condition*. Subjects read the passage silently, then took the same reading comprehension test. The procedure was then repeated one more time. Results showed that beginning and intermediate students scored higher in the pre-reading condition than in the other two. There were no significant differences in reading comprehension due to treatment type among the advanced learners. It appeared that advanced readers had less trouble using their background ("behind the eye-ball") knowledge when reading the L2 than beginning and intermediate readers, hence they profited less from prereading activities focusing on prediction of content of the passage. However prereading activities were especially helpful to less proficient readers. Hudson hypothesized that forming an idea of what the text is going to be about helped these readers to override their linguistic limitations.

(5) *Story-specific schema from general schema*. Singer and Donlan (1983)

conducted a study in which high-school students first learned a general problem-solving schema for short stories and a set of general questions derived from this schema. Then they practiced deriving story-specific questions from the schema-general ones. Results indicated that readers who made up such questions themselves recalled more information from the stories than readers who were given questions about the stories before reading them.

(6) *Imagery*. There is evidence that persons with high imagery ability are able to recall and recognize more items of information from texts than low imagers (Anderson and Kulhavy, 1972; Denis, 1982). At the same time, the performance of low imagers can be improved when they are instructed to form visual images while reading (Levin and Divine-Hawkins, 1974; Kulhavy and Swenson, 1975; Steingart and Glock, 1979; Denis, 1982). In addition, Denis (1982) found that high imagers remembered imageable material, such as descriptions/narratives better than low imagers, but there was no difference between high and low imagers in memory for abstract, nonimageable texts. Since both Meyer and Freedle (1984) and Carrell (1984) found that descriptive texts are harder to remember, imaging may be a particularly appropriate technique for this type of text.

(7) *Perspective*. Reading a story from a particular perspective affects recall in that idea units important to that perspective are recalled better than those that are unimportant to it. For instance, persons told to listen to a story about a house from the perspective of a burglar or a prospective home-buyer, recalled different idea units of the story depending on the perspective (Pichert and Anderson, 1977; Anderson and Pichert, 1978; McDaniel, 1984).

Conclusion

Almost a decade ago, a plea was made calling for research directed specifically at real-world use of mnemonic techniques (Ott, Blake and Butler, 1976). Little has been accomplished since then to call for changes in the research agenda for the decade to come. What is needed today, as was needed a decade ago, is a line of research which involves naturalistic observations in real environments where learners use spontaneously generated memorization strategies. The individual components of these strategies need to be examined in controlled studies to determine their unique contributions to successful memorization. This should, then, lead to the development of objective criteria for selecting from among a host of candidates those memory strategies that will contribute to more accurate and longer-lasting memories for second language material.

If we can isolate strategies which contribute uniquely to better recall in L2, we will have won only half the battle. It can only be fully won when learners discover for themselves that certain strategies can enhance their performance, and on the basis of this discovery are willing to continue using these strategies on their own. Good memory entails prior experience and practice, availability of meaningful associations, and efficient encoding and retrieval strategies. In addition, it is important to remember that it entails individual awareness of what truly does and does not improve memory performance and willingness to experiment with different ways of memorizing.

Follow-up Activities

Making Links

1. According to Thompson, "Memory is also central to the acquisition of linguistic skills." Interpret and evaluate this statement by referring to views expressed in the literature in second language acquisition and cognitive science referred to by Wenden in Chapter 1 (e.g. Hunt 1982; McLaughlin 1983); also see *The Natural Approach: language acquisition in the classroom* by S. Krashen and T. Terrell, Pergamon Press, 1983; *Applied Psycholinguistics* by R. Titone and M. Danesi, University of Toronto Press, 1985.

2. Although learners must remember a great deal of vocabulary, students are usually provided with little guidance as to how to learn, remember and use vocabulary.
    (a) Review two of your favorite methods books and/or recent articles from one of the second language journals (e.g. *TESOL Quarterly, Foreign Language Annals*) to determine:
    — what teachers are told about helping L2 learners learn vocabulary
    — what advice learners are given about learning vocabulary.
    (b) To what extent is the advice given by the methods books compatible with the research on memory described in Chapter 4?

Applying the Ideas

3. Think about the last time you had to remember something. What did you do to help yourself remember? What other strategies do you often use to remember? Can they be classified in terms of the mnemonics described in this chapter? If not, could the difference be related to the kind of material to be learned?

4. The mnemonics listed here have been used to remember vocabulary. Find out whether they would also be used for other memory tasks and if so, whether and how they vary from task to task.
    (a) Ask your students to list the "tricks" they use to remember (i) a telephone number (ii) directions to a place they've never visited before (iii) a new grammar rule (iv) the pronunciation of a new word (v) the meaning of a word.
    (b) Categorize the data in terms of the mnemonic techniques described in this chapter. Are they similar to those listed for remembering vocabulary in 3? Do strategies vary on the basis of task?

5. Thompson lists several factors that should be taken into account in considering the use of mnemonics in second language learning. Refer to these as well as to your own experience as a language learner to determine the following:
    (a) Which of the mnemonics listed in the chapter do you consider most efficient?
    (b) Which of the mnemonics would you consider most appropriate for particular learners (consider learning style, age, proficiency, educational background)?

6. Though there is still need for more research on the use of mnemonic devices, what is known so far seems to generally support the notion that mnemonics enable learners to memorize vocabulary effectively.
    (a) Summarize the findings regarding the effectiveness of various mnemonics for learning vocabulary in L1 & L2?
    (b) Test the applicability of these findings. E.g. have L2 students try to remember lists of words. First provide them with key words. Then, have them generate their own keywords. Compare the results.
    (c) List topics on which you think future research is needed.

7. Three main factors involved in comprehending and storing information contained in a written text are background knowledge, rhetorical structure, and reading strategies.
    (a) Summarize what research findings reported on in Thompson's article have demonstrated regarding the effects of background knowledge and rhetorical structure.
    (b) Use these findings to evaluate and predict the comprehensibility and recallability of the content of two second language readers — one you find effective and one you do not.
    (c) Test the applicability of the findings. For example, compare student recall on (i) a passage with no title or subtitles and one that has them (ii) a descriptive passage and a cause-effect passage.

8. There are several studies that demonstrate that effective reading strategies can be taught to improve comprehension in L1. We do not know whether they can be taught effectively in L2.

(a) Consider the reading strategies Thompson has described. Which ones do you think might be taught effectively?

(b) Have your students keep a log of what they do to help themselves understand and remember before and after they finish a reading.

(c) Compare their strategies with those listed in the Thompson paper. Are good readers and poor readers distinguished by the strategies they use?

(d) To what extent can good reading strategies help L2 learners override their linguistic limitations?

Chapter 5

Student Processing of Feedback on Their Compositions

ANDREW D. COHEN

While teachers may spend hours marking student papers, the question has been raised as to whether such corrections make a difference. Marzano and Arthur (1977), for example, studied twenty-four 10th-grade English-native-language writers assigned to three treatments, and found that students did not read the teachers' comments or read them but did not attempt to implement the suggestions and correct the errors. In a follow-up study with 141 university students who received one of four correction treatments while studying German as a foreign language, Semke (1984) found that corrections did not significantly increase writing skill. The learners' achievement was enhanced by writing practice alone. In fact, for those students whose purpose for writing is to learn how to shape and reshape meaning in an effective way, the teacher's red marks may serve as a distractor, shifting the focus excessively on to the form of the message (Sommers, 1982).

Furthermore, too much importance may be allotted to the role assumed by the teacher as arbitrator-reader and not enough to that of the student-writer in the developing of composing skills (Cumming, in press). Such an attitude could result in students doing their written assignments so as to please a given teacher (Raimes, 1983). These assignments are consequently relegated to the role of language exercises to be marked right or wrong. Then when the written work is returned embellished by teacher corrections, the students groan, put it away, and hope that somehow they will get fewer red marks next time (Raimes, 1983:141–142). The various critics of the current state of the art would like to see writing of papers as a multi-draft process with continual teacher-learner interaction, however possible this may be in the given teaching situation.

Part of the problem with the current state of affairs seems to stem from the nature of the teacher feedback itself. Several studies have investigated the ways in which teachers respond to student writing (Pica, 1982; Cumming, in press; Zamel, 1985). Pica found that in their corrections, teachers use some of the *same* errors that they are correcting in the students' papers — e.g., sentence fragments and underdeveloped paragraphs. Cumming (in press) found that teachers have been remiss in not incorporating insights from process approaches to feedback (i.e., not including instruction on aspects of composing as well as of written form), and hence have failed to assist students beyond the level of cosmetic adjustments. Zamel (1985) suggests that feedback usually tends to concern itself more with accuracy in form — i.e., surface-level features of writing — than with meaning. She conducted a survey of the responding styles of fifteen teachers of English as a second language. Not only did she find an emphasis on form rather than on meaning, but also a number of weaknesses in the feedback. The teachers both misread the text and consequently gave misguided feedback, or offered recommendations and corrections that were unclear or imprecise. Zamel further claimed that learners would rarely read through the comments more than once and that they rarely wrote subsequent drafts incorporating the teachers' corrections.

Research into feedback on compositions has mainly concerned itself with the "best" means of teacher correction on written work (e.g., Hendrickson, 1980; Cardelle and Corno, 1981), rather than with the issue of how students actually respond to each of these methods. To my knowledge, only two studies so far have looked at how native-language writers themselves respond to such external feedback on their written work.

Recent research was conducted by Hayes and Daiker (1984) with seventeen native-English writers during the second semester of a college freshman English course. The students were interviewed for approximately one hour each while they reacted aloud to feedback on a paper as if they had just received it back in class. At first they were just asked to react and then were asked questions about things they did not understand. The research report focused on five of the students, all in a class where the teacher was reported to be responding to papers "in keeping with the best pedagogical advice currently offered in our professional literature" (i.e., balancing criticism with positive reinforcement, avoiding abbreviations and correction symbols, noting improvement from paper to paper). The results showed that even in a course with an enlightened, process-oriented teacher, the students may still misinterpret the teacher's comments. The following is a listing of some of the findings:

1. The teacher asked the student to provide greater analysis of a given literary text, and the student thought he was supposed to provide a summary.
2. The student thought that "sentence fragment" meant that the sentence was out of place.
3. Because marginal comments were not anchored to the text by a circle or an arrow, the student did not know what to do with them. In one case, this involved the word "What?" In another, "good use of rhet. quest." was interpreted to mean "rhetorical quest" or search.
4. Short comments like "unclear," "explain," "be more specific" were generally found to be of little help to the students.

Another study (Kreizman, 1984) had ten native-Hebrew high school writers indicate for each teacher correction whether they understood it and whether they could implement it, with or without further explanation by the teacher. If a teacher's explanation was given, the students were asked to indicate how helpful it was. They were also asked to indicate whether they would be willing to ask for an explanation in the instances where none was provided. Kreizman found that when the students received their papers back, their primary interest was in their grade — that they only did a minimal reading of the teacher's comments. She also found that there were learners who listened to the comments that the teacher directed at the whole class and felt that therefore they were not obliged to read comments on their own paper.

In the field of second-language research, an early study I conducted alluded to this problem but no formal research appears to have yet been conducted on this topic. The study involved three Chinese-speaking ESL students (Cohen and Robbins, 1976) and included the request that the students indicate what their reactions were to the feedback when they received it. One of the students, a poor performer, Hung, reported that he did not keep track of the errors he made, nor did he seem interested in knowing about them — particularly if the grade was low: "The teacher always tell us to write papers and when she turn them back, if I get a bad grade — I never care about English that much anyway — so I just never go into it." It appears that much of the feedback was unclear to Hung. For example, when he was asked about a third person singular *s* deletion ("Now that he come to my mind . . ."), Hung replied: "If I read through the paragraph, it's hard for me to detect this errors. I guess if you mark it, then I probably might know the error on that one. If I read about twice or three time, I probably can't even detect it." Hung reported that he especially directed his attention to those forms that he thought were *correct* — the ones that had not been marked by the teacher: "Sometimes I try to experiment a little which way . . . I just turn in the paper and to see which way is not marked."

These studies prompted this survey which undertook to obtain verbal report data from students of first- and second-language regarding the way that they relate to teacher comments on the papers they write. The study sought to determine whether there was justification in providing students access to a repertoire of processing strategies for dealing with feedback. The justification would be that without such a repertoire, most students would ignore teacher feedback. Furthermore, such a repertoire would have to include choices that fit the learners' background, learning style, and level of language. The questions being investigated included the following:

1. What does teacher feedback tend to deal with and what form is it presented in?
2. How much of this feedback do students process, how do they go about doing this, and what forms of feedback might be difficult for them to interpret?

Research regarding learner strategies (see Rubin, this volume) and especially research dealing with metacognition in second language learning (see Wenden, 1986) have demonstrated that learners are able to describe their choice of strategies, their setting of priorities, and the way they evaluate the effectiveness of these strategies. This study relied on the students' ability to provide basic information regarding the set of strategies they use in processing teacher feedback on papers.

Methods

Subjects

The subjects were 217 students from New York State University at Binghamton. They were all studying in courses in which the writing of papers and the receiving of teacher feedback on them was an integral part. Sixty of the students were in freshman English rhetoric courses — two classes in basic writing (Rhetoric 100), one slightly more advanced (Rhetoric 110), and one the standard freshman composition course (Rhetoric 115); 34 in English as a second language classes — two beginning classes (ESL 101) and an intermediate one (ESL 201); 109 in French as a foreign language classes — two beginning classes (French 101), four continuation classes (French 102), and one intermediate class (French 151); eight in an intermediate German as a foreign language course (German 251); and six in an advanced Hebrew as a foreign language course (Hebrew 103).

The subjects were drawn from a variety of language classes and levels in order to see if papers written in different languages at different levels would produce differences in teacher comments characteristic of that language and/or level.

Instrument and Data Collection Procedures

A questionnaire was designed that would be brief (one page) yet informative regarding the form and substance of teacher feedback, and the ways in which learners dealt with this feedback (see Appendix). It asked the respondents to think of the last paper that they received back from their teacher — presumably a day or two before receiving the questionnaire. (The nature of the writing assignment was not specified with regard to formality or genre.) This survey questionnaire was not administered at the same time that the students were given their papers back so as to avoid the possibility that the questionnaire would influence the students' handling of teacher's comments. Thus, the intent was not just to describe the processing of teacher comments among those who make use of them, but also to find out how many students do not look at the comments or do so only sparingly. This meant foregoing think-aloud and introspective approaches, whereby learners would be asked to provide verbal report as to what they were doing at the very moment they were responding to teachers' comments — in favor of a retrospective approach (also see my article on verbal report techniques, this volume).

Findings

The majority of the students (81%) reported reading over all or most of the composition. Yet there were still 17% who reported reading only some of it, and 2% who said that they did not read it over at all. A similar distribution of responses was found for the item regarding thoughtful attention to teacher corrections — 80% reporting that they attended to all or most of the corrections, and 20% who attended to some, few, or none of them (see Table 1). It was also found that those students who were less likely to read through the entire paper and to attend to the corrections were the ones who rated themselves as poorer learners (see Table 2).

The students reported the most frequent type of teacher comment to be in the form of single words (average: 37%). Twenty-six percent were reportedly in phrases, 20% symbols, and only 17% in complete sentences. The teachers' comments across language classes and levels were reported to deal primarily with grammar (83% reported either "some" or "a lot") and with mechanics (74% indicated either "some" or "a lot"). Teachers apparently devoted considerably less of their time to vocabulary (47% "some" or "a lot"), organization (44% "some" or "a lot"), and content (32% "some" or "a lot") (Table 1). A crosstabulation of reported teacher comments by class showed that teachers of the more advanced classes did not provide more comments regarding vocabulary, organization, and content than did the teachers of the beginning classes (Table 3). For example, the English rhetoric teachers were all reported to provide limited feedback regarding the use of vocabulary, and in Rhetoric 110 there was also limited feedback

TABLE 1. *Frequencies of Student Responses to Feedback Questionnaire* (*data in percentages; n = 217*)

1. Percent of paper read over:
    all of it 47%   most of it 34%   some of it 17%   none of it 2%.
2. Percent of teacher's corrections given thoughtful attention:
    all of them 39%   most 41%   some 16%   few 2%   none 2%.
3. Average percent of teacher's comments reported to be:

single words	37%	(s.d., 28.10)
phrases	26%	(23.27)
symbols	20%	(26.33)
complete sentences	17%	(23.27)

4. The extent to which teacher's comments dealt with:

	a lot	some	little	none
grammar	41%	42%	14%	3%
mechanics (spelling, punct.)	37	37	22	4
vocabulary	13	34	38	15
organization	16	28	28	28
content	9	23	34	34

5. Student attention to teacher's comments on:

	a lot	some	little	none
grammar	59%	30%	10%	1%
mechanics (spelling, punct.)	44	37	16	1
vocabulary	35	44	17	4
organization	40	34	17	9
content	29	32	25	13

6. What Students did when they went over the teacher's comments:
    Made a mental note: 41%,
    Figured out the corrections: 4%,
    Wrote down points: 9%,
    Rewrote the paper incorporating the points: 9%,
    Referred to other papers: 1%,
    Looked over the corrections: 2%,
    Did nothing: 2%,
    Made a mental note and wrote down points: 9%,
    Made a mental note and referred to other papers: 2%,
    Figured out the corrections and made a mental note: 8%,
    Figured out the corrections and wrote points: 4%,
    Figured out the corrections and rewrote the paper: 2%,
    Wrote down points and rewrote the paper: 5%,
    Referred to other papers and rewrote the essay: 1%,
    No comment: 1%.
7. Teacher comments that students could not understand:
    17% had examples. (See text for sample comments.)
8. Student self-rating as learner:
    excellent 19%   good 70%   fair 11%   poor 0%.
9. Student self-ratings in the different language skills:

	excellent	good	fair	poor
writing	12%	55%	29%	4%
reading	26	59	13	2
listening	30	53	15	2
speaking	11	41	39	9

TABLE 2. *Extent of Reading over Paper and Attending to Corrections by Self-Rating as Learner*

(Mean ratings, one-way analysis of variance; n = 214)

| | Self-Rating as Learner | | | | |
	Excellent	Good	Fair	F Ratio	df
Reading over Paper	3.43	3.29	2.92	3.22	215
	* └———————————┘				
Attending to Corrections	4.45	4.16	3.63	7.24	214
	** └———————————┘				
	* └————————┘				

* *P* < .05.
** *P* < .01 (Scheffé multiple-range test).

TABLE 3. *Focus of Teacher Correction by Class (data in percentages)*

		Mechanics		Grammar		Vocabulary		Organization		Content	
Class	N	HI	LO	HI	LO	HI	LO	HI	LO	HI	LO
Rhet 115	(21)	67	33	55	45	6	94	60	40	35	65
Rhet 110	(16)	38	62	56	44	31	69	38	62	31	69
Rhet 100	(11)	50	50	73	27	20	80	70	30	60	40
Rhet 100	(12)	75	25	64	36	33	67	58	42	55	45
ESL 201	(15)	80	20	87	13	71	29	67	23	69	31
ESL 101	(12)	75	25	83	17	46	54	50	50	58	42
ESL 101	(7)	100	0	86	14	71	29	86	14	50	50
Fr 151	(20)	78	22	95	5	56	44	22	78	11	89
Fr 102	(10)	70	30	80	20	30	70	40	60	10	90
Fr 102	(8)	88	12	100	0	50	50	63	37	25	75
Fr 102	(18)	83	17	100	0	67	33	24	76	29	71
Fr 102	(6)	67	33	100	0	80	20	17	83	33	67
Fr 101	(21)	80	20	100	0	57	43	38	62	19	81
Fr 101	(16)	94	6	86	14	53	47	25	75	14	86
Ger 251	(8)	67	33	100	0	63	37	33	67	33	67
Heb 103	(6)	67	33	83	17	67	33	67	33	17	83

regarding organization and content. By the same token, the teacher of the more advanced French course was reported to provide limited feedback concerning organization and content.

Students reported attending extensively to teacher comments regarding grammar (89% reported "some" or "a lot") and mechanics (83% indicated "some" or "a lot"). Students also reported giving considerable attention to the areas of vocabulary (79% "some" or "a lot"), organization (74% "some" or "a lot"), and content (61% "some" or "a lot") — areas in which the number of teacher comments was noticeably limited. Those students who rated themselves as better overall learners also reported attending more to vocabulary, grammar, and mechanics than did those rating themselves as poorer learners (Table 4). Furthermore, those rating themselves as poor writers paid significantly less attention to the teachers' comments regarding grammar than did students who gave themselves higher self-ratings (Table 5).

TABLE 4. *Attention to Type of Teacher Comment by Self-Rating as Learner*

(mean rating, one-way analysis of variance)
Self-Rating as Learner

Type of Teacher Comment	Excellent	Good	Fair	F Ratio	df
Mechanics	4.64	4.23	4.05	5.61	199
Grammar	4.79	4.45	4.13	7.56	204
Vocabulary	4.52	4.04	3.90	5.23	184
Organization	4.20	4.04	3.90	0.55	164
Content	3.86	3.73	4.00	0.62	150

* *P* < .05
** *P* < .01 (Scheffé multiple-range test)

TABLE 5. *Attention to Type of Teacher Comment by Self-Rating in Writing Ability*

(Mean rating, one-way analysis of variance)
Self-Rating in Writing Ability

Type of Teacher Comment	Excellent	Good	Fair	Poor	F Ratio	df
Mechanics	4.46	4.28	4.27	3.88	1.27	199
Grammar	4.68	4.50	4.49	3.78	4.00	205
Vocabulary	4.16	4.14	4.02	4.00	0.34	185
Organization	3.82	4.07	4.10	3.89	0.38	165
Content	3.20	3.82	3.87	3.57	1.85	151

* *P* < .05
** *P* < .01 (Scheffé multiple-range test)

With regard to how students reported processing the feedback, by far the largest single group (41%) reported simply "making a mental note of the comments." Four percent reported "figuring out the corrections" as their sole strategy, 9% reported "writing down points," 9% reported "rewriting the paper incorporating the points," 1% reported "referring to other papers," 2% reported "looking over the corrections," 2% reported doing nothing, and 1% had no comment. Some students reported combining two strategies — "making a mental note" with "writing down points" (9%) or with "referring to other papers (2%); "figuring out the corrections" with "making a mental note" (8%), with "writing down points" (4%), or with "rewriting the paper" (2%); "writing down points" with "rewriting the paper" (5%); and "referring to other papers" with "rewriting the essay" (1%) (see Table 1).

In the English rhetoric and ESL classes, students were required to rewrite their papers. However, relatively few students from these seven English classes reported incorporating teacher comments in their revision — and most of these students were from only three of the classes. For example, in Rhetoric 110 the teacher called for two drafts, and conducted a 15-minute conference on the first draft. Three-quarters of the students reported revising their paper based on feedback from the teacher. In the more advanced Rhetoric 115, forty-two percent of the students reported revising based on the teacher's comments. In ESL 201 (intermediate level), the teacher called for three drafts, and conducted a one-half-hour session on the second draft. Her students were also requested to keep a notebook of mispellings and of grammar rules pertaining to their errors, and to refer to this notebook when proofreading papers. All the students in this class (n = 15) did report attending to most or all of the corrections, yet only four of them reported revising their paper based on the teacher's comments, while another four reported making only a mental note of these comments. In the other English rhetoric and ESL classes, revision based on teacher feedback was more limited. In the classes in other languages, revision was not required and was, in fact, negligible, according to student report.

When we look at student processing strategies in terms of self-reported writing ability, we see that the students who rated themselves as better writers were also more likely to rely exclusively on making a mental note of teacher comments. Fifty-six percent of those who rate themselves as excellent writers reported that they just made a mental note, while only 23% of the small group of those designating themselves as poor writers did so. Those rating themselves as poor writers were also the most likely to rewrite their paper (22%) or to write down points as well as rewriting (22%) (see Table 6).

TABLE 6. *Choice of Processing Strategy by Self-Rating in Writing Ability*

(data in percentages)

	Self-Rating in Writing Ability			
	Excellent (n = 27)	Good (n = 117)	Fair (n = 60)	Poor (n = 9)
Made a mental note	56	38	43	23
Figured out the corrections	0	4	5	0
Wrote points	4	8	15	11
Rewrote the paper	7	8	10	22
Referred to other papers	0	1	3	0
Looked over the corrections	0	2	5	0
Did nothing	0	2	0	11
Made a mental note and wrote points	7	12	5	0
Mental note and reference to other papers	4	2	3	0
Figured out corrections and mental note	7	11	4	0
Figured out corrections and wrote points	7	5	0	0
Figured out corrections and rewrote paper	4	1	4	0
Wrote points and rewrote paper	4	4	3	22
Reference to other papers and rewrote	0	2	0	0
No comment	0	0	0	11

Seventeen percent of the students indicated at least one teacher comment that was not understood. The students suggested that most of their queries were handled in class at the time the papers were passed back, or, in some cases, in private consultation with the teacher. The following is a list of comments (in quotes) which students indicated to be unclear to them, followed in some cases by student comment:

"This could be clearer." (ESL 101)
"needs transition" I didn't understand this comment. (ESL 101)
"arrows" Not clear how to interpret them. (Hebrew 103)
"not clear" What isn't clear? (Rhet 115)
"confusing" What is confusing? (Rhet 115)
"avoid 100% statements." (Rhet 115)

Thus, in this sample, teacher feedback that was difficult to interpret involved vague statements about clarity or confusion, use of arrows without explanation, allusion to transition without an example, and admonitions regarding the strength of claim the writer was making.

In summary, this study sought answers to certain questions regarding the handling of teachers' feedback on papers written in first- and second-language classrooms. The survey nature of the study provided data on a large cross-section of students. The results indicated the following:

1. Whereas most students read over all or most of a paper returned to them and attended to all or most of the corrections, still a fifth of the students surveyed did so only sparingly or not at all. The self-rated poorer learners were also less likely to read through the paper and attend to the corrections.
2. For the students who were attending to comments, these comments were being transmitted primarily in the format of single words or short phrases, dealing primarily with mechanics and grammar, both in the elementary and in the more advanced courses. When students indicated that they did not understand teacher comments, these comments tended to be in the form of single words or short phrases — e.g., "confusing" or "not clear."
3. Not only did students report paying considerable attention to teacher comments concerning mechanics and grammar, but they also reported paying much attention to comments regarding vocabulary, organization, and content — areas where teacher comments were reportedly lacking. Those rating themselves as better learners paid more attention to comments on vocabulary, grammar, and mechanics than did poorer learners. Also, poorer writers paid less attention to grammatical comments than did the other students.
4. With regard to the nature of student processing of feedback, the most popular strategy by far seemed to be that of simply making a mental note of the teacher's comment. The rewriting of papers was reportedly limited, and more prevalent among students who rated themselves as poor writers.

Discussion

This study suggested that learners have a limited repertoire of strategies for processing teacher feedback. The learners in this study mainly just made a mental note of the teacher's comments, as opposed to writing down points for future revision, referring to other papers, and especially, revising their paper with the incorporation of teacher comments. Self-rated poorer learners and poorer writers in particular appeared to have an even more limited repertoire of strategies. Although it has been claimed that feedback is only valuable if the composition is subsequently revised (e.g., Gorman, 1979:198), it would appear that such revision takes place only infrequently.

Learners were asked whether they read over their paper when they got it back in order to see if they refreshed their memories enough to give the teacher's comments a meaningful context for interpretation. They were asked whether they attended to comments (and if so, to which ones) in order to see if a selection process was going on. The fact that 80% of a cross-section of students from various first- and second-language classes did read over their papers when they were returned, and that a similar percent attended to the teacher's comments on the papers, showed that these basic steps in processing were generally going on. Yet this study demonstrated that we cannot assume these basic steps are taken. As it turned out, one-fifth of the students performed these activities sparingly, if at all, and students who were perhaps in greatest need of input from the teacher — namely, those who rated themselves as poorer learners — were also least likely to read over their papers and to attend to the corrections,

The self-rated better learners indicated among their repertoire of strategies a willingness to pay more attention to the basics of writing — mechanics, grammar, and vocabulary, with those viewing themselves as good writers indicating special attention to comments concerning grammar. This would suggest that while writing may be a creative process, successful creativity does not take place at the expense of basic matters of form. In this study, it was also the case that those most likely to report themselves as just making a mental note were those rating themselves as better writers. It may be that a good mental note on one item is worth more than making a list of ten items, if genuine learning goes on in the former case but not in the latter. It may also be that those rating themselves as good writers do not really need the teacher's comments in order to improve their writing. Either these students had already concluded from their previous learning experiences that input has little effect on growth and improvement in writing (Vivian Zamel, *personal communication*) or perhaps they had gotten to be better writers by doing more than making a mental note at an earlier stage in their learning.

In contrast to the situation with self-rated better writers, a quarter of those rating themselves as poor writers did, in fact, report both writing down points and rewriting their papers incorporating comments. It may be that the poorer students wrote down more points and did more rewrites because they were asked by the teacher to do so. This says nothing about the quality of these points or of the rewrite, which may constitute nothing more than a time-consuming copying task with little genuine learning going on.

The results of this survey would suggest that the activity of teacher feedback as currently constituted and realized may have more limited impact on the learners than the teachers would desire. The results show that sometimes it may be too abbreviated in nature, too general, and possibly not focused enough in the areas where learners want feedback for it to have much impact on the learners. For example, while teachers were reported to respond primarily with single words or phrases, students reported that it was especially these short comments that were sometimes the most uninformative (e.g., "not clear," "needs transition," and so forth). In addition, even in the more advanced courses that were supposedly focusing on discourse more than on mechanics and grammar, teachers' comments were not reported to deal more with vocabulary, organization, or content than were the more beginning courses. This finding is consistent with Zamel's (1985) finding that teacher feedback tends to concern itself more with accuracy in form than with meaning.

The fact the students reported paying considerable attention not just to grammar and mechanics, but to comments regarding vocabulary, organization, and content as well, suggests that there may be somewhat of a mismatch between the type of information sought by the learners and that provided by the teachers. It may be that teachers mark for mechanics and grammar more because these areas are the easiest to respond to, or the ones that are most conspicuously in need. Comments relating to the other three areas may demand a higher degree of judgment and most likely take more time. Means of providing stylistic feedback to students beyond that which is provided by the teacher have been suggested. One such technique is that of "reformulation," wherein non-native writers compare their best, most revised version of a paper with a version prepared by a competent native writer. The native writer is requested to preserve all the ideas found in the non-native paper, while expressing them in his or her own words (see Cohen, 1983). Successful use of a technique such as this one usually requires some learner training.

With respect to the research design, it is possible that the study itself produced certain reactive effects. For example, knowing that they would give out a student questionnaire assessing feedback procedures, several teachers may have altered their feedback somewhat. Furthermore, some of the students (particularly the foreign ones) may have been reluctant to criticize their teacher even though the questionnaires were answered anonymously. If there were such effects, however limited, then the payoff to teacher feedback may be even more limited than this survey suggests. In any event, it may be concluded from this study that there is room both for learner training regarding the various strategies available for handling teacher feedback and for teacher training with respect to more effective feedback for student writers. In addition, those students who rate themselves as poorer learners in general and poorer writers in particular may stand to benefit the most from such learner training.

Notes

1.   I gratefully acknowledge the feedback I received from Vivian Zamel, Anita Wenden, Joan Rubin, Alister Cumming, Craig Chaudron, Ann Raimes, Tom Robb, and Steven Ross at various stages of this effort. My thanks also go to Marsha Bensoussan for coordinating the data collection, to the students who made this research study possible, and to the following teachers: Victoria Belankaya-Hagopian, Dick Boswell, Valerie Chambliss, Danielle Datta, Roger Davis, David Howland, M. Lakich, Samuel Morell, Laura Paykin, Susan Ratchford, David Sibbitt, Bet Tricomi, Jacqueline van Baelen, Larry Wells and James Wright.

Appendix. Feedback Questionnaire

Please think of the last essay(s) that your teacher corrected and returned to you. You will be asked questions about what you did with this feedback from your teacher. Please answer as honestly as you can.

1. How much of the essay did you read over when you got it back?
   All of it_____. Most of it_____. Some of it_____. None of it_____.

2. How many of the teacher's corrections did you give thoughtful attention to?
   All of them_____. Most_____. Some_____. Few_____. None_____.

3. Please describe the type of comments the teacher made. What percent were symbols_____, single words_____, phrases_____, complete sentences_____. (Please enter approximate percentages, totalling 100%.)

4. To what extent did these comments deal with:

	a lot	some	little	none
mechanics (spelling, punct.)				
grammar				
vocabulary				
organization				
content				

5. If you attended to the teacher's comments, how much attention did you give to items involving:

	a lot	some	little	none	not applicable
mechanics (spelling, punct.)					
grammar					
vocabulary					
organization					
content					

6. Please describe what you did when you went over the teacher's comments. For example, did you just make a mental note of the feedback? Did you write down points to consider for revision or for future use? Did you rewrite the essay incorporating the feedback?_____

7. Were there any teacher comments that you did not understand? If so, what were they like? (E.g., "Be more precise here.")_____

8. How would you rate yourself as a learner?
   excellent____ good_____ fair_____ poor_____

9. How would you rate yourself in the different skills?

	excellent	good	fair	poor
writing				
reading				
listening				
speaking				

10. Native language_____
11. Name (optional)_____.
12. Class_____
13. Teacher_____

Follow-up Activities

Making Links

1. Cohen's paper questions our assumptions about the effectiveness of teacher feedback on compositions. His findings suggest three reasons why it may not make a difference. What are they? Referring to the research on feedback in second language learning and to theories on information processing, discuss whether you would expect this type of feedback to lead to learning, i.e. more facility in the written language?

2. Cohen lists several factors that might determine whether and how L2 students attend to and process teacher feedback on composition. What are they? Refer to readings in L2 theory and your classroom experience to suggest others.

Applying the Ideas

3. How do you process the feedback you receive on (a) your academic work (b) your teaching? e.g. do you consider it useful? attend to the feedback? What strategies do you use to deal with it?

4. Cohen's study suggests that feedback on compositions should vary from student to student.

(a) Analyze the feedback you gave on one set of student compositions. Refer to the categories listed in questions 3 & 4 of Cohen's survey instrument to categorize your comments (e.g. symbols, phrases, . . . dealing with mechanics, grammar, vocabulary . . .).

(b) Note whether and how your feedback may differ from student to student and try to determine why this is so.

5. The following reasons have been put forth to explain why students do not pay attention to teacher's feedback — they are interested only in the grade (cf Kreizman, 1984); they feel the teacher's comments to the whole class are sufficient; they consider that the teacher's feedback has little effect on their growth and improvement. Administer Cohen's questionnaire to your students.

(a) Have them also indicate their reasons for the answers they give to 1, 2 and 5, i.e. why do they (or do they not) reread the essay? consider (or not consider) the teacher's comments?

(b) Compare the students' answers to the questions regarding the feedback the teacher gives (i.e. 3, 4, 5 and 7) with the analysis you completed (question 2). Were students' perceptions consonant with your practice? What are the implications of some of the discrepancies in perception for your teaching practice?

(c) Note the reasons your students listed for not paying attention to teachers' feedback and use them together with the reasons listed above to devise a second survey instrument dealing with student views on the utility of feedback. Have them complete the survey. Then, discuss the reasons for their opinions. In the context of the discussion, have them consider alternative viewpoints and approaches to dealing with feedback on their compositions.

6. The students in Cohen's sample reported using 14 different strategies.

(a) Which would you consider most effective? Why?

(b) Together with a group of teachers, brainstorm for the kinds of strategies you would recommend that second langauge writers use in dealing with feedback on their compositions.

(c) Use this list to develop a survey instrument to determine which strategies students use to deal with feedback on composition. Administer it to your students.

(c) Note the responses of good writers and poor writers. Are they consistent with the students' assessment of themselves made in response to 9 of the Cohen survey instrument, i.e. are the students who categorized themselves as good writers distinguished by the strategies they use?

(d) Have students bring a copy of the survey instrument to a writing conference and discuss with them which strategies might be appropriate for dealing with their specific writing difficulties.

7. Data obtained through structured questionnaires, such as the one you used in 6, has been criticized because it forces respondents to choose from one of several alternatives. Moreover, one does not know how respondents may have interpreted the questions. Finally, when respondents retrospect, they may report doing what they think they do or should do. The validity of information obtained in this way can, therefore, be determined by obtaining self-reports from a small group of students as they complete a task or just after it.

(a) Conduct a follow-up interview with one or two of the students who completed the survey you developed and administered (6) to determine the consistency of students' responses.

(b) During this interview have them think aloud or self-observe as they go over the comments on a composition. Analyze and compare the data obtained from both kinds of student accounts. E.g. is it consistent?

(c) How would the insights gained about these students influence your teaching strategies? course content?

Chapter 6

The Learning Strategies of ESL Students[1]

ANNA UHL CHAMOT

Introduction

What can I do to help my students become proficient in English? All ESL teachers have asked this question and have tried to find answers through a variety of means. They have espoused one method or another, tried eclectic combinations of methods, or even eschewed methodology completely.

If learning is to take place, it usually involves the collaboration of two people — a teacher and a learner. The teacher cannot do it all alone, and most learners find the difficulties of doing it all alone overwhelming. Of course, it is true that many second language learners are able to acquire facility in social language use through exposure to the new language in communicative contexts, and it has been suggested that this type of "natural" second language acquisition is a largely unconscious process (Krashen, 1982). Teachers find, however, that this type of communicative competence is not sufficient for students to participate successfully in the mainstream curriculum. Students also need to develop academic competence, or the ability to use the second language as a learning tool (Saville-Troike, 1984). In trying to develop their students' communicative and academic competence, ESL teachers may wonder why some of their students seem to learn rather easily, while others apparently find learning English fraught with difficulties.

This chapter addresses these issues by describing a study which investigated ways in which some good language learners made conscious efforts to learn English more efficiently. After describing how the learning strategies of these good language learners were identified, some suggestions are provided for teachers on how these examples of personal learning strategies could be used to help more linguistically naive students discover some special tricks and shortcuts to make second language learning easier.

Learning strategies are techniques, approaches, or deliberate actions that students take in order to facilitate the learning and recall of both linguistic and content area information.[2]

Background and Literature Review

Investigation of students' learning strategies is a relatively new endeavor in the field of second language learning. Studies of second language learners have classified learning strategies in various ways, making it difficult in many cases to compare strategies reported in one study with those reported in another.

The study of learning strategies outside the field of second language learning has a much larger body of literature and a longer history of identification, classification, and training of learning strategies. Therefore, our review of the literature (O'Malley, Russo and Chamot, 1983) looked at research on the use of learning strategies not only in second language acquisition and learning but also examined studies of learning strategies for learning tasks in a first language. A valuable insight gained from reviewing these studies was identification of a classification scheme that was capable of subsuming the various types of learning strategies identified by second language researchers.

Brown and Palinscar (1982) classified general learning strategies as meta-cognitive or cognitive, and this distinction is also useful in classifying the strategies used by second language learners. In Brown and Palinscar's view, metacognitive strategies involve thinking about the learning process, planning for learning, monitoring of learning while it is taking place, and self-evaluation of learning after the learning activity. Metacognitive strategies can be applied to virtually all types of learning tasks, whereas cognitive strategies are more directly related to a specific task and learning objective and may not be applicable to different types of learning tasks. Cognitive strategies involve manipulation or transformation of the material to be learned; in other words, the learner interacts directly with what is to be learned. Cognitive strategies can vary in the amount of learner interaction or transformation involved; greater involvement is thought to result in increased learning. A third type of learning strategy identified in the literature on learning tasks in a first language involves affective and social components. McDonald *et al.* (1979) found that students trained to use a cooperative learning strategy for reading comprehension outperformed those who worked individually, and a subsequent study found that cooperative learning was most effective when students with differing cognitive styles were paired (Larson and Dansereau, 1983). In the field of second language learning literature, this third type of strategy is generally referred to as affective (see, for example, Naiman *et al.* 1978, and Rubin and Thompson, 1982).

Learning strategies in the second language literature can also be classified within these three general categories, that is, as metacognitive, cognitive, or social-affective in nature.

The research already accomplished in second language learning strategies, which is described in detail in Chapter 2 indicates quite clearly that at least some students do apply particular strategies to learning a second language, and that these strategies can be described and classified.

Description of the Study

A two-phase study was designed to explore further the identification, classification, and application of learning strategies to English as a second language. The first or descriptive phase of this study was undertaken in order to discover what learning strategies high school ESL students use on their own to facilitate their learning of English (O'Malley *et al.*, 1983; 1985). The second phase of the study was experimental in design, and is reported elsewhere in this volume by the principal investigator of the study, J. Michael O'Malley (see also O'Malley *et al.*, 1985). This chapter reports on the descriptive phase of the study, in which we observed classes and interviewed students and teachers to find out what learning strategies students were using to help them learn English.

Objectives. The purposes of the descriptive ESL learning strategies study were to:

- identify the range and variety of learning strategies used by high school ESL students who were good language learners,
- classify the learning strategies identified into a framework that could be used by researchers and teachers, and
- discover which strategies were associated with particular language learning activities and whether there were differences in strategy use between beginning and intermediate level students.

Subjects. The subjects of the study were 70 ESL students and 22 of the teachers in three suburban high schools in northern Virginia. Except for five Vietnamese students, the students interviewed were from Central and South America and Puerto Rico. They had been classified by their school as at the beginning or intermediate level of ESL, and had been nominated by their teachers as "good" language learners.

The teachers interviewed and observed had volunteered to participate in the study. All held secondary teaching certificates and had a minimum of two years of teaching experience. Teachers employed a variety of methodologies, ranging from audiolingual to grammatical and communicative approaches in ESL classes, and from lecture to demonstration and small group hands-on activities in content classes.

Instruments. The instruments used in the data collection were class observation guides and interview guides for teachers and students. The class observation guide, besides calling for identifying information on the teacher, school, subject (e.g., ESL: Grammar, ESL: Reading; Biology, etc.), and proficiency level of students, also asked for information on the following aspects of the class:

Source	Did the strategy originate from the student or the teacher?
Activity	What instructional activity was the strategy used on? Vocabulary? Grammar drills? Listening comprehension?
Setting	Was the strategy used when whole group instruction was being delivered, when small group activities were taking place, or when an individual student was interacting on a one to one basis with the teacher?
Materials	What instructional materials were used by the teacher and/or students at the time of the strategy use?
Approach	What did the teacher and/or students say or do as the strategy was being implemented?

The student interview guide (see Table 1) was designed to elicit from students the types of learning strategies they used for specific English learning tasks. The guide for interviewing teachers had a similar format and elicited the learning strategies they either overtly taught or had observed their students using for the same learning tasks.

Methodology. Class observations were conducted of ESL classes and selected content area classes for a four day period immediately prior to the interviews. Pairs of researchers took notes following the class observation guide described above, and then compared observation notes in order to establish reliability.

TABLE 1. *Student Interview Guide*

1 — PRONUNCIATION
Your teacher wants you to pronounce several words. He/she says them aloud. Then you must repeat them, using the same pronunciation as your teacher.

My questions are:

1.   Do you do this activity in your class?
2.   Do you do this outside of class?
3.   What special ways do you have to make sure that you copy the teacher's pronunciation? (How do you remember the pronunciation?)

2 — ORAL DRILLS/GRAMMAR EXERCISES
Your teacher asks you to: (Pick an appropriate example)

1.   Repeat a sentence
2.   Memorize a dialogue
3.   Change verb tenses (give example)
4.   Change positive to negative (give example)
5.   Answer questions (give example)

My questions are:

1.   Do you do this in your class?
2.   How do you remember what the teacher says?
3.   Do you use any special techniques or ways to help you understand the sentences?

3 — VOCABULARY LEARNING
You are asked to learn the meanings of ten new words in English.

My questions are:

1.   Do you do this in your class?
2.   Do you have any special tricks to help you learn and remember new vocabulary words?

4 — INSTRUCTIONS/DIRECTIONS
In this situation, your teacher asks you to understand directions on how to do something in (chemistry lab, physical education class, driver's education, home economics, or shop class). You must understand what the teacher says, remember the steps needed to do the activity, and then actually do it yourself.

My questions are:

1.   Do you do this type of activity in any of your classes? Outside of class?
2.   Do you use special tricks to help you understand or remember?
3.   What do you do if you forget what to do next as you are doing the activity?

5 — COMMUNICATION IN A SOCIAL SITUATION
You are talking to some people who only speak English. You must listen to what they say, understand the meaning, and speak yourself.

My questions are:

1.   What do you do that helps you understand?
2.   What do you do that helps you remember new words or phrases?
3.   What do you do that helps you talk?

6 — OPERATIONAL (FUNCTIONAL) COMMUNICATION
You want to find a part-time job. Or you need to buy a present in a store. Or you need to make an important telephone call for information.

My questions are:

1.   Do you do this type of activity outside of school?
2.   Do you prepare beforehand? If so, how do you prepare?
3.   How do you understand what is said to you?
4.   How do you make yourself understood?

7 — TEACHER PRESENTATION/LECTURE (RECALL/ANALYSIS)
The teacher talks for ten or fifteen minutes about the early history of the United States. You are expected to understand, get the main idea, and then answer questions.

My questions are:

1.   Do you do this in your class?
2.   What do you do that helps you understand the teacher?
3.   What do you do to remember the main idea and details?
4.   What do you do that helps you answer questions?

8 — TEACHER PRESENTATION/LECTURE (INFERENCE)

Your teacher: (pick the appropriate example)

a)   Says several sentences in the presentation that have words you do not know. You have to figure out what they mean. How do you do this? Do you have any special tricks to help you?
b)   Tells you the first part of a story. You then have to give a good ending. Do you have any special ways that help you predict or guess the ending?

9 — STUDENT ACADEMIC ORAL PRESENTATION
You have to give an oral presentation in class, for example, a book report, a history report, or a report on a science project. Afterwards the class asks you questions.

My questions are:

1.   Do you do this in any of your classes?
2.   What helps you to prepare the report?
3.   What helps you to present the report?
4.   Do you have any special tricks that help you answer questions after the report?

In the interviews, students were asked about their use of learning strategies for language activities in the classroom and also outside of school, and teachers were asked what learning strategies they taught their students to use or observed them using in and outside of the classroom.

Teachers were interviewed individually, and students were interviewed in small groups of three to five. Hispanic students classified at beginning level of ESL were interviewed in Spanish so that their lack of English proficiency would not hinder them from participating in a full discussion of their own learning strategies. Each interview lasted for about 45 minutes.

The questions posed by interviewers asked students to describe any special techniques or tricks they used in understanding and remembering English in nine specific oral language activities. Seven of these activities involved typical classroom ESL learning tasks such as vocabulary, pronunciation, oral grammar drills, listening comprehension, and oral reports. The remaining two activities students were questioned about pertained to their use of English in communicative situations outside of school (see Table 1).

All interviews were taperecorded and then summarized by the researcher who had conducted the interview. The interview summaries consisted of a verbatim transcription (or translation for interviews conducted in Spanish) of each student's learning strategy descriptions, and brief identification of the student's level (beginning or intermediate) and the learning activity associated with the strategy described. Names were given to the strategies described by students by using the names suggested by students themselves or identified in the learning strategies literature (e.g., Brown and Palinscar, 1982; Rubin, 1981). In a few cases, neither of these sources appeared to capture the essence of the strategy reported by a student, so a collective decision on a descriptive strategy name was made by all four researchers. Interrater reliability was established by having another member of the research team make an independent transcription of the student strategy description portions of the tapes; the transcriptions were then compared and any discrepancies resolved through a third listening by the research team.[3]

Results of the Descriptive Study

Class observations yielded limited information about learning strategies because classes tended to be teacher directed and students had few opportunities to engage in active learning with observable strategies. This finding was not surprising, as it confirmed what previous researchers had discovered about the inadequacies of classroom observation for identifying learner-generated mental strategies (Naiman et al., 1978; Cohen and Aphek, 1981). Rubin (1981) suggests that observations are not particularly effective because teachers tend to focus on correct answers rather than the process by which the answers are obtained. An examination of the strategies identified in the literature (see, for example, Brown and Palinscar, 1982; Rubin, 1981) and described by language learners shows that many are mental activities with little external behavior, and are therefore not observable.

Teacher interviews were also somewhat disappointing because teachers tended to confuse learning strategies with teaching strategies; they could describe in detail how they taught, but in most cases were uncertain how students actually went about learning the material presented. Many teachers knew very little about the kinds of English acquisition experiences their students had outside of school.

On the other hand, student interviews were extremely productive of accounts of strategy use. What emerges is the fact that the best way to get at what strategies learners actually use as they go about their learning tasks, is to ask them. And indeed, the most valuable data gathered in the descriptive study were through student interviews, and for this reason, the results reported below refer exclusively to the strategies identified in the student interviews.

Students were not only aware of but anxious to talk about the ways in which they learned English. The 70 students interviewed reported a total of 638 instances of learning strategy use. In many cases, a combination of strategies was reported for a single language task or activity.

Many of the strategies reported matched those identified in the review of literature in both first and second languages (e.g., Bialystok, 1981; Brown and Palinscar, 1982; Levin, 1981; McDonald *et al.*, 1979; Naiman *et al.*, 1978; Rubin, 1981; Wittrock, 1983). Some additional strategies were also described by students and new labels and definitions were developed for these. All of the strategies previously identified in the literature and the additional ones suggested by the students could be classified as metacognitive, cognitive, or social-affective. Table 2 provides the list of learning strategies reported by students, and the definitions adopted to describe them. This table also shows how the reported strategies were classified into the metacognitive, cognitive, and social-affective classification scheme. Although Rubin (see Chapter 1) classifies clarification/verification as a cognitive strategy, our review of the cognitive psychology literature indicates that cognitive learning strategies are characterized by internal conceptual manipulation or transformation of the material to be learned (Brown and Palinscar, 1982; Brown *et al.*, 1983). Questioning for clarification is an external act that may not involve the student in this type of direct operation on the learning task. Therefore, we classified questioning for clarification, along with cooperation, as a social-affective learning strategy requiring interaction with another person.

Examples of Learning Strategies Described by Students

Excerpts from the student interviews reveal students' conscious use of strategies in their efforts to learn English. The following examples (translated from Spanish) are typical of the comments made during the interviews:

For Self-management: "I sit in the front of the class so I can see the teacher's face clearly." "It's a good idea to mix with non-Hispanics, because you're forced to practice your English. If you talk with a Chinese who is also studying English you have to practice the language because it's the only way to communicate."

For Advance Organization: "You review before you go into class. You at least look through each lesson. I don't try to totally understand it; I look over it."

For Self-monitoring: ". . . I just start talking. What happens is that sometimes I cut short a word because I realize I've said it wrong. Then I say it again, but correctly."

For Delayed Production: "I can more or less understand whatever is said to me

TABLE 2. *Learning Strategy Definitions*

Learning Strategy	Description
Metacognitive	
Advance Organizers	Making a general but comprehensive preview of the concept or principle in an anticipated learning activity.
Directed Attention	Deciding in advance to attend in general to a learning task and to ignore irrelevant distractors.
Selective Attention	Deciding in advance to attend to specific aspects of language input or situational details that will cue the retention of language input.
Self-management	Understanding the conditions that help one learn and arranging for the presence of those conditions.
Advance Preparation	Planning for and rehearsing linguistic components necessary to carry out an upcoming language task.
Self-monitoring	Correcting one's speech for accuracy in pronunciation, grammar, vocabulary, or for appropriateness related to the setting or to the people who are present.
Delayed Production	Consciously deciding to postpone speaking to learn initially through listening comprehension.
Self-evaluation	Checking the outcomes of one's own language learning against an internal measure of completeness and accuracy.
Cognitive	
Repetition	Imitating a language model, including overt practice and silent rehearsal.
Resourcing	Defining or expanding a definition of a word or concept through use of target language reference materials.
Directed Physical Response	Relating new information to physical actions, as with directives.
Translation	Using the first language as a base for understanding and/or producing the second language.
Grouping	Reordering or reclassifying and perhaps labelling the material to be learned based on common attributes.
Note-taking	Writing down the main idea, important points, outline, or summary of information presented orally or in writing.
Deduction	Consciously applying rules to produce or understand the second language.
Recombination	Constructing a meaningful sentence or larger language sequence by combining known element in a new way.
Imagery	Relating new information to visual concepts in memory via familiar easily retrievable visualizations, phrases, or locations.
Auditory Representation	Retention of the sound or similar sound for a word, phrase, or longer language sequence.
Key Word	Remembering a new word in the second langauge by (1) identifying a familiar word in the first language that sounds like or otherwise resembles the new word, and (2) generating easily recalled images of some relationship between the new word.
Contextualization	Placing a word or phrase in a meaningful language sequence.
Elaboration	Relating new information to other concepts in memory.
Transfer	Using previously acquired linguistic and/or conceptual knowledge to facilitate a new language learning task.
Inferencing	Using available information to guess meanings of new items, predict outcomes, or fill in missing information.
Social-affective	
Cooperation	Working with one or more peers to obtain feedback, pool information, or model a language activity.
Question for Clarification	Asking a teacher or other native speaker for repetition, paraphrasing, explanation and/or examples.

now, but the problem is in talking. I need to study more so that I can talk better. I talk when I have to, but I keep it short and hope I'll be understood."

For Imagery: "Pretend you are doing something indicated in the sentences you make up about the new word. Actually do it in your head."

For Auditory Representation: "When you are trying to learn how to say something, speak it in your mind first. Then say it aloud. If it is correct, you can keep it in your mind forever."

For Transfer: "For instance, in geography class, if they're talking about something I have already learned (in Spanish), all I have to do is remember the information and then try to put it into English."

For Inferencing: "Sometimes all the words of the sentence make the meaning of the new word. I think of the whole meaning of the sentence, and then I can get the meaning of the new word."

These examples represent a small part of the extensive comments and descriptions of individual strategies elicited in the student interviews.

Table 3 summarizes differences and types of strategy use by beginning and intermediate level students. Metacognitive strategies, which accounted for about 30% of strategy usage, involved thinking about one's own learning style, planning for language learning opportunities, monitoring of oral production, and self-evaluation after a language interaction, and were applied to a variety of different language activities. Cognitive and social-affective strategies, which accounted for about 53% and 17% respectively of strategy usage, were more directly linked to the task at hand and involved strategies such as repetition, notetaking, imagery, contextualization of words and expressions, transfer of previously acquired information, inferencing to guess meanings of new items, and cooperation with friends or family members.

Differences in individual strategy use were also found between beginning and intermediate level ESL students. Metacognitive strategies favored by intermediate level students were primarily self-management, advance preparation, and self-monitoring strategies; whereas beginning level students relied heavily on metacognitive strategies such as selective attention and delayed production.

Cognitive and social-affective strategies favored by different proficiency levels of students showed many similarities but some important differences in emphasis. Both levels favored such tried-and-true strategies as repetition, notetaking, questioning for clarification, and cooperation. However, translation and imagery were used less by intermediate students than by beginners, and contextualization was a strategy which students with greater proficiency in English were able to use advantageously. In general, intermediate level students reported using meta-cognitive strategies more frequently than did beginning level students. This indicates that a certain basic proficiency in a second language may be a prerequisite for students to be able to reflect on their own learning style, plan for learning opportunities, and make reasonably accurate comparisons of their own output to that of a native speaker model. Krashen for example, found that monitoring is used primarily by students who have had greater exposure to the new language.

Of particular interest to teachers is the relationship of individual strategies to specific language learning activities. We found that some types of language activities attracted greater strategy use than others, and we also found differences

TABLE 3. *Number of Learning Strategies Used by Beginning and Intermediate Level Students*

Learning Strategy Type	Learning Strategy Classification	English					
		Beginning		Intermediate		Total	
		n	%	n	%	n	%
Metacognitive							
Planning	Advance preparation	24	21.4	20	25.0	44	22.9
	Self-management	22	19.6	18	22.5	40	20.8
	Selective attention	25	22.3	13	16.3	38	19.8
	Directed attention	15	13.4	10	12.5	25	13.0
	Delayed production	8	7.1	2	2.5	10	5.2
	Advance organizers	1	0.9	0	0.0	1	0.5
Monitoring	Self-monitoring	8	7.1	10	12.5	18	9.4
Evaluation	Self-evaluation	9	8.0	7	8.8	16	8.3
Subtotal		112	100.0	80	100.0	192	100.0
Cognitive							
	Repetition	45	20.0	21	18.8	66	19.6
	Note-taking	43	19.0	20	17.9	63	18.7
	Imagery	31	14.0	11	9.8	42	12.5
	Translation	29	13.0	9	8.0	38	11.3
	Transfer	23	10.2	12	10.7	35	10.4
	Inferencing	21	9.3	11	9.8	32	9.5
	Resourcing	11	5.0	7	6.2	18	5.3
	Contextualization	7	3.1	11	9.8	18	5.3
	Elaboration	9	4.0	2	1.8	11	3.3
	Auditory representation	3	1.3	2	1.8	5	1.5
	Grouping	1	0.4	3	2.7	4	1.2
	Recombination	1	0.4	1	0.9	2	0.6
	Deduction	1	0.4	1	0.9	2	0.6
	Key word	0	0.0	1	0.9	1	0.3
	Directed physical response	0	0.0	0	0.0	0	0.0
Subtotal		225	100.0	112	100.0	337	100.0
Social-affective	Cooperation	34	47.0	18	49.0	52	48.0
	Questions for clarity	38	53.0	19	51.0	57	52.0
Subtotal		72	100.0	37	100.0	109	100.0
Total		409	100.0	229	100.0	638	100.0

in strategy use between proficiency levels. Table 4 summarizes the degree of strategy use by language activity. Students used most learning strategies for vocabulary and least for listening activities requiring inferencing. In examining the differences between learning strategy use for a particular learning task between beginning and intermediate level students, the task in which the greatest difference was found was oral presentation. A greater percentage of intermediate level students used strategies for oral presentations than did beginning level students, but this finding can be explained by the fact that the schools' curriculum did not require oral presentations until students reached the intermediate level of ESL. Beginning level students simply were not required to make oral presentations, and so did not report strategies for them.

Discussion

The most interesting finding of the descriptive study was that both beginning and intermediate level high school ESL students were able to describe their use of a

TABLE 4. *Number and Percentage of Strategy Uses Among Beginning and Intermediate Level Students for Different Learning Activities*

| | English Proficiency | | | | | |
| | Beginning Level | | Intermediate Level | | Total | |
Learning Activity	n	%	n	%	n	%
Listening Comprehension:						
Inference	34	8.3	12	5.2	46	7.2
Oral Presentation	22	5.4	30	13.1	52	8.2
Operational Communica-						
tion	46	11.2	17	7.4	63	9.9
Instructions	42	10.3	25	10.9	67	10.5
Social Communication	42	10.3	28	12.2	70	11.0
Listening Comprehension:						
Analyzing	49	12.0	24	10.5	73	11.4
Oral Drills	52	12.7	21	9.2	73	11.4
Pronunciation	51	12.5	37	16.2	88	13.8
Vocabulary Learning	71	17.4	35	15.3	106	16.6
Total	409	100.0%	229	100.0%	638	100.0%

wide range of learning strategies. In fact, our original list of strategies suggested by a review of the literature (O'Malley *et al.*, 1983) was nearly doubled after our interviews with the subjects in the study.

Also of great interest was the degree of metalinguistic awareness displayed by many of the students interviewed, which indicated some sophistication in their ability to compare their first language to their second, to transfer linguistic knowledge, and to evaluate their degree of success in using the new language communicatively. Students were aware of paralinguistic factors and of style and register differences between the type of English they heard in the classroom and from English speaking peers. Many students commented on the differences between Spanish and English, and seemed to be aware of the limitations of translation. Some students realized that their knowledge of Spanish was an asset in their deliberate transfer of language skills to English, while others complained that their lack of formal Spanish hindered them in learning similar formal features in English.

The classification system which we found most useful for organizing the learning strategies identified has three main categories: metacognitive, cognitive, and social-affective strategies. This framework can provide a classification basis for other researchers and for teachers who wish to integrate learning strategy instruction into their curriculum.

Although there were some differences in types of strategies used by beginning and intermediate level students, both groups favored repetition as the most frequently used strategy. This rote strategy requires less mentally active engagement with the learning task than strategies that were favored least, such as elaboration, auditory representation, or grouping. (One can copy words or repeat them orally without attending to their meaning, but other strategies require one to understand the meaning of a word in order to engage in the strategy.) This indicates that students could benefit from training in additional strategies that they might not think of using on their own, and that might be more effective for learning.

The two language activities for which students reported the most strategy use were vocabulary and pronunciation. These are relatively discrete language tasks, unlike integrative language tasks such as listening comprehension or oral communication. Whether this was because students viewed language as a collection of words to be pronounced correctly and so concentrated their strategic efforts in these two areas, or whether they were merely unaware of the application of learning strategies to integrative language tasks is unclear and warrants further research.

Implications for Practice

To return to the question asked at the beginning of this paper, "What can I do to help my students learn?", some clear implications for teaching can be drawn from the findings of this study. The fact that students identified as good language learners by teachers do use conscious learning strategies not only in ESL classrooms but also in out of classroom acquisition environments is an indication that teachers could profitably direct students to utilize learning strategies for a variety of language learning activities. Intervention by the teacher could help less able students profit from the strategies used by more able students, and even the more able students could be provided with opportunities to refine and add to their learning strategies so that they became as efficient as possible.

As a first step, teachers could attempt to discover what strategies their students are already using. Possible ways of achieving this are through the use of student diaries of language learning experiences in which students are directed to record and classify their language learning experiences according to the conscious strategies they employ. Teachers could also conduct interviews with individual students or with small groups in order to question them about the strategies employed for specific language learning tasks, and also, in order to get at metacognitive strategies, ways in which they plan, monitor, and evaluate the language learning they experience.

Two major benefits could be expected from such a teacher-generated activity: students would likely become more metalinguistically sophisticated as they practiced retrospective analysis of themselves as language learners, and teachers would become sensitized to the learner's perspective and to the various factors, both in the outside of the classroom, which affect the learning process. Hosenfeld (1979), in fact, suggests that a teacher's first act should be to identify the students' learning strategies so that instruction can be adapted accordingly. In our interviews with teachers we discovered that some of them had never stopped to consider what might be going on in their students' minds as they were learning English. Once the idea of student learning strategies was presented, however, teachers expressed great interest in discovering those strategies and capitalizing upon them in their teaching approach.

Another promising idea suggested by Hosenfeld (1979) is that teachers compare the learning strategies for a given task between good and poor learners, and then set up small group language tasks in which an able student is instructed to "think aloud" during the task so that the less able students an expand their own learning strategy repertoires as they listen.

When teachers provide students with learning tools that they can use on their own outside of class, they can make more effective use of the learning opportunities that they encounter. Learning strategies can even be used to elicit what Krashen (1982) terms "comprehensible input" from native English speakers.

Metacognitive strategies such as self-management and self-monitoring can be practiced in communicative situations in which the learner wishes to gain the maximum amount of comprehensible speech from others. Cognitive strategies such as contextualization of new words by deliberately using them in conversation and thus invoking reactions to or comments on their communicative value and sociolinguistic appropriateness is yet another way of eliciting comprehensible input. Social-affective strategies that can be used in acquisition environments might include cooperation with peers or other English speakers to obtain feedback or pool information, and the use of questioning not only for clarification (such as requesting repetition, paraphrasing, or explanation), but also as a means of eliciting further native speaker input. What the teacher can do is to provide students with practice in useful strategies for the negotiation of conversational encounters outside of class. This should be encouraged by teachers through assignment of language encounters in the community outside the classroom.

In conclusion, what this study has perhaps shown most clearly, is that second language learners are not mere sponges acquiring the new language by osmosis alone. They are thinking, reflective beings who consciously apply mental strategies to learning situations both in the classroom and outside of it.

Notes

1. This study was conducted for the U.S. Army Research Institute for the Behavioral and Social Sciences in Alexandria, Virginia, under Contract No. MDA-903-82-C-0169. The views, opinions, and findings contained in this report are those of the author, and should not be construed as an Official Department of the Army position, policy, or decision, unless so designated by other official documentation.
2. They are obviously not the same as teaching strategies, which are those techniques and maneuvers that teachers use to improve the effectiveness of their teaching. Politzer (1965), however, has pointed out that learning strategies are the reverse side of the coin of teaching strategies: a successful learning strategy user has in fact become a successful self-teacher.
3. Addition details on methodological procedures can be found in O'Malley et al., 1985.

Follow-up Activities

Discussing the Issues

1. Chamot says, "If learning is to take place, it involves the collaboration of two people — a teacher and a learner." What do you consider the role of learners to be in second language learning? of teachers? What does this study suggest in this regard?

Interpreting the Data

2. Chamot's findings are summarized in Tables 3 and 4. Examine these data for differences and similarities that you perceive to be significant. Discuss the insights your analysis may provide regarding the second language learning process.

Applying the Ideas

3. The literature in metacognition notes that the differences between cognitive and metacognitive strategies is not always clearcut. In Table 2, Chamot provides a list of cognitive and metacognitive strategies reported by students in her study and the definitions adopted to describe them.

(a) What do the definitions suggest regarding the differences between the two types? i.e. how would you distinguish one type of learning strategy from another?

(b) Why would the students in her study have used cognitive strategies more frequently than metacognitive strategies? than social-affective?

4. Chamot's data suggests that strategy use is, in part, influenced by the level of the student's proficiency and by the language task. What are the implications of this for the classroom teacher?

5. Make a list of some of the questions you have regarding the difficulties your students may have completing particular academic tasks and how they deal with these difficulties. Use (and adapt as necessary) Chamot's interview guide to find answers to your questions.

6. Hosenfeld (1979) states that a teacher's first act should be to identify students' learning strategies so that instruction can be adapted accordingly. And, as Chamot suggests, learning diaries can be used to gather this information.

(a) Ask your students to keep a learning journal focusing their entries on different language learning tasks and experiences (e.g. writing a composition, reading a newspaper, listening to TV).

(b) Ask them to describe the difficulties they encounter in each instance and to indicate how they will deal with these difficulties.

(c) Use the list provided by Chamot to analyze their entries.

(d) Indicate the insights derived from the diaries and how they will determine what you teach and how.

7. According to Chamot, learning strategies can be used to elicit what Krashen (1982) terms "comprehensible input".

(a) List several varied contexts in which second language learners need to use (i.e. read, listen to, speak or write) their second language.

(b) Consider the strategies listed by Chamot and Rubin and indicate which ones could be used to elicit comprehensible input in each context.

Chapter 7

Strategies of Two Language Learners: A Case Study

ROBERTA G. ABRAHAM and ROBERTA J. VANN

Beginning with the premise that no single learning strategy, cognitive style or learner characteristic is sufficient to explain success in language learning, Naiman *et al.* (1978) emphasized that many factors must be considered simultaneously to discover how they interact to affect one's success as a language learner in a given situation. In their research, Naiman and his colleagues attempted to identify "(1) the strategies and techniques the learner consciously develops and employs and (2) certain learner characteristics, in particular personality and cognitive style factors, which are likely to influence the use of strategies and techniques and thereby, indirectly, learning outcomes" (p. 4). Their results to some extent supported their view that success in language learning is related to a number of personality and cognitive style factors, and that these may have an effect on learning and communication processes. However, limitations in their methodology left many unanswered questions about the nature of these relationships.

While Naiman and his colleagues examined factors leading to the success of high school students learning a foreign language, we were interested in students (both successful and unsuccessful) in a different setting; an intensive English as a second language (ESL) program at a university, where "success" means passing the Test of English as Foreign Language (TOEFL) and being able to function adequately in a university environment. To learn more about the relationships among learner background, learner strategies, and this kind of success, we set up a case study of fifteen students in the program. Using some of the instruments employed by Naiman *et al.*, some developed by other researchers, and others that we designed ourselves, we collected data on (1) background factors that subjects brought to the learning situation, (2) their observed use of learning and communication strategies,[1] and (3) their reported methods for developing language proficiency.

In this article, we compare two of the learners in our study — one successful and one unsuccessful. After an overview of the study, we report and discuss our data from these two learners. We then propose a model relating strategy use to background factors.

Description of Study

Method

Our fifteen subjects were selected from intermediate classes (levels 3 and 4 in a 6-level program) to represent the population of our program in terms of native language, cultural background (Arab, Latin American or Asian), and sex. It is important to note that when we selected our subjects we did not know which of the learners would succeed or fail. However, after they left the program, we arranged them in three groups — very successful, moderately successful, and unsuccessful —

as determined by their rate of progress through the program[2] and final evaluations of their performance by their instructors.

The background variables we investigated were language and educational/ professional background, motivation for studying English, cognitive style, and intelligence. Information on background and motivation was obtained in a series of taped interviews with questions adapted from those provided in Naiman *et al.* (1978). Cognitive styles (field independence/dependence and reflection/ impulsivity) were assessed with standard instruments and intelligence by means of Raven's Standard Progressive Matrices. The complete interview protocol and a brief description of the other instruments are provided in the Appendix.

Strategies were identified in two ways. First, we observed those used during the interviews. Second, we presented subjects with four tasks typical of those assigned in their English classes — a verb tense exercise, an article usage exercise, a cloze test, and a composition. Subjects were asked to think aloud as they carried out each task, and from these "process descriptions," we noted their use of strategies.[3]

Additionally, as part of the interview, we asked the subjects questions about means they used to develop proficiency in English. Their answers provided a valuable perspective on their approaches to language learning.

Data in this study were gathered by two Asian women, both fluent English speakers and students in the graduate TESL program at Iowa State University. Cognitive learning and communication strategies that subjects used in the interview and the think-aloud tasks were coded according to the general scheme proposed by Rubin (1981, this volume), with certain modifications.

Comparison of Two Learners

The two subjects reported on here, Gerardo and Pedro, came, respectively, from the upper and the lower groups described in the preceding section. These subjects were chosen because they shared enough background factors (native language, positive attitudes toward the U.S., willingness to take risks in using English, etc.) to make observations about their differences meaningful. Table 1 provides detailed information on their backgrounds.

Data for these subjects were collected by the same research assistant.

Strategies

Observed Interview Strategies. The strategies the two subjects used in the interviews are summarized in Table 2.

It is apparent that in the course of the interview, Gerardo used many more strategies that could directly or indirectly contribute to learning than Pedro did, even when length of the interview is taken into account. Gerardo also used a greater *variety* of strategies.

Comparison of strategy use by category is also illuminating. With respect to cognitive learning strategies, both subjects used more clarification/verification strategies than any other type, demonstrating considerable persistence in communicating with the interviewer. Comparisons within this category, however, disclose important differences as well as similarities. While both subjects frequently

TABLE 1. *Background Information on Subjects*

	Gerardo (successful)	*Pedro* (unsuccessful)
First Language	Spanish	Spanish
Country	Ecuador	Puerto Rico
Motivation (reported)	strong	strong
Age	33	20
Intelligence	above 95th percentile (Raven's)	75 percentile (Raven's)
Formal Education/ work experience	bachelor's degree/ college instructor	high school diploma
Prior study in English	7 years, 2 hrs./week; no contact with native speakers	1 hr./day through secondary school; little interest in classes, preferred to "talk to girls on the beach"
Entering MEPT[1] score	6	31
Preferred mode (reported)	written	oral
Cognitive style	field independent (GEFT[2] = 15) reflective (MFFT[3] = 1st of 15 subjects)	field dependent (GEFT = 5) reflective (MFFT = 2nd of 15 subjects)
Weeks in Program	24	40
Final TOEFL[4]	523	473
Final TSE[5]	120	180

[1]MEPT = Michigan English Placement Test
[2]GEFT = Group Embedded Figures Test Score
[3]MFFT = Matching Familiar Figures Test ranking
[4]TOEFL = Test of English as a Foreign Language
[5]TSE = Test of Spoken English

asked for clarification of meaning (IA1) and for questions to be repeated (IA2), Gerardo used several strategies far more frequently than Pedro. Three of these involved repetition and paraphrase (IA3, IA4, and IA5). Gerardo was also much more concerned than Pedro with the correctness of forms (IA6):

| Interviewer: | [Where do you use English outside of class?] |
| Gerardo: | In the dinning room? dining room . . .? Dinning room or dining room? |

Finally, on a number of occasions when Gerardo had difficulty in understanding the interviewer, he clarified meaning through visual/textual representation, e.g., spelling a word or reading from the interview protocol (IA7). Pedro did not use this strategy at all.

In monitoring, both subjects paid attention to word choice (IB1). However, Gerardo showed more concern with correcting grammar/morphology (IB2):

| Interviewer: | [Is pronunciation still a problem for you?] |
| Gerardo: | Yeah. *I can't . . . pronunciation* good. *I can't pronunciation. I cannot, I cannot . . . pronounce.* |

In the categories of inductive and deductive inferencing, Gerardo again used more strategies. As an example of inductive inferencing, he frequently repeated key words in questions, apparently in an effort to extract the main idea (IC1):

TABLE 2. *Observed Strategies in Interviews*

			Gerardo (successful)	*Pedro* (unsuccessful)
Elapsed Time			142 min.	52 min.
Strategies				
I.	*Cognitive Language Learning Strategies*			
	A.	*Clarification/Verification*		
		1. Asks for meaning	16	10
		2. Asks to have statement/question repeated	9	9
		3. Repeats part of word or phrase, asks for more	13	1
		4. Paraphrases to confirm understanding	9	1
		5. Repeats word or phrase in question to confirm he heard it correctly	13	1
		6. Asks for correct form or verification that form is correct	23	1
		7. Uses visual representation of language during interview to clarify/verify	9	—
			92	23
	B.	*Monitoring*		
		1. Vocabulary	4	10
		2. Grammar/Morphology	15	4
		3. Pronunciation	2	—
			21	14
	C.	*Inductive*		
		1. Confirms key words in question and then answers	11	2
		2. Guesses meaning of word from cognate	1	—
		3. Guesses meaning of word from context	1	—
		4. Gives inappropriate answer because he has incorrectly guessed meaning of question	19	4
			32	6
	D.	*Deductive*		
		1. Classifies	1	—
		2. Tests hypothesis	1	—
		3. Uses morphological rules	3	—
		4. Infers morphology by analogy	1	—
		5. Compares English with native language	2	—
			8	0
	E.	*Practice*		
		1. Repeats correction/verification immediately	29	8
		2. Uses new or troublesome form later	18	—
		3. Uses word supplied by interviewer	9	3
		4. Plays with language	7	—
		5. Practices sound	5	—
			68	11
	Total Cognitive Language Learning Strategies		221	54

II.   *Communication*
   A.   *Content Clarification/Verification*

1.	Asks for more information or, after intervening discussion, asks for repetition of question	41	18
2.	Goes back to question asked on earlier day to ensure that he was understood	1	—
3.	Corrects interviewer's understanding of his statement	—	2
		42	20

   B.   *Production Tricks*

1.	Uses synonyms, paraphrase, repetition or example to communicate idea	7	1
2.	Appears to make up word	2	2
3.	Shows example of what he is describing	—	1
		9	4

   C.   *Social Management*

1.	Repeats or paraphrases interviewer's repetition of answers to confirm interviewer's understanding	19	2
2.	Jokes	15	1
3.	Relates his experience to that of interviewer	6	—
4.	Thanks interviewer for correction	5	—
		45	3

Total Communication Strategies	96	27

Summary

Total number of strategies used	317	81
Number of different strategies	32	19

Interviewer:	Do you remember *what kind of homework* you had to do?
Gerardo:	*What kind homework?*

Notable also was high willingness to guess at the meaning of interview questions, evidence of which were his large number of inappropriate responses (IC4). In these cases, the interviewer usually tried to get him back on track, and lengthy dialogues in which meaning was negotiated often ensued.

An example of deductive inferencing is found in the following use of morphological rules (ID3):

Interviewer:	[asking whether Gerardo ever feels helpless in trying to learn English]
Gerardo:	I think I don't understand exactly means of the "helpless."
Interviewer:	"Helpless" means —
Gerardo:	*No help.*
Interviewer:	No help, yeah. You feel like you can't do anything about it.

Gerardo:	All right, yeah. [pause] *That is meaning, that I don't need help*, for example?
Interviewer:	No . . . [gives more explanation]
Gerardo:	*I know "help." I know "less." L-E-S-S. Helpless. Help-less. Helpless.*
Interviewer:	Means nobody can help you. You feel like nobody can help you. There is nothing I can do to help you.
Gerardo:	Yeah. Yeah.

(This discussion continued until Gerardo seemed satisfied he understood, thus providing evidence — as did many other exchanges — of Gerardo's perseverance in learning.)

Gerardo also used many more practice strategies. In addition to repeating new or troublesome forms (IE1, IE2, IE3), he sometimes appeared to play with words (IE4) in a manner reminiscent of that of children learning their first language:

| Interviewer: | [How do you practice speaking?] |
| Gerardo: | I have a friend from Haiti, especially no — no speak . . . Spanish very well, so *speak English, only speak English, they speak English only*, so I talk with him. |

With respect to communication strategies, both subjects frequently raised questions about the general content of topics covered in the interview and asked to have questions repeated after the conversation had digressed (IIA1). However, Gerardo used more production tricks to make himself understood (paraphrasing etc.) than Pedro. For example, in the exchange cited earlier when Gerardo was trying to discover the correct pronunciation of "dining room," the communication was interrupted. As a result, the interviewer went on to another question, having failed to understand that Gerardo meant he used English in the dining room. To make sure she had the correct information, Gerardo went back to the earlier topic, but this time using different vocabulary (IIB1):

| Gerardo: | [pause] Cafeteria. |
| Interviewer: | [after thinking a bit] OK. OK. You speak English when you eat. |

This episode also provides another example of Gerardo's persistence.

Finally, Gerardo used many more social management strategies, all of which had the effect of encouraging the interviewer to talk more. His repeating to confirm that the interviewer had understood him (IIC1) and his joking (IIC2) provided evidence of his desire to keep the conversation flowing. His thanking her for correction (IIC4) probably prompted her to teach him other facts about grammar, something she did not do with any other subject.

Think-Aloud Task Strategies. Performance and strategies for Tasks 2, 3, and 4 are summarized in Table 3.[4]

In looking at the strategies used on these tasks, it is important to keep in mind that the nature of the task is likely to affect strategy use. For example, one would expect Task 2, on article use, to elicit more deductive and inductive strategies as subjects applied rules or used key words or their ears to test answers. Task 3, the

TABLE 3. *Performance and Strategies in Tasks*

		Gerardo (successful)	*Pedro* (unsuccessful)
Elapsed Time			
	Task 2 (Articles)	14 min.	8 min.
	Task 3 (Cloze)	32 min.	8 min.
	Task 4 (Composition)	44 min.	13 min.
		90 min.	29 min.
Scores			
	Task 2	21/23 correct	12/23 correct
	Task 3	19/33 correct	3/33 correct
	Task 4 (score is rank out of total of 15 subjects)		
	Rater 1	3/15	12/15
	Rater 2	1/15	13/15
	Rater 3	3/15	15/15
Strategies			
I.	*Cognitive Language Learning Strategies*		
A.	*Clarification/Verification*		
	Task 2	11	5
	Task 3	31	1
	Task 4	17	17
		59	23
B.	*Monitoring*		
	Task 2	3	0
	Task 3	6	3
	Task 4	28	6
		37	9
C.	*Inductive*		
	Task 2	3	9
	Task 3	17	6
	Task 4	5	3
		25	18
D.	*Deductive*		
	Task 2	6	9
	Task 3	13	0
	Task 4	0	1
		19	10
E.	*Practice*		
	Task 2	3	3
	Task 3	0	0
	Task 4	5	2
		8	5
	Total Learning Strategies	148	65

II.   *Communication*
    A.   *Content Clarification/Verification*

Task 2	1	0
Task 3	11	2
Task 4	11	10
	23	12

    B.   *Production Tricks*

Task 2	2	2
Task 3	2	3
Task 4	1	4
	5	9

    C.   *Social Management*

Task 2	4	0
Task 3	7	2
Task 4	9	1
	20	3

Total Communication Strategies	48	24

Summary
    Totals by task

Task 2	33	28
Task 3	87	17
Task 4	76	44
Total strategies used	196	89
Total strategies/minute	2.2	3.1

cloze test, would also be expected to elicit inductive strategies, and, because of its unfamiliarity and relative difficulty for most subjects, both learning and communicative clarification/verification strategies. Task 4, the composition, required subjects to read a description and interpret a diagram of an auto accident and then to imagine themselves as policemen writing accident reports from inferences of what actually happened. This task, an unfamiliar and challenging assignment for all fifteen of the subjects, would seem to require a relatively larger number of clarification/verification strategies than would a more straightforward task, and, because it was a writing assignment, more monitoring (rereading and editing).

For all three tasks, tallies indicate clear differences between subjects. Gerardo, the better performer, used more strategies, no doubt partially because he spent more time working. On the other hand, Pedro used his time more efficiently, at least in the sense of squeezing in more observable strategies per unit of time than Gerardo did. As in the interview, the two subjects also demonstrated different patterns of strategy use. Pedro used fewer than half as many communicative strategies as Gerardo, and proportionately even fewer learning strategies. Within the learning strategy category, Pedro used far fewer monitoring strategies. These differences and others become more apparent as one looks at a detailed description of strategies by task.

On Task 2, which requires subjects to fill in blanks with correct articles, both subjects relied on the similarity of Spanish and English article function. However, procedure and attention to detail differentiated one from the other. Pedro, using fewer than half as many clarification/verification learning strategies (IA) as Gerardo, plunged into the task without reading the directions. Consequently, he did not realize that some of the blanks were not to be filled. On the other hand, he used *more* inductive and deductive strategies than Gerardo on this task. He often relied on "the sound," testing out his answers before writing them by saying them aloud (IC). (Gerardo also used this strategy, but to a lesser extent than Pedro.) As did many of our subjects, he cited the " 'an' before words beginning with vowels" rule, an indication of his deductive reasoning (ID). But for Pedro, this rule superseded all others: he began the exercise by scanning the page for all words beginning with vowels and writing "an" in the preceding blanks, even when the noun was plural. He also invented a rule: "Use 'the' at the beginning of sentences." This explains to some extent his relatively large tally of deductive strategies (ID) on this task. In contrast, Gerardo's use of deduction in this assignment was characterized by his moving from the general — sometimes stating what rule was not operating — to more specific rules reminiscent of the charts on article usage sometimes used in ESL classes. As is evident from Table 3, the two subjects did not differ markedly in their use of other strategies on this task.

Task 3, the cloze test, was a less familiar and sometimes frustrating experience for subjects, but elicited a variety of strategies not observed in earlier tasks. While Gerardo asked the research assistant for extensive clarification of the assignment (IIA), Pedro proceeded with confidence: "I know what I have to do." This accounts for the dramatic difference between the two subjects in the number of clarification/verification communication strategies used. Gerardo took four times as long as Pedro, apologized for "thinking slowly," and checked his answers. In contrast, Pedro charged through the assignment, skipping paragraphs and leaving blanks: "When I understand nothing, I continue." Pedro seemingly regarded his practice of not checking his work as a *positive* strategy: "When I do something I am sure . . . I don't go again because it puts me in very unsurance." Likewise, there was a major contrast in the number of clarification/verification learning strategies (IA) the subjects used, e.g., Gerardo more often asked for the meaning of a given expression. Regarding inductive strategies, Pedro repeated key words before blanks, once again used sound, and relied on clues from previous discourse (IC). While Gerardo also used these inductive strategies on this task, he differed from Pedro in using a number of deductive strategies in which syntactic structure determined his response, for example, "necessary an adjective in this case because there is a noun."

On Task 4, one of the obvious differences among our fifteen subjects was their relative frustration or ease with the notion of playing a role they had never assumed and writing from implicit rather than explicit knowledge of an event. However, both subjects reported on here seemed relatively comfortable with the assignment. Their differences lay primarily in the care with which they completed it.

Gerardo, who was sucessful in writing the composition, spent a relatively long time preparing to write. As he read the directions, he asked rhetorical questions. For example, after reading "You are a traffic officer," he asked "I?" In addition, rather than asking for specific information about the assignment from the research assistant, he explained: "I don't know what a police report looks like, but I'm trying to build the accident." Pedro, on the other hand, began without hesitation, skipping part of the directions: "I don't read all the aspect. I know what I need to do. I look the picture."

While both subjects were interested in clarifying and/or verifying new vocabulary (IA), they contrasted in their responses to unfamiliar words. Pedro tended to simply ask for explanations of key words, such as "skid" and "shoulder," while Gerardo was careful to delineate the boundaries of his understanding: "I know the meaning of shoulder, but in this case?"

Monitoring (IB) on Task 4 included rereading and editing, but the two subjects differed dramatically in their use of this strategy. Both during and after writing, Gerardo made extensive changes in his work, while Pedro, although saying that he reread and edited this assignment, spent only ten seconds doing so.

Means of Developing Proficiency (reported). In the interviews, both subjects reported that they created situations for using English outside of class for reading, writing, and conversing. Both said they watched TV and listened to the radio. Neither felt shy about practicing English, and both claimed to welcome correction.

Both reported participating in class, an activity they thought important, although for somewhat different reasons. For Gerardo, "It's necessary . . . the teacher tell me if I'm wrong or I'm right [in use of vocabulary and grammar]," while for Pedro, "I need to talk in class and increase my vocabulary."

Gerardo reported paying attention to grammar in class (listening to the teacher, doing homework) and then trying to use rules in speaking and writing. In contrast, Pedro indicated that he disliked metalanguage ("When the teacher says 'past participle, present progressive', sometimes I feel I don't understand . . . I feel very strange"). Later he admitted, "I don't pay a lot of attention [to grammar]." In grammar class, he preferred examples to rules. Outside of class, he showed little concern with grammatical correctness ("I don't care if I talk bad").

Gerardo reported perseverance in trying to communicate or understand an idea — "I think that is . . . how I can — I learn English", whereas Pedro said he sometimes abandoned a topic when he was having trouble explaining it — "forget it, depends the people really don't understand, say 'forget it' ".

Discussion and Conclusion

From the data on subjects' use of strategies and from their reports in the interview, we can infer their approaches to learning English, that is, their conscious or unconscious plans or systems for this endeavor. In one respect they were similar. Both seemed to feel it was important to create opportunities to use English. Gerardo's social management strategies in the interview provide direct evidence of this; however, Pedro's reports of strategy use indicate that he, too, arranged his life to include a great deal of conversation in English. Their reported participation in class also seemed to be motivated by their perceived need to use English in order to learn it.

However, there are at least two important differences in approach between these subjects. One lies in their efforts to achieve grammatical correctness. While both subjects were interested in communicating (and used strategies which enabled them to do so), Gerardo was clearly much more concerned with form than Pedro. In the interview, he asked for and practiced correct forms much more frequently than Pedro; in the think-alouds, he often monitored and checked over his work, whereas Pedro seldom did this. In their reports of how they learned, Gerardo said he tried to use new rules of grammar to improve his speaking and writing, while Pedro admitted (with what might even have been a touch of pride) his lack of concern about either rules or correctness.

The other difference, probably unconscious, lies in their flexibility in using strategies. There is some indication of this in the interview, where Gerardo used a greater variety of strategies than Pedro. Even more evidence emerges from the think-aloud tasks. Here, Gerardo's ability to match his choice of strategy to the demands of the task was probably an important factor in his success on each one. He also showed flexibility in his use of time, spending a great deal of it on aspects of the tasks where he thought it was important, but cutting short a lengthy explanation from the interviewer that he felt to be unnecessary. In contrast, Pedro seemed to organize his approach to all tasks in the same way, quickly determining what needed to be done and then doing it in the simplest and most straightforward (and often superficial) way possible.

The data on these subjects also provide some clues to their language learning philosophies, that is, their beliefs about how language operates, and, consequently, how it is learned. Gerardo appeared to take a broad view: his flexibility, variety of strategies, and concern with correctness suggest a belief that language learning requires attention to both function and form, the latter including vocabulary, morphology, and grammar. He knew that he had to discover how the forms enable a person to communicate; he also recognized that they should be used with precision in an academic or professional setting. In contrast, Pedro's view of second language learning was relatively limited. He appeared to think of language primarily as a set of words and he seemed confident that if he could learn enough of them, he could somehow string them together to communicate. The exact way in which they should be combined (and, indeed, the actual forms the words should take) was relatively unimportant. Acting in accordance with this view, Pedro had adopted certain positive strategies that enabled him to be successful in unsophisticated oral communication; however, when he encountered the demands of academic written English, he failed.

To their patterns of strategy use (demonstrated in the interview and think-alouds) and the approaches and philosophies that appear to underlie them, we can link background information about the subjects. In Gerardo, a combination of maturity in learning (a factor including both age and educational/professional background) and intelligence likely disposed him to take the approach to language learning noted above, and allowed him to better assess the demands regarding English in an academic situation. Likewise, our observations of his persistent efforts to determine and communicate meaning, learn new forms, and explore language rules suggest that both tenacity and curiosity, at least with regard to language learning, may be influential personality traits. At the same time, his field independence may explain his ease in focusing on details within the linguistic system.[5] His preference for the written mode was likely related to his use of appropriate and effective strategies in dealing with written tasks. Since the program in which these subjects were enrolled, and TOEFL as well, emphasizes use of written language, this combination was probably important in Gerardo's success in this setting, though it might have worked against him in circumstances where oral language was more important.

For Pedro, there is evidence of a combination of background factors leading to his narrow philosophy of language learning; out of this grew an approach and strategies that led to failure in an academic setting. One relevant background factor was probably lack of maturity in learning (his age together with his more limited educational background, including, by his own admission, his less than scholarly attitude). His earlier needs to use English for rather basic communication (talking to girls on the beach) may also have contributed to his equation of language learning with vocabulary acquisition. Pedro exhibited little persistence or curiosity about the forms of English except in learning vocabulary. His most salient personality characteristic, particularly evident in the think-aloud sessions, was his haste. Always in a hurry to finish his work, he plunged in without pausing to read the instructions and re-emerged without taking time to look over what he had done. (That he tested as reflective on our cognitive style test for reflection/impulsivity seems anomalous and suggests that the measure may be inappropriate in this context.) Another important background factor may have been his field dependence, which may have led to his difficulty in paying attention to detail.

Pedro's preference for the oral mode probably predisposed him to use effective oral communication strategies and thus to exchange ideas with others more efficiently than Gerardo. However, his inability or unwillingness to switch to strategies appropriate for writing was probably at least partly responsible for his failure in an academic program.

Given the above observations about these two subjects, we propose the following model for second language learning (see Fig. 1).

We suggest that learners have, at some level of consciousness, a *philosophy* of how language is learned. This philosophy guides the *approach* they take in language learning situations, which in turn is manifested in observable (and unobservable) *strategies* used in learning and communication. These factors form a hierarchy shown in the "B" box in the model, and they directly influence the degree of success learners achieve.

However, the "B" factors should not be considered in isolation. Combinations of variables in the learners' background (factors in the "A" box in the model) are also important, because they affect each of the "B" factors. Additionally, influences in the environment surrounding the second language learning experience ("C" factors, including formal or informal instruction and practice) may be important in modifying the "B" factors, and, hence, have an indirect effect on degree of success. The model, therefore, permits many combinations of factors, both "winning" and "losing".

Our model results from our attempt to redress the limitations of earlier studies by considering the importance of background variables in understanding the strategies used by a particular learner and from our reliance on more than one method and context for eliciting strategy use. However, the model needs to be tested and refined. In order to do this, future researchers need to resolve a number of problems.

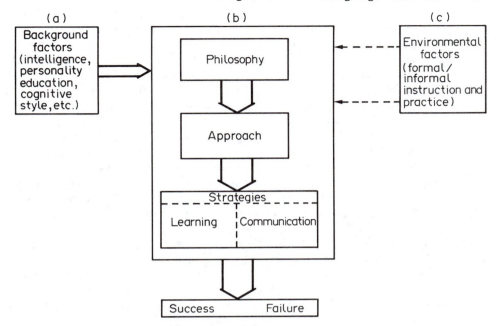

FIG. 1. Model of Second Language Learning

1. Tools for systematically assessing background variables are lacking. One of these variables is personality, although gaining information about this will undoubtedly prove complex because of cross-cultural considerations. Also needed are appropriate measures of cognitive style; our experience here with the Matching Familiar Figures Test for reflectivity/ impulsivity suggests that it does not always provide information that is valid in the language learning setting. (Other researchers, for example, Naiman *et al.*, 1978, have had similar experiences with other measures.) Other styles should also be investigated. Finally, ways of obtaining detailed and reliable information about educational background would be helpful, particularly insights into the kinds of strategies which previous teachers have encouraged students to use.

2. Present instruments to elicit data on "B" factors are at best cumbersome, requiring extensive time for administration and analysis of results. New tools need to be developed which can yield comparable information in less time, making widespread testing more feasible.

3. Classification systems of strategies need further development and standardiz-ation. In the past few years, other taxonomies besides the one used here have been proposed (see, for example, Tarone, Cohen, and Dumas, 1983, and Faerch and Kasper, 1983). While each provides useful insights, it is difficult to compare results from studies using different bases for categorizing strategies.

Using improved instruments and methods, more "winning" and "losing" combinations need to be described. Since there are undoubtedly many of each, a number of case studies will probably be required before meaningful generalizations about the successful and the unsuccessful learner can be made.

As suggested by other authors in this volume, one reason for studying learner strategies is to discover whether poor learners can be trained to use strategies which will lead to greater success. In our model, this training would become an optional "C" factor which may alter a learner's philosophy and approach. Our research suggests that in planning such training it is important to consider a learner's "A" factors: training that might be congenial and therefore effective with one set of characteristics may be so alien to another that it proves counterproductive. As an example, for a field dependent learner with an oral mode preference, such as Pedro, forcing the application of deductive learning may be ineffective. Instead, it may be more useful to train such a learner to employ monitoring strategies based on what "sounds right" instead of rules to edit for correctness.

The language learners we have pictured here are no doubt in many respects familiar figures to experienced ESL teachers. Yet, until now all of us have had to rely too much on impressionistic descriptions of good or poor learners and the causes of their success or failure. The methods used in this study have allowed us to provide considerable documentation of what these two students actually did in the process of learning/using English and to relate these data to their background characteristics. We look forward to combining these insights and others gained from further analysis of our data with those of other researchers in order to better understand the relationship of factors which contribute to success or failure in language learning.

Notes

1. As noted by Rubin (this volume), learning strategies "contribute to the development of the language system which the learner constructs and affect learning directly" while communication strategies, used when there is a discrepancy between "the learner's knowledge and the learner's communicative intent" may contribute indirectly to learning by permitting greater opportunity for language use. In this paper, we have also included in the category of communication strategies attempts by the learner to establish rapport with the listener.

2. Rate of progress through our program was determined by the students' performance on the Michigan English Placement Test (MEPT), given at eight-week intervals during their enrollment. Although the MEPT was designed as a placement rather than an achievement test, we have successfully used it, along with independent teacher evaluations, to make promotion and retention decisions within the program.

    There are potential problems in using the MEPT increase per week as an indication of rate of progress, since students at low levels tend to progress faster than students at higher levels. However, in this study, the correlation between entrance scores and rate of increase was only .09, indicating that there was no significant relationship between the level at which these students began and their rate of progress through the program.

3. Both of our methods of identifying strategies have limitations. The first, observation of strategy use, requires some type of verbalized evidence and thus is more effective with extroverted subjects. The second, thinking aloud, can elicit only information of which subjects are consciously aware, and, like the first, is more productive with subjects who are willing and able to share their thoughts. However, it has been used to advantage by Emig (1971) and Perl (1979) in first language composition, and by Cohen and Hosenfeld (1981) in second language learning. The latter note that students with only a small amount of training are able to provide illuminating comments on their thought processes as they work through problems in language use.

4. Data from Task 1 are missing for one of these subjects, so this task is not discussed here. In general the same subcategories of strategies were used in analyzing data from these tasks as from the interviews, except that social management strategies also include the subjects' comments about the task or their relationship to the task, and inductive strategies include using "what sounds right" as a means of judging appropriate linguistic response. In reporting data from the think-aloud tasks, we have not broken down the counts beyond the broad category level, since

the nature of the think-aloud procedure sometimes prevents the analyst from subcategorizing strategies accurately. For example, in our study, when a subject changed "step" to "steps," it was not possible to tell whether he was monitoring his pronunciation or grammar/morphology. Similar problems occurred in subcategorizing other strategies. Therefore, reporting by main categories permits a more faithful picture of our subjects than would an expanded table.

5. Fillmore (1983), in a study of individual differences among children learning English as a second language, noted a group characterized as both good students and good language learners who "tended to be both analytical and curious" (p. 163). Gerardo seems to resemble these learners in certain respects.

Appendix. Instruments Used for Assessing Background Factors

1. Interview Protocol

    Language Background

    1.   Where were you born?

    2.   Where did you spend your childhood?

    3.   What languages were spoken in your home?

    4.   What do you regard as your native language?

    5.   What languages were spoken in your neighborhood?

    6.   Which was the first foreign language you learned?

    7.   When did you start and how long did you study?

    8.   Where and under what circumstances did you learn? a. When you studied . . .(at school/at home, etc.), what did you study, mainly grammar, for example? b. What kind of textbooks did you use? c. Did the teacher speak in the foreign language most of the time? d. Did you have to speak a lot yourself or did you mainly read and/or translate? e. Do you remember what kind of homework you had to do? f. Do you remember what you had to practice, what was really difficult for you? g. Did you have any contact outside the classroom/your home with speakers of that language? h. Did you have the chance to listen to the radio or see films in the foreign language/in class or outside?

    9.   Which other languages have you studied or tried to study?

    10. Which of these languages do you still speak/use?

    11. Could you tell me how you know these languages now? (see card)

    12. Are you satisfied with your achievement in . . . (the different languages) or would you like to know more?
         Satisfied   More   Other
         Language: Language:

    13. Some people say they have a gift for languages, others say they haven't. Would you regard yourself as strong or weak in languages?
         Strong   Weak   Medium

    (1) Do you think you have a good ear for languages?
         Yes   No   Other

    (2) Do you have a good memory?
         Yes   No   Other

    (3) Do you like to take the language apart and analyze it?
         Yes   No

(Do you like to figure out the language on your own or would you rather have the teacher tell you rules, etc?)

Present Living Conditions

1. Where do you live in Ames? How do you feel about living where you do?

2. What languages do you speak with the person you live with? If you don't speak English with this person, are there others you speak English with? How many hours per day do you spend with this person? Does this person correct your English? If so, how often? What kinds of conversations do you have in English?

3. For what other activities do you use English outside of IEOP? E.g. church, movies, talking with friends, shopping, business, reading for pleasure, reading for other classes, writing letters, etc.

4. Why are you in IEOP?

5. Why did you come to this particular program?

6. When do you want to leave IEOP? What are your plans after IEOP? Are there any reasons why you need to finish IEOP very quickly?

IEOP Classes/Students Goals

1. Compared to language classes in your country, do you regard IEOP classes as formal or informal? Explain what you mean. Do you feel comfortable in this environment?

2. Are any of your IEOP classes different in atmosphere from the others? How do you feel about those classes?

3. What language skill do you think IEOP emphasizes most? In other words, what do you think IEOP teaches students about English? E.g. do you think your teachers want you to be able to understand English more than to speak it, etc?

4. What would *you* like to get out of your English training in the long run?

5. What classroom activities do you like best in IEOP? Give examples. What do you like least?
    If you could change one classroom activity in order to make learning English easier or more interesting for you, what would it be?
    What aspects of English are easy or difficult for you? Why?

Students' Insights into the Language Learning Process

1. Do you think you have any special abilities which help you in learning English? If so, what are they? Do you think you lack certain abilities which would help you be a better learner of English? In other words, what abilities do you wish you had?

2. Have you developed any special techniques or study habits which help you learn English?

3. What grammatical parts of English are most difficult for you? Which parts are easiest?

4. Do you have any idea why this/these parts of English are easy or difficult for you?

5. When you learn new grammar points would you like to be given a rule in English, in your native language, or no rule at all (just examples)?

6. When the teacher introduces a new word, do you learn better when you see it written down or when you hear it?

7. When the teacher introduces a new word, would you prefer a translation of the word into your native language or an explanation of the meaning in English?

8. In speaking, if you don't know a word or expression in English, do you find other words in English to express your idea, say the word or idea in your language, look up the word in a bilingual dictionary, or just forget about trying to express your idea? In writing . . .?

9. Do you participate often in class? Why or why not? Do you mind being called upon by the teacher when you don't have your hand up? Do you like to be able to call out answers without raising your hand? Does it bother you if other students call out without raising their hands? Do you feel that the teacher calls on you often enough or would you like to be called upon more often?

10. When you don't understand something in class, what are you more likely to do? a. Ask the teacher for help or clarification, b. Ask another student for help, c. Try to find help from a textbook or dictionary, d. Not worry about the problem at all.

11. Do you mind being corrected? Are there certain circumstances when you prefer not to have your English corrected?

12. When you make a mistake, do you prefer to be interrupted right away or would you rather finish your response?

13. What do you do when you are corrected? (Do you repeat the correction?)

14. Do you correct other students when they make an error? Do you do it silently or aloud?

15. Many language learners feel very negative about their learning experiences. They say they feel (a) discouraged (b) frustrated (c) impatient or (d) confused by the difficulties of the language learning task. Have you experiences any of these feelings?

16. Other language learners say that the new language feels (e) funny or crazy to them and that they feel (f) ridiculous expressing themselves in the language. Do you ever feel this way about English?

17. Some people feel very (g) shy and (h) helpless when they actually *use* the language. Is this experience familiar to you when you use English?

18. If you had some of these feelings in the past, but no longer have them, what did you do to overcome these feelings?

So far we have talked about what you'd like to learn, how you would go about doing it and how your native language might influence your learning other languages. Considering all this, would you say that you have developed any language study habits (gimmicks, tricks, ways, techniques) that you would find useful in learning the new language?

(1) in learning the *sound system*
    e.g. reading aloud to yourself (in front of a mirror), repeating words silently to yourself after the teacher, etc.

(2) in learning the *grammar*
    e.g. memorizing rules through humorous rhymes, etc., forming hunches about regularities and rules and then applying them, etc.

(3) in learning *vocabulary*/words
    e.g. by constant repetition, by finding relations between words, writing down words, etc.

(4) in developing *listening comprehension*
    e.g. by listening to records, to the radio, etc.

(5) in learning to *talk*
    e.g. through contact with native speakers, by insisting on constant correction or by imagining dialogues in your mind or by talking to yourself, etc.

(6) in learning to *read*
    e.g. by reading popular magazines or books on your own

     (7)   in learning how to express yourself in *written* form
            e.g. by writing to pen pals.

2.   The Raven's Standard Progressive Matrices test (see Raven, Court, and Raven, 1983) was used to assess nonverbal intelligence. This test is language free, and, according to its developers, culture free. It has previously been used in ESL research by Flahive (1980), Oller and Chesarek (reported in Oller, 1981), and d'Anglejan and Renaud (1985).

3.   Cognitive Style Measures

    a.   The Group Embedded Figures Test (GEFT, see Witken *et al.*, 1971) was used to assess field independence/dependence. The GEFT measures the degree to which a subject is able to break up an organized field, separating one part from its background. Subjects who are able to do this easily are *field independent*, while subjects who cannot are *field dependent*. Scores range from 0 to 18, with higher scores representing greater field independence.

    b.   The Matching Familiar Figures Test (MFFT, see Kagan *et al.*, 1964) was used to assess reflection/impulsivity. The MFFT presents subjects with tasks that require hypothesis making and testing. Subjects who respond with the first answer that occurs to them, even though it is often incorrect, are *impulsive*, while subjects who consider several possible answers before making their decision are *reflective*. In this study subjects were ranked along the continuum between reflectivity and impulsivity.

Follow-up Activities

Making Links

1. Consider the various components of Abraham and Vanns model of language learning.
    (a) What assumptions about language learning underly the model?
    (b) How do these assumptions differ from those implicit in Krashen's monitor model? Bialystok's model (*Language Learning* 28 1978)? How are they similar?

Interpreting the Data

2. Compare the strategies Chamot's subjects reported using with those used by the two learners described by Abraham and Vann. Explained the differences or similarities you may note in terms of mode of verbal reporting, taxonomy used to classify the strategies, age, task and other factors you may consider relevant.

3. Examine the data summarized in Tables 2 and 3 to determine how the two subjects differ in their patterns of strategy use.
    (a) How do Abraham and Vann account for these differences? Can you suggest other reasons?
    (b) Would Gerardo's approach to language learning (and his strategies and implicit philosophy) have led to success in an informal context where oral/aural skills were more important?

Applying the Ideas

4. According to Abraham and Vann, their model of second language learning permits many combinations of winning and losing factors.
    (a) Choose four learners from among those you are presently working with — two whom you consider successful and two who are not.
    (b) Referring to Abraham and Vann's model, predict reasons for their success or lack of it. Then, use the procedures they developed to test your insights.
    (c) Evaluate the procedures. What are their strengths? weaknesses? What changes would you make when you use them again?

5. The results from the think-aloud academic tasks (e.g. the cloze, writing) completed by students in the Abraham and Vann study revealed that strategies may also be determined by the task.
    (a) Choose two or three different types of language learning tasks typically used in a second language classroom (e.g. a cloze, evaluating another student's composition, writing sentences with new vocabulary, a fill in the blanks grammar exercise).
    (b) During student-teacher conferences, have students think aloud as they complete these tasks in their second language.
    (c) Note differences and similarities in strategies utilized for the various tasks.

Chapter 8

How to Be a Successful Language Learner: Insights and Prescriptions from L2 Learners

ANITA L. WENDEN

> . . . the adult learner, however, uninstructed he may be, has thought about words and their meanings and the business of communication. And in learning a second language, the adult student almost inevitably thinks about what he is doing and reflects on the nature of the process. (Lewis, 1948: 29–30)

Earlier research on learner strategies has focused exclusively on what learners do or report doing to learn a second language, i.e. their strategies and strategic knowledge (cf Rubin, this volume). There is almost no mention in the literature of second language learners' reflections on the assumptions or beliefs underlying their choice of strategies — what Lewis refers to as the nature of the process (of language learning). Moreover, the few references are limited to acknowledging that language learners hold such beliefs and that they are important. For example, in summarizing the findings of research on the strategies of "good" language learners, Omaggio (1978: 2) did indicate that good language learners have "insight into the nature of the task (of learning)". Hosenfeld (1978) referred to students' "mini-theories" of second language learning and called for research about student assumptions, how they develop, and how they operate. Riley (1980) described a technique that can be used to have students reflect on their learning in order to discover the assumptions they hold about it. He pointed out that making these views explicit can help learners improve their learning skills. In this volume, Abraham and Vann refer to the beliefs learners are assumed to hold about the nature of language; Holec describes learners' "representations", or the assumptions they have about the role of teachers, students, and materials. However, these beliefs have been inferred from the learners' use of strategies. To date, except for Horwitz (this volume), no one has attempted to identify learners' explicit beliefs in any systematic way.[1]

The purpose of this paper is to report on an investigation of one particular subset of these beliefs, i.e. what learners think about how best to approach the task of learning a second language — their explicit prescriptive beliefs.[2] Answers were sought to the following questions: do language learners hold such beliefs? What are they? Are the beliefs reflected in what learners say they do to learn a second language? And finally, what is the significance of such beliefs?

Procedures

A group of 25 adults who had lived in the United States for no longer than two years and who were enrolled part time (5 hours a week) in the advanced level classes of the American Language Program at Columbia University were selected and interviewed (Appendix 1). The questions that formed the main body of the semi-structured interview required learners to report on social contexts in which they heard or used English. They were also asked to talk about language learning activites in which they engaged in the classroom and outside — with emphasis on activities outside the classroom. (See Appendix 2 for a list of topics covered during the interview.) The interviews, which averaged ninety minutes in length, were tape recorded and transcribed. Guidelines for analyzing the transcripts for recurring statements of beliefs were developed by adapting procedures from content analysis. (See Appendix 3 for a brief description of content analysis and the criteria developed to identify statements of explicit belief, and Appendix 4 for a coded transcript.)

Findings

Twelve explicit statements, representing learners' prescriptive beliefs, were identified, defined and categorized into three main groups on the basis of the general overall approach to language learning advocated by each one. In this section, the beliefs that make up each group will be explained and illustrated with examples from students' transcripts.[3] Next, the approaches of three learners, representative of each group, will be analyzed to determine the possible relationship between learners' explicit beliefs and their approach to language learning. Finally, the significance of such beliefs will be discussed.

Views on Language Learning

Fourteen of the twenty-five learners made explicit statements about how best to approach language learning. Five of the statements stressed the importance of using the language, i.e. especially of speaking and listening. Four pointed to the need to learn about the language, especially grammar and vocabulary. Three others emphasized the role of personal factors.[4]

Group 1: Use the Language

1. *Learn the natural way.* This statement means that it is not necessary to be in a classroom to learn a second language. One simply utilizes it in the social contexts in which one finds oneself to fulfill the functions necessary to communication in the context. Moreover, while opportunities to use the language should not be avoided, this does not mean that learners should force themselves to use it. Stating his view on using new words, a young Israeli who stressed the importance of "living the language" explained:
   "I don't think I have to use it. If it happens to me to use it, I use it. I don't force myself to use a word, cause if it's compulsive, it's not natural."
Describing his stay with a British Family, Miguel says:
   "Everything was natural. The relationship with him (i.e. his landlord) was as with a family. We watched TV and talked about what we saw."
And later referring to his courses in the Business School at Columbia University:
   "I took two courses in business — micro economics and accounting. . . . I read,

studied, listened to lectures and took notes in English. I thought about the meaning of the subject. I did not think about the language. I was trying to learn the natural way."

2. *Practice*. This second theme stresses the *necessity* of using the language *as often as possible*. There is a note of intensity not present in the preceding theme, e.g. "I tried this way not only to study very hard, but to take every opportunity (to speak) . . ."; "I tell myself . . . if you are here you must speak."; "You have to do everything in English . . ."; "Practice. That's the secret." Learners varied on what the result of intensive practice would be. For some practice was necessary or one would forget or lose one's sense of English. Others felt that with practice one would learn "automatically", "get accustomed to speaking," "understand better," and/or "learn to think in English."

3. *Think in your second language*. This third theme emphasizes the need to focus directly on the meaning of the communication when using the language. One should not first plan the utterance in one's native language and then translate. Says Laszlo, "Even when someone asks me a question, I concentrate on the meaning. I don't plan what I have to say. I try to eliminate my native language so the idea and word are almost simultaneous. This is the best way not to think in your native language. You must think in the language you are learning . . ." Ilse's view is similar. Reflecting upon a listening strategy she had used during her first month in the United States, she says: ". . . (it's) also very important to get the sound and keep it. Then to transfer everything into thinking."

Generally, it was felt that thinking in the second language would enable one to learn better: "I thought the less we think, speak, read Portuguese, the better we can get in English . . ." And, more specifically, it was felt there was a kind of reciprocal relationship between using the language and thinking in the language: "You hear it, you speak it, you learn to think in the language . . . If you have to think in English, you speak better."

4. *Live and study in an environment where the target language is spoken*. For most learners this guideline meant that one should be in the country where the target language was the main or official language of communication. And so, if one wanted to learn English, for example, one should go to the United States or Britain. On the other hand, one learner decided it might be even better to go to a country where neither his native language nor the target language was the main language of communication but where one could expect to meet speakers of the target language. He felt that it would be easier to become a part of a community of TL speakers living abroad (in his case, Americans) than it was to do so in their country of origin.

Learners had different reasons for stressing this guideline. For some, living in a target language community provided one with the opportunity to practice:
" . . . you learn to speak English when you learn here because you have to practice . . . because everywhere you have to speak English and have to listen . . . I think if you don't go to the place, you don't learn the language."

Others, such as Ryuichi, a Japanese business man, felt that if his "hearing is a little better" it is because "now, he understands America . . ." So even if he can't understand some words, he can guess. ". . . It's not related with the improvement of language . . ." In other words, being in the target language country, one could better understand the culture and once that happened one would better understand the language.

For Ilse, however, "It's not important to know the culture. But when you are in the culture it's easier to learn and when everything is in this language, then it's better. You learn it better . . . not easier." Learning better meant learning the language more authentically: "When you are in a country, you get everything . . . not only grammar and vocabulary . . . It's mixed up more."

5. *Don't worry about mistakes.* Of course most learners wanted to learn to speak accurately, but learners who made this statement believed that excessive concern about accuracy would get in the way of using the language. ". . . if you don't speak and if you don't write because of your mistakes, you'll have to wait twenty years before you say something. It's better to talk." Asked what advice he would give a friend coming to study English Oshi said, "Speak as much as you can . . . don't care about mistakes." Or (Oshi again), "Just say it. Never be concerned about English structure."

Group 2: Learn About the Language

1. *Learn grammar and vocabulary.* Learners who made this statement considered grammar and vocabulary fundamental to successful learning for they are the building blocks of English: "I'm watching my English by learning more vocabulary . . . because without words . . . English consists of words and I think I should learn more vocabulary." Or, "Grammar background is important to learn. Without grammar background you can't improve. There are some limitations." One learner spelled out these limitations: "If I don't pay attention to constructions, I may translate all the words, but I don't know what they're talking about."

2. *Take a formal course.* Learners had different reasons for recommending the taking of a formal course. For some it is the "best way" because "it's systematic." One proceeds "step by step from easy to hard" and in that way does not "miss some basic material" (which was usually grammar, vocabulary and in some cases the "right pronunciation").

Taking a course was also a means of ensuring that one learned correct English:

> "The course gives me the right base . . . If you learn to play tennis or to use a weapon, if you don't have the right base to use it, you make mistakes all the time and afterwards you get to making mistakes and you'll never be good cause someone who makes mistakes sticks to them. They'll never get rid of them. Anyway, someone who wants to learn the language has to take a course for the direction."

3. *Learn from mistakes.* This view on mistakes is different from the view presented in the previous category in that it emphasizes the importance of feedback as a way to learn, i.e. mistakes brought to one's attention should be reflected on so that they may be avoided in the future. In some cases feedback comes from friends or a teacher: "When I make a mistake they correct me (his friends). It is a good way to learn from those mistakes." Or "the best way is to write the sentence and let the teacher correct you . . ." And, in others, one becomes aware of one's mistakes oneself. One simply speaks out and contrasts what one has said with what native speakers say and note the differences. Of this strategy, Jairo says:

"... I think it's a good way to learn ... Though it (i.e. what one says) may not always be right. But, if I don't speak out my mistakes I'll never learn ... I'll never find out the right way ..."

Alternately, in the very act of speaking out one becomes aware of one's mistakes. Says Oshi:

"Don't care about mistakes, grammar or rules of English. Speak according to the order of your thinking; it will be wrong. You will notice it is different (from English). Then I'll think according to the English way. I'll speak naturally English. I can change the order of thinking ..."

4. *Be mentally active.* This statement stressed the need for deliberate, conscious effort on the part of the learner. For Jose, this means paying alot of attention: "It's very important that you have attention. Without attention, I couldn't understand." Laszlo adds a note of intensity to the same notion when he says, "My mind is always open to accept information about the language ... I always concentrate because I have to learn." Moreover, when one doesn't understand, it is important to ask: "This is the best way to learn — ask always." Finally, being mentally active means acting upon or transforming what one has received or asked about: "I just don't take it as it comes. I change it in my mind. There's always movement."

Group 3: Personal Factors are Important

1. *The emotional aspect is important.* It is understood that *feelings* have a strong influence on language learning and that they must be taken into account. "I think one problem for me and perhaps everyone learning a language, you have to be stimulated to learn." In some cases, feelings can facilitate learning: "If the discussion is interesting, one's mind is awake and one is open to learn — even unconsciously." And in others learning is inhibited unless feelings are overcome: "I was not ashamed to ask. That was the main point. I had to overcome this shame or fear."

2. *Self-concept* can also facilitate or inhibit learning. Cida reports, "My theory was similar to the theory I had working with adults. They become like children when they're in school ... they regress. I decided when it happened to me I wouldn't worry. But still it wasn't easy to endure and live through it ..." And so, referring to her landlady, she acknowledges, "She treated me like a child — she only made me regress further."

3. *Aptitude for learning* is a third personal factor considered necessary for learning. Says Ryuichi, "I think the improvement of language is due to some inheritance ... I think the most important thing is our personal ability to learn English. In my case, I have no personal ability, so I think it will take a long time ... there is no good way to speed up my learning ..."

Table 1 provides an overview of the themes in terms of frequency. Of the 14 students who actually made explicit statements about their prescriptive beliefs, nine stressed the importance of practice and seven the importance of learning grammar and vocabulary. The following four beliefs (3–6) were referred to by five of the students and the others (7–8, 9, 10–11, 12) by four, three, two and one respectively.

Table 2 presents the beliefs in terms of category. It shows which learners referred to which category of beliefs and how often.

As represented in Table 2, the data suggests that beliefs related to using the language were the most popular. Seven learners (1–7) referred predominantly to

TABLE 1

Prescriptive beliefs by frequency

1.	Practice	9	7.	Feelings are important	4
2.	Learn grammar/vocab.	7	8.	Be mentally active	4
3.	Learn the natural way	5	9.	Learn through your mistakes	3
4.	Think in SL	5	10.	Don't mind mistakes	2
5.	Live in the TL env't	5	11.	Language aptitude counts	2
6.	Take a course	5	12.	Self-concept counts	1

n = 25

TABLE 2 *Prescriptive Beliefs of Individual Learners by Category*

Beliefs	1	2	3	4	5	6	7	8	9	10	11	12	13	14
1. USE THE LANGUAGE														
Learn the nat'l way	6*		1	6			2							1
Practice	3	2	1	1	4	6	1	1	1					
Live in the SL env't	1	3			1	1		1						
Don't mind mistakes**	1		4											
Think in SL		3		1	1						1			1
2. LEARN ABOUT THE LANGUAGE														
Take a course				1		1	1			2		1		
Learn G/V					1			2	3	5	2	1	1	
Learn from mistakes			1							2				2
Be mentally active		2			1					3	1			
3. PERSONAL FACTORS COUNT														
Feelings										2	1		1	4
Language aptitude				2			2							
Self-concept												1		

*numbers indicate the frequency of the statement
SL: second language; G/V: grammar and vocabulary
**The expression "don't mind" means don't "worry about" NOT "ignore".

this set of beliefs while four learners (9–12) referred predominantly to beliefs related to learning about the language (i.e. Group 2) and only two (13 and 14) predominantly to beliefs related to personal factors (Group 3). One learner (8) referred equally to beliefs from each category.

Moreover, most of the students (except 5, 8 and 14) seemed to have a preferred set of beliefs. In other words, of the seven who referred most frequently to the importance of using the language, one (1) referred to this set of beliefs exclusively and five (i.e. all but 5) referred to only one other belief — from Group 2. Of the four learners who stressed the importance of learning about the language, two learners referred to this category of beliefs exclusively (i.e., 10 and 12). One (9) referred to only one other belief — from Group 1. And though learner 11 referred to beliefs from all three categories, his references to Group 2 were more frequent. As for learners referring predominantly to the importance of personal factors, one of the two (13) referred to only one other belief (in Group 2).

Behavioral Profiles

To illustrate the possible relationship between the explicit beliefs of these learners and what they said they did to learn English, differences in the characteristic approaches of three learners will be outlined. Miguel (from Spain) stressed the importance of using the language to learn. During the interview he referred exclusively to this set of beliefs mentioning four of the five themes that make it up. Eunn Jin (from Korea) stressed the importance of learning about the language and, also, referred exclusively to this set of beliefs. During the interview, she mentioned recurringly two of the four themes that define this view. Finally, Cida (from Brazil) emphasized personal factors and in her interview talked in detailed about the importance of emotional stimulus and self concept.

Differences will be described in terms of strategies, attending pattern, criteria used for evaluating the effectiveness of a language learning activity, and planning priorities.

Strategies

Learners who emphasized the importance of using the language would often utilize communication strategies. In explaining why it was not difficult for him to speak with the British family with whom he spent a summer, Miguel said he did not think before speaking. He looked for the words he needed to "build up" short sentences at school or used words his landlord had used. He also "spoke as clearly and slowly as he could" or "used many explanations or drawings". To understand the language, he "asks questions and listens with all five senses" or uses visual cues to help himself understand, "Actions represent the meaning of speech . . . (I) heard 'demonstration' and saw the action (on TV); then the announcer said 'this is a demonstration' . . . " When reading the newspaper, he used pictures and headlines and focused on news from Spain. While such strategies may have led him to focus on specific words (e.g. "demonstration"), the primary purpose was to get at the overall meaning of the discourse.

On the other hand, learners who emphasized the importance of learning about the language tended to use cognitive strategies that helped them to better understand and remember specific items of language. In explaining how she dealt with unfamiliar words encountered while reading, Eunn Jin said, "I looked up all the words I didn't know and made a notebook. (Miguel had said he refused to make such a word list.) I tried to memorize ten words a day." She also "consulted grammar books to understand." Her approach to using the words also placed a primary emphasis on remembering rather than on communicating. She says, "But you can't remember the words if you don't use them. So I tried to use the words I learned. It was hard in Korea, but I used them when I had the chance." Of the 23 strategies she referred to using during the interview, 16 were cognitive strategies. Learners in this group also used cognitive strategies to learn from their mistakes.

Learners who stressed the importance of personal factors were not distinguished from the others in terms of their strategies.

Attending Pattern

As they interacted in a variety of social settings, learners who emphasized the importance of using the language attended primarily (though not always exclusively) to the meaning and social purpose of the interaction, not to language form. In describing his strategy for understanding the newspapers he read, Miguel said, "I didn't think about grammar. I tried to catch the meaning." As for learning vocabulary, he said, "Everything was natural. When I went to a restaurant, I had to order. So I looked at the menu and learned words that way." And later, he added, "In a conversation your partner speaks to you and you have to answer. You become very interested in the subject and you remember words you learned. You learn new ones. In this way you understand better." For Miguel and learners who approached language learning as he did, the focus of their attention was on the purpose of the communication.

Learners who stressed the importance of learning about the language were much more conscious of language form. They said they approached communication situations very consciously with the primary (but not exclusive) intent to learn about the language. In Eunn Jin's case, this meant paying attention to grammar and vocabulary. She said, "Now I understand more easily, and so I try to catch the grammar. When I read, I also pay attention to the grammar. I feel uncomfortable if I can't get it exactly." And referring to watching TV, she said, "Now, when I watch TV and listen to the news, I pay attention to the vocabulary."

Learners who said personal factors were important were not distinguished from the others because they tended to attend to language form or the social purpose of a communication. Rather they tended to remember the feelings associated with various language learning activities and contexts of learning. Referring to her first days in the country, Cida said, "I was crazy 'cause I didn't know how to express myself . . . I felt depressed and did not think I could learn." Of the impact made by her landlady's constant attempts to correct her, she said she was "ashamed"; she made her feel like a child . . . "When you are a foreigner adapting and you have problems feeling confident, she only made me regress further . . ." She disliked her ESL classes, especially the methodology and was sensitive to her American classmates' attitudes towards foreigners . . ." I feel they don't like to listen to foreigners and I'm the only foreigner in my concentration . . ."

The analysis did not indicate that learners could be distinguished by the specific *aspects* of language form they actually reported noting. All learners referred more frequently to vocabulary and less so to items of syntax or phonology. Nor did learner attention to their proficiency prove to be a distinguishing characteristic among the three groups of learners. All of them were more preoccupied with how well or poorly they used the language, especially their oral/aural skills and not with how much they knew about it. However, the learners who stressed the importance of personal factors tended to look beyond proficiency to themselves as the cause for a lack of improvement or a generally undesirable level of proficiency. They referred to character traits ("I'm lazy . . ."); age ("At my age, it's hard to remember."); social role ("I'm too busy now. I have no time to study."); physical state ("If I'm tired, I can't learn.")

Evaluation Criteria

To explain why they considered a particular language learning activity or context helpful to learning, those interviewees who believed that using the language was important referred most often to whether or not they had the opportunity to use the language. Thus, Miguel said that living with his landlord was "good" because of the opportunity to speak English. His business courses were also "a good experience" because he talked and read in English, i.e. he used the language. On the other hand, he soon left one ESL class because "there were only Spanish students." The implication was that he would not be able to use the language since he, too, was Spanish. He left a university in Connecticut for the same reason, "The problem was that the campus was far from the city and after the first semester, all the American students left. There was no opportunity to practice. I didn't like that." Secondarily, students who emphasized the importance of using the language noted whether the context facilitated understanding. For example, Miguel found watching TV a useful experience because of the many non verbal clues it provides for understanding what is said. Finally, other learners with the same set of views also thought a language learning activity useful when the English they heard in that particular setting was "real" or authentic (i.e. not classroom English).

On the other hand, learners, such as Eunn Jin, who believed in learning about the language, noted whether the context or activity provided an opportunity to hear "good or proper" language. She, as did other learners who held a similar set of views, also referred to the complexity and level of difficulty of the learning or communication task, e.g. the kind of topics discussed, the sophistication of the language used, in evaluating their contexts of learning. For those who wished to be challenged, this was an asset and for others it was a disadvantage. They found that they could not perform satisfactorily and that this inhibited their learning. Finally, some learners who held this view referred to the fact that they could have their errors corrected as an advantage.

In evaluating their learning activities, learners who felt personal factors were important to learning were distinguished by their preoccupation with affective criteria. They noted the relevance of what they were learning. They also mentioned the qualities of the teacher and the social environment (i.e. their classmates, the classroom atmosphere. . .). Cida, for example, found speaking with a social work colleague a useful learning experience because she "stimulated her to learn" and tried to make her feel confident. A discussion class she was taking was also evaluated as useful because the students were supportive. The social work classes she audited for language learning purposes were also considered useful because she could learn vocabulary related to her profession, i.e. they were relevant.

Planning Priorities

Learners representative of Group I (use the language) and Group II (learn about the language) could be distinguished on the basis of their language learning priorities. The former group had emphasized the importance of aural/oral skills. Of course, they did not all refer explicitly to a decision to focus on aural/oral skills. However, the description of the activities they engaged in and the strategies they utilized indicated a preoccupation with speaking and understanding. The latter group tended to give priority to learning about the language. For some learners, this was an implicit decision, but for others, like Eunn Jinn, the decision was quite explicit. She decided, as a result of a frustrating experience in a reading class in Korea, that it "was important to learn grammar and vocabulary first." And that was what she did and continued to do as indicated by the focus of her strategies and learning activities despite the fact that she had more serious problems with the use of the language.

Implications

How should this listing of learners' explicit prescriptions about how best to learn a second language be interpreted? What does it reveal to us about this group of second language learners? What could similar investigations reveal about other groups of second language learners?

First of all, it shows us, as Lewis stated (p. 1), that language learners do think about the nature of the process (of language learning) and are able to articulate some of these beliefs. The Piagetian view of the three types of self-regulation in learning provides insight into the significance of this ability. According to Piaget (1976), there are three primary types of self-regulation — autonomous, active, and conscious regulation.[5] In the autonomous stage, individual learning remains unanalyzed and learners are totally preoccupied with the goal. They do not try to represent to themselves the nature of what they are doing. They have not yet generalized on their experience or attempted to abstract what is salient. On the other hand, in the fully conscious stage, processes are carried on exclusively on the mental plane. Hypotheses are constructed and their results imagined and on the basis of these speculations, they may be revised or rejected. It is the intermediate stage, of active regulation, that is of special relevance in this discussion of the explicit beliefs of language learners. In this stage, learners move beyond exclusive preoccupation with the task and seek to understand principles behind it. There is awareness of one's actions and of a need to systematize, consolidate, and generalize knowledge. Successful procedures begin to be noted and "theories-in-action", i.e. the implicit ideas or changing modes of representation underlying action (Karmiloff-Smith and Inhelder, 1974/75: 196), are created and tested.[6] At the outset, theories-in-action are implicit. However, eventually, learners are able to describe them. From this perspective, then, the beliefs identified in this study can be interpreted as representing their "theories-in-action." The beliefs point to the fact that these learners have begun to reflect upon what they are doing in order to understand the principles behind it and so, to their developing potential to regulate their learning.

This study also raises the following questions about learner beliefs:

1. How comprehensive and representative is the set of beliefs described in this study?
In her study (this volume), Horwitz used a structured questionnaire of 34 items.

These items represented the views of 100+ foreign language teachers and second language learners, elicited through a free-recall task or check list based on the outcome of the free recall. Of these 34 items, fifteen could be classified in terms of the categories reported on in this paper. However, only in five cases were these items restatements of beliefs I have already listed. Some provided further elaboration on some of these beliefs. There were six different items referring to views on language aptitude. Others were themes that might eventually develop into separate sets of beliefs, e.g. the role of culture, the nature of language. These differences point to the need to develop a more comprehensive and representative set of beliefs.

2. How are beliefs formed? As I have already mentioned, the students' reports did reveal five factors that appeared to influence or trigger the formation of their beliefs. Moreover, the actual number of factors seemed to vary from learner to learner. The genesis and development of beliefs should also be investigated.

3. Are learners' beliefs reflected in their practice? Analysis of the self-reports of the language learners in this study have suggested some possible relationships between belief and behavior. These provide us with an initial set of hypotheses. However, more definitive statements about such a relationship will require the development of some type of scale. A well tested and comprehensive set of beliefs could provide the basis for devising such an instrument. At the same time, one should be cautious about quickly attributing what learners do exclusively to their beliefs. Some learners will not necessarily be able to refer explicitly to their beliefs, if they hold them at all. For example, in this study, four learners did not. Then there may be other factors, such as purpose, influencing their practice. These also need to be determined.

These questions need to be answered if we wish to better understand this facet of the language learners' cognitive abilities. It is intended that the preliminary classification and the procedures outlined in the study serve as a starting point for researchers who wish to do so.

Teachers will have recognized the similarity between learners' explicit beliefs and some of the topics of discussion that have come up and, in some cases, been hotly debated in second language methodology classes. In recent decades, for example, we have been led to reconsider the best context for language learning. Is it the "natural way"? and if so, what are the implications for classroom teaching? There is also controversy on the significance of errors and how best to deal with them. Learners who stated that feelings and self-concept are important echo the concerns for affective factors reflected in methodologies that encourage a more holistic approach to second language learning and teaching (e.g. counseling-learning). In other words, the beliefs listed by the learners in this study point to learning-teaching issues that classroom teachers must confront and resolve. They provide us with learners' views on these methodological questions and can be a source of insight into their learning difficulties and to the overt and hidden resistance to some of the activities we organize to help them learn. Therefore, teachers are also encouraged to use the procedures outlined in this study to discover the prescriptive beliefs of their own students and, then, to translate this knowledge into "teaching strategies" which will enable learners to approach second language learning autonomously and skillfully.[7]

Notes

1. For references to research on learner beliefs or "theories" in areas other than L2 learning see Trepanier, 1982; Steinberg, 1980; Lambert, 1984; Brown and Baker, 1984).
2. The findings reported on in this paper were the outcome of an analysis that constituted phase three of a study originally undertaken to investigate and classify learners' statable or declarative knowledge about various aspects of their language learning. The first two phases of the study sought to determine what aspects of their language learning experience learners were capable of talking about other than their strategies and what insights this knowledge could provide on their use of strategies. The results of these two phases have been described in Wenden, 1986a.
3. Self-reports quoted have been edited for syntax. Ideas which may not have appeared in sentence form and which may have been interrupted by a question from the interviewer have been rewritten as complete sentences to facilitate comprehension. Terms used by learners to express these ideas, however, have not been changed.
4. Some of the learners also referred explicitly to the belief that language learning was unconscious. However, this belief was not included in the findings because it is not prescriptive in nature. Moreover, seven of the learners who made this statement are not included among the fourteen whose beliefs are to be analyzed because they referred only to this belief (that language learning is unconscious) and to no other.
5. While Piaget was primarily concerned with the cognitive development of children over time, Brown *et al.* (1982: 119–120) refer to a study which illustrated how an adult progressed through the three stages within a single problem solving session. In other words, while these notions have been based on the observation of the learning of children, they can be applied to the learning of adults as it evolves in one domain and in response to one task, such as language learning.
6. Karmiloff-Smith and Inhelder (1974/75) distinguish between "theories-in-action" and hypotheses, stating that the latter connote the idea of expressly trying to verify. This notion is not implied by "theories-in-action".
7. See Wenden (1986b) for classroom activities which help learners examine and evaluate beliefs about language learning.

Appendix 1. Profile of Learners

Country of Origin

Country	Number of learners	Country	Number of learners	Country	Number of learners
Argentina	1	Columbia	1	Korea	1
Austria	1	Hungary	1	Portugal	1
Brazil	3	Israel	1	Spain	1
Sri Lanka	1	Italy	2	Taiwan	1
China	1	Japan	8	Yugoslavia	1

English Proficiency

Level	Number of learners
ESL-advanced I	3
ESL-advanced II	6
ESL-advanced III	13
English	3

Education

Level	Number of learners
High school	3
BA degree	19
MA degree	3

Length of Stay in English Speaking Country

Number of years	Number of learners
½ year or less	8
½ year–1 year	10
1 year–1½ year	4
1½ year–2 years	3

Age

Age	Number of learners
47–40	2
39–31	7
30–26	9
25–23	7

n = 25

Appendix 2. Interview Procedures and Topics

In order to facilitate retrospection and to reduce the possibility of faulty reporting due to memory lapses, the following procedures were implemented before the actual interview.

1. A few days before the interview, participants were given a list of questions to think about. The questions were related to various aspects of their language learning. They were also asked to complete a Grid of Daily Activities. The grid indicated the social settings in which they usually found themselves during a typical week an the language they used in each one. Learners' reports were focused on the settings in which they used English, e.g. a favorite TV program, reading novels, taking a pottery class, studying for the TOEFL test, taking flying lessons.

2. To help interviewees feel at ease and to give them confidence in their ability to talk about their learning, actual discussion of the social settings on their grid was preceded by questions about topics language learners generally talk about quite readily (e.g. why they came to the United States; their reactions to the culture; their previous second language learning experience).

3. Before reporting on a specific setting, interviewees were asked to recreate/describe it. Then, questions dealing with the following topics were asked about each one:

(1)   why they participated in the given social setting

(2)   what strategies they used to express themselves, to understand what was said, and to think in their second language
(3)   what they noticed about the language
(4)   how they dealt with their errors
(5)   how they felt in that situation and why
(6)   whether they felt the situation contributed to their language learning and why.

When the social settings listed on a grid had been discussed, more general questions were asked to test the consistency of their answers. These questions dealt with the same aspects of learning discussed in the main body of the interview, but they were not context bound and, in some cases, presented learners with hypothetical situations, e.g. advice they would give a friend coming to the United States to study.

Appendix 3. Methodological Notes

According to Kerlinger (1973), content analysis is a way of studying and analyzing written communications in a systematic and objective manner. Instead of observing people's behavior directly or even interviewing them, the researcher takes the communications people have produced and asks questions of these communications. In some cases the communications have not been produced for research purposes. That is letters, diaries, newspaper editorials can be content analyzed. In other cases, the written communications are prepared especially with a research purpose in mind. In this study, for example, written transcripts were analyzed. These transcripts were based on semi-structured interviews which had learners retrospect on various aspects of their language learning.

How is content analysis done? First, it is necessary to define the area or "universe of content" that is to be analyzed. In this study, it was learners' prescriptive beliefs about language learning. A unit of analysis must also be determined. In this study, I used the "theme," i.e. any proposition or statement learners made about how best to learn English.

The following criteria were developed to identify the themes or explicit statements of belief:

1.   The themes were *generalizations* learners made about themselves, all language learners or about various aspects of language learning.
2.   They were either used to *justify* why learners did what they did, or to *describe* on a more abstract level the *essence of an experience* or a learner's *characteristic approach*.
3.   Sometimes they were *spontaneous contributions* on the part of the learner, or they were a *response to a probing question* by the interviewer (e.g. why?) checking for clarification or consistency.
4.   They often appeared in the following *verbal contexts*:
    — "I think . . ."; ". . . It's important to . . ." (statements of opinion)
    — "The best way to learn is . . ." (superlative or comparative statements)
    — "You have to . . ." (the imperative mode)
    — ". . . is . . ." (a definition about what it means to learn English)
    — "if . . ., then" (a hypothetical statement).
5.   The statement might be expressed *recurringly* throughout the interview either using the same phraseology or restated in other words.
6.   The statement might be *explained in great detail* and/or with a tone of conviction.

Appendix 4. Coded Transcript

The speaker is a Hungarian immigrant to the United States. He had had no formal training of English in Hungary.

str 1: cognitive strategy   str 2: strategy of communication
att flg: attending to feelings   att com: attending to communication
thry: theory   evl: evaluative criteria

Q: Would you like to discuss your friends? How did you learn from them?
A: [Whenever I didn't understanding anything, I asked, I inquired and they explained.] str 1 & 2*
      [I was not ashamed to ask.] att:flg [That was the main point.] thry . . .
Q: Do you remember what you asked about?
A: Concrete words . . . mostly the everyday English I couldn't read in a book.
Q: What did you do after they explained it to you?
A: [I kept it in mind.] str 1 [I practiced.] str 1 I . . . hard to explain. I tried to keep it in mind . . . and [to use it to build up a sentence . . .] str 1
Q: By yourself or . . .?
A: By myself and in conversation. I tried to use it to practice to give a deep trace in my mind . . . not

only the isolated word that I learned but I tried to put it in a sentence and [I acquired, I remembered . . .] evl

Q: When you wanted to say something, what did you do? Some people think carefully first; others just talk . . .

A: Yeah. [I always concentrate on what I say.] att:com [But I don't put into form before hand, so I try to do the same in English, whatever level it is. I try to eliminate my native language so the idea and the word are almost simultaneous . . .] str 1 & 2

Q: You did that from the very beginning?

A: Yes. I tried . . . [It's the best. A language has to reflect the reality and not in another language.] thry . . . so I remember in Hungary at the very beginning, [I used the method where I connect the English word to the object and not to the Hungarian word, so I made an associative relation — the object and the English word.] str 1

*The distinction between a cognitive strategy and a communication strategy is not always so clear. The same strategy may contribute to learning and facilitate communication.

Follow-up activities

Making Links

1. According to Wenden, some of the specific beliefs that constitute each main view outlined in her study point to teaching/learning issues that come up and are hotly debated in L2 methodology classes. She cites three.
   (a) What are they? Can you list others?
   (b) Which second language teaching methodology (or methodologies) is most similar in its approach to the three main categories of beliefs described in the study, i.e. "use the language"? "learn about the language"? "personal factors are important"?
   (c) Which of these categories of beliefs best illustrate the approaches to language learning utilized by the successful and unsuccessful learners described by Abraham and Vann? the beliefs of learners you've worked with?
   (d) Predict what the expectations of students holding beliefs from the various categories would be about classroom methodology, curriculum, student role in L2 learning.

Applying the Ideas

2. It has been suggested that the explicit beliefs of learners represent their theories-in-action, i.e. their attempts to articulate the principles that underlie their language learning behaviors. Reflect on your beliefs about L2 learning.
   (a) Do they represent what you actually did to learn your second language? how you teach a second language?
   (b) How were your beliefs formed? i.e. what factors other than experience may have been the source of your beliefs?
   (c) Referring to the studies in this section for guidance, devise procedures for researching the origins of learner beliefs on L2 learning. Also consult texts on qualitative research methodology for further suggestions.

3. Several of the students interviewed by Wenden pointed to the utility of the semi-structured interview as a means of raising awareness about the learning process. They felt the interview helped them to clarify and assess their approach to learning. As one student said, "It's like therapy."
   (a) Have your students list the activities or social settings where they usually use English (i.e. hear, speak, read, write). Using the interview topics listed by Wenden, have them discuss their language learning experience in one or several of these social settings, in small groups. See Wenden's procedures for hints on how to lead such an interview. For further background read books on administering interviews and/or survey questionnaires (e.g. Kahn, R. and Connell, C. The Dynamics of Interviewing I)
   (b) Tape record the discussion and, then, play it back to the group.
   (c) Students can be asked to clarify and/or defend their views.
   (d) Varying views and/or approaches to similar language tasks can be identified and evaluated.

Chapter 9

Surveying Student Beliefs About Language Learning

ELAINE K. HORWITZ

Introduction

Language learning is the subject of many strong opinions.[1] Each month the academic journals report language teachers' and researchers' latest ideas on foreign language aptitude or child-adult learning differences, and even casual chatter at cocktail parties draws spirited controversy. Many Americans believe strongly, for example, that children are better language learners than adults or that second language learning is mainly a matter of learning many new vocabulary words. ESL students also hold a wide variety of beliefs about language learning. These beliefs have varying degrees of validity and numerous origins, often differing radically from the current opinions of second language scholars; in many cases, the term "myth" might be a more accurate characterization. Some beliefs are likely influenced by students' previous experiences as language learners. An unsuccessful learning experience could easily lead a student to the conclusion that special abilities are required to learn a foreign language and that s/he does not possess these necessary abilities. Other beliefs are probably shaped by students' cultural backgrounds. In the typical ESL classroom where there is a native teacher and students of many cultural backgrounds, differing beliefs about language learning may well be a significant source of culture clash.

Although we know that students come to ESL classes with many preconceived ideas about language learning, we know very little about the nature of these beliefs, the beliefs that specific types of students hold, or how these beliefs affect language learning strategies. This paper will report on the development of an instrument to assess student beliefs about language learning and report on the responses of one group of ESL students to this inventory. Its aim is to sensitize teachers to the types of beliefs students hold and to the possible consequences of these beliefs for second language learning and instruction.

Importance of Studying Student Beliefs

ESL teachers often encounter student resistance to some of their instructional activities. Some students want more opportunities for free conversation and complain about pattern drills while others distrust communicative approaches and insist that their every utterance be strictly corrected. Teachers are likely to find similar instances of student concern or dissatisfaction whenever instructional activities are inconsistent with students' preconceived beliefs about language learning. When language classes fail to meet student expectations, students can lose confidence in the instructional approach and their ultimate achievement can be limited.

Even when student beliefs do not manifest themselves overtly in class dissatisfaction, they still can have a strong impact on the students' ultimate success in language learning. A large proportion of language learning goes on outside of the classroom and is therefore not subject to the teacher's direct intervention. Yet, how students control this learning is crucial to their success as language learners. Chamot and O'Malley note:

> . . . (language) learning strategies enable students to take command over their learning and to apply procedures that will assist them in retaining and using important language skills. Productive use of learning strategies, though, is an acquired skill.[2]

The question raised here concerns the impact that student beliefs have on the students' acquisition and use of effective language learning strategies. A student who believes, for example, that one must never say anything in English until it can be said correctly will probably avoid speaking most of the time. Indeed, Wenden (this volume) supplies preliminary evidence that student beliefs about language learning can influence their language learning strategies. In interviews with language learners, she finds numerous instances where students are not only able to enumerate their beliefs about language learning, but, even more importantly, they describe learning strategies consistent with these beliefs. In other words, what students think about language learning can affect how they go about doing it. Therefore, knowledge of student beliefs about language learning is an important step toward understanding the etiology of learning strategies.

The Development of a Language Learning Belief Inventory

The Beliefs About Language Learning Inventory (BALLI)[3] was developed to assess student opinions on a variety of issues and controversies related to language learning. The 34 Likert-scale items have both research and training purposes (ESL Student Version, Appendix A). As a research instrument, it is currently being used to assess the beliefs of students and teachers about language learning (1) to understand the nature of student beliefs and the impact of these beliefs on language learning strategies (2) to understand why teachers choose particular teaching practices and (3) to determine where the beliefs of language teachers and their students might be in conflict. As a teaching instrument the BALLI has served as a useful stimulus in teacher workshops and in discussions with language learners as to how to improve their language learning strategies.[4]

In order to elicit a wide-range of beliefs, the development of the inventory proceeded in several stages. First, in a free recall task, four groups of approximately 25 language (both English and foreign language) teachers of different cultural backgrounds were asked to list (1) their beliefs about language learning (2) other people's beliefs about language learning, and (3) their students' beliefs about language learning. (The decision to use teachers at the onset was based on the assumption that their beliefs would be more salient to them.) Interestingly, the lists were rather short and contained a great deal of overlap.

After idiosyncratic beliefs were eliminated (for example, one Spanish teacher reported that one of her students believed that speakers of Spanish first thought in English and then translated their thoughts into Spanish), a 30-item list of beliefs was compiled from the teachers' free-recall protocols. Foreign language teacher educators from a variety of culture groups including those commonly represented in ESL classes then examined the list and added beliefs, either their own or ones they had encountered. Finally beliefs were added which arose in focus group discussions between the researcher and groups of ESL and foreign language students. To facilitate comparisons between second and foreign language learners, two versions of the questionnaire were written; one in standard English for use with American foreign language students, and the other in simplified language for use with ESL students. The two versions were then pilot tested (each with the appropriate subject group) for clarity and comprehensiveness with 150 first-semester, foreign language students and 50 intensive English students at The University of Texas at Austin.

The resulting inventory assesses student beliefs in five major areas: foreign language aptitude, the difficulty of language learning, the nature of language learning, learning and communication strategies, and motivations. Subjects are asked to read each item and then to indicate a response ranging from strongly agree to strongly disagree. As an inventory, the BALLI does not yield a composite score; rather, responses to the individual items are important both as descriptions of student (and teacher) views of language learning and as discussion stimuli.

Beliefs of a Group of ESL Students

This section will discuss the responses of three classes of ESL students to the major topics addressed by the BALLI. (To help teachers use the BALLI with their own classes, the corresponding item numbers are noted with each topic.) The 32 students were at the intermediate level in the Intensive English Program at The University of Texas at Austin and represent cultural backgrounds typical of students in intensive English programs. There were 26 males and 6 females. Their countries of origin are listed in Table 1. Responses to the BALLI may be broken-down by sex, country of origin, or other demographic variables; however,

TABLE 1. *Countries of Origin*

Country of Origin	Number of Students
Costa Rica	1
El Salvador	1
Ghana	1
Indonesia	2
Japan	2
Korea	1
Lebanon	1
Malaysia	6
Mexico	6
Republic of China (Taiwan)	4
Saudi Arabia	2
Venezuela	5

such an analysis will not be reported here because of the small size of students representing each group.

There are no clearcut right and wrong answers to the BALLI questions. For example, the question of whether children are better language learners than adults is the subject of controversy among respected researchers. It is not the purpose of this paper to identify "incorrect" student opinions; rather, it seeks to describe specific beliefs and discuss the potential impact of these beliefs on learner expectations and strategies.

Foreign Language Aptitude. BALLI items 1, 2, 6, 10, 11, 16, 19, 30, 33.

These items concern the general existence of specialized abilities for language learning ("Some people are born with a special ability for learning a foreign language", "Everyone can learn to speak a foreign language.") and beliefs about the characteristics of more (children, bilinguals, women, my countrymen) or less successful language learners (adults, monolinguals, men, "people who are good at mathematics or science"). In other words, these items address the issue of equal potentiality for language learning: Are some people more likely to be successful than others, and if so, who are these more successful learners?

These ESL students generally endorse the concept of foreign language aptitude or special abilities for language learning. Eighty-one percent either strongly agreed or agreed with the statement: "Some people are born with a special ability to learn a foreign language". Like many Americans, they feel overwhelmingly (84%) that it is easier for children than adults to learn a foreign language. And interestingly, almost one-third (31%) said that they themselves possess a special ability for foreign language learning, although the largest group of students (50%) selected a neutral response. These responses indicate that relatively few of these students have particularly negative assessments of their own language learning abilities. Accordingly, the majority (almost 85%) agreed that everyone can learn to speak a foreign language.

Two beliefs, common to Americans about the type of people who generally excel at language learning, were not supported by this group of ESL students. No one endorsed the statement that people who are good at mathematics or science are not good at learning foreign languages, and only 18.5% agreed that women are better than men at learning languages. The first result is especially important since many of the sampled students intended math- or science-related study. Interestingly, they were enthusiastic about the language learning abilities of their fellow countrymen, only 9% disagreed and over 40% agreed with the statement "people from my country are good at learning foreign languages". The analysis, currently being undertaken, of BALLI responses from a large sample of students will permit an examination of how particular cultural groups feel about the language learning abilities of their compatriots, the measure of a group language learning self-image.

Since a belief that some people are unable, or at least less able, to learn a second language can lead to negative expectations by the student, these results about foreign language aptitude are very encouraging. The students, for the most part, do not believe that they personally lack the capacity to learn a language. On the other hand, the two students (6% of the total sample) who strongly disagreed with the statement "I have a special ability for learning a foreign language" probably represented a minority appearing in most ESL classes and are the cause of some concern. These are the students who feel that they lack some ability necessary to learning languages; and therefore, they probably expect to do poorly in language study.

The Difficulty of Language Learning. BALLI items 3, 4, 5, 15, 25, 34.

These items concern the difficulty of learning English as a second or foreign language ("If someone spent one hour a day . . .," "Some languages are easier to learn than others", "English is a language of_____difficulty."). Items 25 and 34 assess the relative difficulty of different language skills, and item 5 surveys student expectations for their own success.

These ESL students overwhelmingly believe (75%) that some languages are easier to learn than others and that English, the language they are trying to learn, is at least of average difficulty. Over one-third of the respondents judged English to be a difficult language while nearly one-half (47%) called it a language of medium difficulty. None of the subjects called English "a very easy language" although 12% judged it an "easy" one.

The questionnaire next asked respondents to estimate the length of time necessary to learn a language. In response to the question "If someone spent one hour a day learning English, how long would it take them to speak the language very well?", their estimates varied over the entire range of possibilities including less than a year (16%), one to two years (12.5%), three to five years (31%), and five to ten years (19%). In addition, 19% supported the statement, "You can't learn a language in one hour a day".

Student judgments about the difficulty of language learning are critical to the development of students' expectations for and commitment to language learning. If they underestimate the difficulty of the task, they are likely to become frustrated when they do not make progress as quickly as they expect. On the other hand, a belief that it will take ten years or more to learn a language could be discouraging and cause them to make only minimal efforts since good results are so far from hand.

The Nature of Language Learning. BALLI items 8, 12, 17, 23, 27, 28.

This category includes a broad range of issues related to the nature of language learning. Items 8 ("know about English-speaking cultures") and 12 ("learn in an English-speaking country") concern the role of cultural contact and language immersion in language learning. Item 27 determines if the learner views language learning as different from other types of learning while items 17 (vocabulary) 23 (grammar) and 28 (translation) concern the learner's conception of the focus of the language learning task.

Many people believe that learning another language is merely a matter of translating from English or learning grammar rules or vocabulary words. These respondents, in particular, shared some of these opinions about language learning. Although 69% agreed that learning a language differs from learning other school subjects, many of the respondents endorsed statements indicative of a restricted view of language learning. For example, over half of the students endorsed the BALLI items that the most important part of learning a language is learning vocabulary words or grammar rules. On the other hand, these students generally (63%) rejected the idea that learning English is mainly a matter of learning to translate from their native languages (although 16% did agree — but not strongly — with this statement). And consistent with their decision to study in the United States, these students view cultural knowledge and a second language environment as highly facilitative of language learning. They feel very strongly (94%) that "it is best to learn English in an English-speaking country," and sixty-three percent feel that it is necessary to "know about English-speaking cultures in order to speak English."

A belief that learning vocabulary words and grammar rules is the best way to learn English will almost certainly lead students to invest the majority of their time memorizing vocabulary lists and grammar rules at the expense of other language learning practices. In some cases, students may never have had their views about language learning challenged. In one discussion group, a student asked if it were true that some people can speak a foreign language without first translating from their native language. He was told that there are many documented cases of such individuals and that researchers agree that fluent speakers do not translate. After the discussion, he thanked me for my answer, and said he was going to think about his approach to studying English. Even though he had been studying English for eight years, it had never occurred to him to do anything other than translate, although he had often wondered how some of his fellow classmates were able to speak in English without prior preparation.

Learning and Communication Strategies. BALLI items 7, 9, 13, 14, 18, 21, 22, 26.

A number of BALLI items concern the process of learning a language and the practice of spontaneous communication in the classroom; items 18 (repeat and practice) and 26 (tapes) refer to learning strategies, and items 7 (excellent pronunciation), 9 (correct), 13 (practicing with Americans), 14 (guess), 21 (timid), 22 (mistakes) concern communication strategies. These questions are probably the most directly related to a student's actual language learning practices.

First, in reference to traditional learning strategies, these students strongly endorse (75%) the use of audio-tapes or cassettes. They also overwhelmingly agreed (over 95%) that it is important to "repeat and practice a lot". The students are also fairly supportive of practices commonly associated with a communication-centered approach to language teaching. Sixty-five percent agreed that it is "o.k. to guess if you don't know a word in English", and only slightly over a quarter (27.5%) felt that beginning students will probably be unable to correct errors if they are allowed to make them early on in language learning. The vast majority (81%) also agreed that they enjoy practicing English with the Americans they meet. However, thirty-eight percent of the students endorsed the statements, "You shouldn't say anything in English until you can say it correctly". Although the majority of these students support practices necessary for participation in communicative activities (their willingness to guess, for example), these responses also reveal a substantial minority of students who due to their concern with correctness will probably have difficulty accepting the communicative approaches now common in ESL classes in the United States. These results, taken together with the responses to the two following questions, underline the importance of preparing students to participate in — what may be to them — nontraditional language learning activities. Ninety percent of the students agreed that "it is important to speak English with an excellent pronunciation," and 44% stated that they feel "timid" when speaking English with other people. This group of students, therefore, feels positively about speaking English, but their shyness and over-concern with accent will probably inhibit their communication attempts.

Motivations. BALLI items 20, 24, 29, 31, 32.

These items concern desires the students currently hold associated with the learning of English. Whether these motivations contributed to their initial study of English is unknown since this study was undertaken while they were already in the process of learning English.

Ninety-one percent of all respondents agreed (75% strongly) that they wanted to learn to speak English very well. The majority of students (78%) also associated the ability to speak English with better job opportunities although the responses to this question were less firm than to the previous one (only 28% strongly agreed). These students also expressed a strong desire for friendships with Americans. Almost 90% stated that they would like to have American friends, and over half said that they would like to learn English so that they can get to know Americans better. It seems, then, that this group of students is strongly motivated to learn English and have both instrumental and integrative reasons for doing so.

One caveat should be noted. Although these responses show a strong willingness to talk with and to get to know Americans, there is no evidence that these students actually know how to establish such contacts. Indeed, when they discussed the BALLI with their teachers, they expressed great disappointment in their ability to meet Americans. Wanting cultural contacts is very different from knowing how to establish them, and the ESL teacher may want to help in this regard so that the students' integrative motivation is not frustrated.

Conclusion

The BALLI has proven very successful in the identification of many student beliefs about language learning. Some of the results reported here may surprise ESL teachers, others probably confirm their experiences and intuitions. Other studies using the BALLI are currently in progress. One study concerns the beliefs of various groups of ESL students and will compare the beliefs of students by sex, country of origin, and language learning context (second versus foreign). A second study examines the beliefs of American students of foreign languages. A third study seeks to discriminate anxious and nonanxious foreign language students based on their beliefs about language learning. The BALLI should also prove useful in future research on the acquisition and use of learning strategies. It would be interesting to determine, for example, the relative importance of student beliefs about language learning (as compared with other learner variables) on their selection of learning strategies or the connection of specific beliefs to specific learning strategies. Researchers may also want to study the interaction of beliefs with other learner variables such as attitude, motivation, or cognitive style to better understand why and how these variables impact on language learning.

In their ground-breaking *Good Language Learner* study, Naiman *et al.* (1978) cogently pose the basic rationale for studying the strategies of language learners:

> All forms of language learning would be greatly improved if we had a better understanding of the language learning process itself. What is happening to learners in language classes? Why is it that some are successful and other fail?

The ultimate purpose of studying learner strategies is, of course, an applied one; researchers and teachers hope to determine which strategies are most effective and help students adopt more productive learning procedures. Presumably, erroneous beliefs about language learning lead to less effective language learning strategies. From this point of view, knowledge of student belief systems may be particularly useful. In the past two decades, researchers have connected a myriad of cognitive style (such as field dependence/independence)[5] and affective variables (such as attitude and motivation) to successful second language achievement. Although these discoveries have greatly increased our understanding of why some people are more successful than others as language learners, researchers and teachers have met with only limited success in helping other students acquire these characteristics of good language learners. This result is not surprising. Many researchers feel that cognitive style variables are stable from very young in life[6] while affective variables are strongly molded by the social and political contexts of language learning. On the other hand, student beliefs about language learning may be more susceptible to teacher intervention. Both Wenden's work and my own with student focus groups[7] indicates that these beliefs are easily accessible to students. Students who are unaware of their preference for inductive presentations can readily state whether they believe repetition in a language laboratory is important.

Since student beliefs about language learning are often based on limited knowledge and/or experience, the teacher's most effective course may well be to confront erroneous beliefs with new information. This procedure has been very helpful in my work with groups of anxious language learners. Many of these students believe erroneously that they are supposed to understand every word uttered in their foreign language class. When simply told that they are not expected to understand every word and that none of the other students understand every word, they visibly relax and are able to discuss other ways to listen in a foreign language. Similar approaches with other groups of language learners may prove equally effective in modifying their beliefs.

Teachers at the Intensive English Program at The University of Texas, for example, have used the BALLI as a discussion stimulus at the onset of ESL classes to help students develop more effective learning strategies; they report that this discussion not only helped their students clear up some misconceptions about language learning, but also that the activity was one of their most successful discussions as students (and teachers) were vitally interested in the topic. This practice also helps teachers become better aware of their own students' specific beliefs. The results reported here suggest many beliefs that ESL students may hold, but it remains to be determined the extent to which learner beliefs are variable from person to person or setting to setting. (The high percentage of males in the present group, for example, may make the present findings unrepresentative of other groups.) Teachers and administrators would do best to use the BALLI to study the beliefs of their own students rather than to apply the findings of another group.

It is not surprising to ESL teachers that students enter English class with many preconceived ideas about language learning. Indeed, they are confronted with these beliefs on a daily basis whenever a student resists an instructional activity or requests a different teaching approach. However, most of the time, ESL teachers must rely on informal assessments of these beliefs and store in their minds a collection of bits and pieces of private conversations and fragments of class comments. Just as the assessment of the linguistic backgrounds of students insures the most effective language teaching, this paper has suggested that a systematic assessment of student beliefs would greatly facilitate learning in the ESL class.

Notes

1. For the purposes of this paper, no distinction is made between the terms language learning and language acquisition.
2. Chamot A. U. and O'Malley J. M. 1984. Using learning strategies to develop skills in English as a second language, *FOCUS*, September, 1984, National Clearinghouse for Bilingual Education, p. 1.
3. Horwitz E. K. 1983. *Beliefs about Language Learning Inventory*, unpublished instrument, The University of Texas at Austin.
4. Horwitz E. K. 1985. Using student beliefs about language learning and teaching in the foreign language methods course, *Foreign Language Annals*, September, 1985, for a description of the use of the teacher's version of this instrument.
5. S. Messick and Associates 1978. *Individuality in Learning*, San Francisco: Jossey Bass.
6. Messick and Associates.
7. Focus groups are a technique used in marketing research where a researcher poses structured questions to a group of consumers to elicit their opinions about the product or service under study.

Appendix. Beliefs About Language Learning Inventory. ESL Student Version

Below are beliefs that some people have about learning foreign languages.
Read each statement and then decide if you:
(1) strongly agree, (2) agree, (3) neither agree not disagree, (4) disagree, (5) strongly disagree.
There are no right or wrong answers. We are simply interested in your opinions. Mark each answer on the special answer sheet. Questions 4 & 15 are slightly different and you should mark them as indicated.
REMEMBER:
(1) strongly agree, (2) agree, (3) neither agree nor disagree, (4) disagree, (5) strongly disagree.

1.   It is easier for children than adults to learn a foreign language.
2.   Some people have a special ability for learning foreign languages.
3.   Some languages are easier to learn than others.
     English is: (a) a very difficult language
                 (b) a difficult language
                 (c) a language of medium difficulty
                 (d) an easy language
                 (e) a very easy language.
5.   I believe that I will learn to speak English very well.
6.   People from my country are good at learning foreign languages.
7.   It is important to speak English with an excellent pronunciation.
8.   It is necessary to know about English-speaking cultures in order to speak English.
9.   You shouldn't say anything in English until you can say it correctly.
10. It is easier for someone who already speaks a foreign language to learn another one.
11. People who are good at mathematics or science are not good at learning foreign languages.

12.　It is best to learn English in an English-speaking country.
13.　I enjoy practicing English with the Americans I meet.
14.　It's o.k. to guess if you don't know a word in English.
15.　If someone spent one hour a day learning a language, how long would it take them to speak the language very well:
　　　　　(a) less than a year
　　　　　(b) 1–2 years
　　　　　(c) 3–5 years
　　　　　(d) 5–10 years
　　　　　(e) You can't learn a language in 1 hour a day.
16.　I have a special ability for learning foreign languages.
17.　The most important part of learning a foreign language is learning vocabulary words.
18.　It is important to repeat and practice a lot.
19.　Women are better than men at learning foreign languages.
20.　People in my country feel that it is important to speak English.
21.　I feel timid speaking English with other people.
22.　If beginning students are permitted to make errors in English, it will be difficult for them to speak correctly later on.
23.　The most important part of learning a foreign language is learning the grammar.
24.　I would like to learn English so that I can get to know Americans better.
25.　It is easier to speak than understand a foreign language.
26.　It is important to practice with cassettes or tapes.
27.　Learning a foreign language is different than learning other academic subjects.
28.　The most important part of learning English is learning how to translate from my native language.
29.　If I learn English very well, I will have better opportunities for a good job.
30.　People who speak more than one language are very intelligent.
31.　I want to learn to speak English well.
32.　I would like to have American friends.
33.　Everyone can learn to speak a foreign language.
34.　It is easier to read and write English than to speak and understand it.

Follow-up Activities

Making Links

1. Horwitz's inventory assesses student beliefs in five major areas: foreign language aptitude, the difficulty of language learning, the nature of language learning, motivations and strategies. Referring to research and theory in second language acquisition and other related fields, evaluate the validity of these beliefs. Which are myth and which appear to be valid?
2. What are your views on the role of language aptitude in second language learning? e.g. How would you answer BALLI items that refer to foreign language aptitude? Compare your views with the research summarized by Carroll (1981) in "Twenty-five years of research on foreign language aptitude."
3. Complete the rest of the survey. Discuss the reasons for your choices with another teacher.

Applying the Ideas

4. Working with a group of teachers, use the free recall procedure described by Horwitz to list your beliefs and the beliefs of L2 students you have worked with about second language learning, e.g. how best to approach the task; factors that may facilitate or inhibit the process.
　　(a) Categorize these beliefs.
　　(b) Compare your categories with Horwitz's and Wenden's.
　　(c) Utilize these beliefs and those listed by Horwitz and Wenden to devise an instrument to collect data on student beliefs. Consult a book on methodology in behavioral research for guidelines in choosing and developing an appropriate instrument (e.g. Kerlinger, F. N. *Foundations of Behavioral Research* — Holt, Rinehart & Winston, Inc 1973)
5. Discuss the pedagogical utility of the various survey instruments and interview schedules utilized by authors in this section. What classroom activities could you develop around each one? When would you use them? For what purpose?
6. The following are taken from learner self-reports.
　　(a) Read and determine what aspects of their learning, the learners attend to and assess.

(b) Does your analysis suggest categories not included in Horwitz's inventory? In Wenden's (Chapter 8)? If so what are they?

1. . . . Classes in Micro Economics are useful. During these classes I don't think of learning English. I told you I'm trying to learn English the natural way.

2. I speak louder. This is not my character. I don't like it.

3. I think one problem for me and perhaps everyone learning a language is you have to be stimulated to learn.

4. Sometimes I speak awkwardly, but no one notices.

5. Reading novels helped me get real daily life English.

6. . . . there are some words that appear again and again in the reading.

7. Sometimes my friends give me a strange answer and they talk about something different and I guess my pronunciation was wrong.

8. In that class we laughed and joked in English. We made friends. They didn't care about my mistakes. This German class helped me (with my English).

9. I felt I was losing my English. I found I could only use simple words.

10. I don't believe anyone can learn English just from the course in Israel or any other country. That's why I say we have to live the language . . . the best way to learn English it to go somewhere where I don't know anyone who speaks any language but English.

Part Three

PROMOTING LEARNER AUTONOMY

As indicated in Chapters 1 and 2, the educational goal of learner strategy research and its classroom applications is an autonomous learner. Moreover, it was noted that in promoting this goal, both learning skills and learner assumptions should be stressed. These are, indeed, two very important dimensions of this goal, perhaps the most important. For they address in a basic way the "what" of learner training. In other words, what should the objectives be — helping students clarify and assess their beliefs? expand their repertoire of effective learning strategies? learn how to regulate their learning (i.e. define their objectives, choose materials, evaluate outcomes)? These are some of the questions that need to be addressed in providing language learners with the training they will need to become more critical, efficient, and ultimately, more autonomous in their attempts to develop competence in their second language. The approaches to learner training illustrated in this chapter differ on the basis of their answers to these questions.

The studies included in this section further raise and illustrate different ways of dealing with questions concerning "how" learner training should be implemented. Should the purpose and significance of learner training activities be made explicit or remain implicit? Should it precede language training or be integrated with it? And, who is to be responsible for directing or regulating learner training? i.e. should activities be structured and determined by the teacher or should a more non-interventionist approach be taken? Finally, how is it to be evaluated?

Chapter 10
The Effects of Training in the Use of Learning Strategies on Learning English as a Second Language

J. MICHAEL O'MALLEY

Research and theory in second language learning strongly suggest that good language learners use a variety of strategies to assist them in gaining command over new language skills. By implication, less competent learners should be able to improve their skills in a second language through training on strategies evidenced among more successful language learners. With successful training, less competent learners should be able to apply strategies to the acquisition of a variety of different language skills and transfer the strategies to similar language tasks. Teachers can play an important role in this training by conveying strategy applications to students and thereby supporting student efforts to learn the new language.

This study concerns training in the use of learning strategies with minority language students on three critical academic language tasks in English: vocabulary learning, listening to a lecture, and making a brief oral presentation to other students. These three language tasks were selected to ensure that the range of skills presented in the strategy training was representative of tasks found in a high school second language curriculum. The study used natural classroom instruction so that the instructional procedures could generally be applied by most teachers. An experimental procedure with random assignment of students to treatment conditions was used to determine the influence of strategy training. This study was the second phase of an overall investigation of learning strategies and was performed following the study presented by Anna Uhl Chamot in this volume (Chapter 6).

Review of Literature

The design of learning strategies training in second language learning draws upon two types of background research. The first is within the second language learning literature referred to by Rubin (Chapter 2) in her review of the earlier research. Other research discussed by Chamot (Chapter 6) builds on this earlier background and adds specific new information about classifications of second language learning strategies. The classification differentiates strategies that involve planning for, monitoring, or evaluating a learning activity (metacognitive strategies); strategies that entail direct manipulation or organization of new information (cognitive strategies); and strategies that are mediated by social interaction (social-affective strategies).

The second type of literature on which the design of learning strategies training studies can draw is the considerable body of research amassed over the past fifteen years in cognitive psychology (e.g., Sigel, Chipman and Glaser, 1985; Dansereau,

1985; Weinstein, 1978). This extensive volume of literature includes experimental analyses of the impact of learning strategies training on first language reading for native English speakers. Findings from these studies indicate that learning strategies can be taught to learners who are at appropriate levels of maturity (Weinstein and Mayer, 1985), although strategy training may need to be explicit for less skilled learners (Chipman *et al.*, 1985). Within this literature are experimental studies of a number of specific strategies that are adaptable for learning vocabulary in a second language (e.g., Atkinson and Raugh, 1975; Levin, in press; Pressley *et al.*, 1980). These strategies include special techniques such as the keyword method where a person links the new word with its definition via a homonym and a related image. For example, a person learning that "carta" in Spanish means letter could develop an image of a letter in a shopping "cart." While effective, these keywords may be difficult to develop for successive lists of new vocabulary words. The literature also identifies some specific types of strategies that should be included in any strategy training effort. For example, although cognitive strategies serve as the core for most strategy training, present evidence suggests that a combined meta-cognitive/cognitive training approach is superior in producing transfer of strategies to new tasks (Brown and Palinscar, 1982).

Despite the progress made in understanding the application of learning strategies to reading and second language vocabulary, none of the studies discussed above has used experimental procedures to determine the effectiveness of strategy training with integrative second language skills. Vocabulary learning is a discrete language skill that fails to represent the range of integrative tasks typical of language use. The potential for applying strategy training to second language tasks therefore has been uncertain. Research is needed that analyzes the effects of strategy training on integrative language tasks such as listening and speaking. Furthermore, much of the prior research on learning strategy training has not used a regular classroom teaching situation to present the training and consequently has had little direct utility for instruction. Because the strategy training has been presented over a short duration, except for studies by Cohen and Aphek (1980, 1981), students have had few opportunities to try the strategies on subsequent learning materials. And finally, few of the studies have been concerned with individual differences among students in the use and application of learning strategies, and none of the research has investigated strategy training with students of English as a second language.

The study of learning strategy training presented here used an experimental approach that builds upon their prior research but focuses on language tasks such as listening and speaking in addition to vocabulary. The students in the study were learning English as a second language at the high school level and were at the intermediate level of English proficiency. The study used a natural teaching approach as contrasted with the one-to-one training that is customary in experimental studies. Furthermore, the strategies selected for training were intended to appeal to teachers for their ease of use by students, direct application to instructional materials typically used in second language classrooms, and obvious relationship to language learning. The training was designed to include opportunities to apply strategies to new but similar materials over successive days in order to facilitate transfer of the strategies to new tasks. And finally, the study was intended to explore individual differences in the use of strategies among students differentiated by ethnolinguistic background. The study followed by one school year the study reported by Chamot elsewhere in this volume.

Purposes

This study examined the effectiveness of strategy training with students of English as a second language (ESL) on three types of academic language tasks: vocabulary learning, listening comprehension, and oral production. The strategies training was specifically designed to produce increased learning for the language tasks selected in training, and to maximize the likelihood of transfer to comparable tasks.

Specific research questions addressed in this study were as follows:

1. What is the effect of learning strategy training on student use of strategies in second language learning?

2. Does strategy training improve learning for integrative language tasks (listening, speaking) as well as for discrete language tasks (vocabulary)?

3. Are there differences in the effectiveness of strategy training for different students?

Method

Subjects. The subjects were 75 high school students enrolled in ESL classes during the Fall 1983 semester. The students were located in three high schools in an Eastern metropolitan area in the United States. The students were all intermediate level in English proficiency (as defined by school district placement procedures), were of both sexes, and were predominantly from Spanish language countries or from Southeast Asian countries, with a few students from other countries in Europe or Asia. Intermediate level proficiency was defined in both school districts as students with limited proficiency in understanding and speaking English, and little or no skill in reading and writing English. The students in this study were not the same as those reported in the study by Chamot.

Instruments. The data collection instruments used in the study assessed vocabulary, listening comprehension, and speaking. For each language skill, there was a pretest, a posttest, and four daily tests presented during training. Each daily test was designed specifically to reflect the instructional materials presented during training. The vocabulary tests contained recognition (multiple choice) and recall (fill in) items, whereas the listening tests were all recognition items. The speaking test consisted of ratings on a two-minute speech on one of three topics: a personal experience, their own culture, or an academic subject. Students were given time to prepare the talks and then tape recorded the talk before a small group of students. The tapes were scored blind by a panel of judges who rated the talks on delivery, appropriateness, accuracy, and organization.

Overview of Treatment. Students were randomly assigned within each school to one of three groups: a metacognitive group, a cognitive group, or a control group. The size of an instructional group within each school was 8–10 students on the average. The metacognitive group received training in the use of one metacognitive strategy, one or two cognitive strategies, and a social-affective strategy, depending on the language learning task. The cognitive group received training on the same cognitive and social-affective strategies, but no metacognitive strategy training. The control group received instruction to work on the language learning tasks using whatever procedure they ordinarily would employ. The control group was given special instruction on reading strategies on content unrelated to the study to ensure that they benefitted from participation. In each of the three schools participating in the study, the three project staff were responsible for implementing a different treatment condition in its entirety. By the conclusion of training in all three schools, each staff member had taught each treatment condition once, thereby controlling for teacher effects.

An overview of the treatment conditions is presented in Table 1, which shows the specific strategies that accompanied each language learning activity and each treatment. For example, the metacognitive group had metacognitive, cognitive, and social-affective strategies. For the vocabulary task, the metacognitive strategy was self-evaluation, and the cognitive strategies were grouping and imagery. With the listening task, the metacognitive strategy was selective attention, the cognitive strategy was note-taking, and the social-affective strategy was cooperation, and so on.

Students were instructed in the use of learning strategies fifty minutes daily for eight days in roughly a two-week period. On any single day, students typically received two of the three language learning activities: vocabulary, listening, or speaking. For the treatment groups, the same learning strategies were always repeated with each language activity, although new content was presented each time a language activity recurred. Students therefore could practice transfer of strategy applications to similar materials. Direct instructions to use the strategies were reduced over successive days of treatment for each activity, until at the posttest only a reminder was given to use the same strategies they had rehearsed before. Pretesting and posttesting consumed the full first and last days out of the ten-day period, leaving eight full days at fifty minutes per day for instruction and interim performance testings. The interim testing consumed on average about 30%

TABLE 1. *Language Learning Activities and Learning Strategies Presented for Each Treatment Condition*

Treatment Condition	Strategy Type	Language Learning Activities		
		Vocabulary	Listening	Speaking
Metacognitive	Metacognitive Cognitive Social-affective	Self-evaluation Grouping, imagery —	Selective attention Note-taking Cooperation	Functional planning — Cooperation
Cognitive	Cognitive only Social-affective	Grouping, imagery —	Note-taking Cooperation	— Cooperation
Control	Activity only with no strategy training	—	—	—

of the total time for instruction. The following description provides an overview of each language learning task, followed by a detailed description of the treatment conditions for each activity. All instructional procedures described were pilot tested on a separate group of intermediate level English as a second language students in a different school from those used in treatment.

Vocabulary Instruction. New vocabulary words were presented in two cycles of two successive days each for a total of four days during the eight days of instruction. The two cycles were essentially identical in presentation except for content. On each of the four days, the vocabulary instruction lasted about six minutes. Thus, the total practice time for learning strategies with vocabulary items was about twenty-four minutes. A short test followed each practice session. For the pretest, there was no prior training on the vocabulary words, whereas on the posttest, training and practice were presented as before with only a brief reminder to use the strategies.

On Day 1 of Cycle 1, students were asked to learn 20 new words. The words were presented under controlled circumstances by limiting both the duration and type of exposure. The type of exposure was either *pictorial*, in which words were given high imagery value by being presented on a slide projector as they were pronounced, or *verbal*, where words were given low imagery value by being defined orally by the teacher after being pronounced. The presentation rate was about five seconds per word for the pictorial words, and ten seconds per word for the verbally presented words. Definitions of the verbally presented words were brief and used vocabulary that was familiar to the students. The verbally presented words varied in content but included nouns, adjectives, and verbs. After the vocabulary presentation was completed, all groups were given an opportunity to study what they had learned for about four minutes. All students, regardless of treatment group, were given equal exposure and study time and were tested immediately following the study period. On Day 2, students were asked to learn 15 new words, plus 5 most commonly missed words repeated from the previous day's presentation. None of these words was repeated into the next vocabulary presentation in Cycle 2.

Cycle 2 was identical in presentation, with 20 new words to be learned on the first day, and 15 new words plus 5 repeated words to be learned on the subsequent day. Thus, a total of 70 new words were presented during the study, 32 of which appeared on the posttest. Posttest words were evenly divided betweeen Cycle 1 (delayed posttest) and Cycle 2 (recent posttest) words, and between high and low imagery words within each cycle. The instruction for each treatment condition is described in the following sections.

Metacognitive Group. The metacognitive group received instruction on the use of one metacognitive strategy and two cognitive strategies accompanying their vocabulary presentation. The metacognitive strategy was self-evaluation, and the cognitive strategies were grouping and imagery. For the *grouping* strategy, students were taught that a long list of words can often be separated into parts that share semantic or other features. Words used in the vocabulary lists had been preselected for obvious grouping on semantic (meaning) similarity. For example, items that can be used in a kitchen, such as a skillet, a kettle, and a mug would be included in a single list. Students were instructed to scan through the list and group the words that to them had common features. For the *imagery* strategy, students were instructed to close their eyes and vividly create a mental image that incorporated all of the key words they had grouped together.

For example, a student might imagine placing each of the objects on the "kitchen" group together in a kitchen, making certain to couple each object with its corresponding label. Recall was to be facilitated by the student reentering the scene and extracting the required word. These students were tested immediately after their study period. The metacognitive strategy, *self-evaluation*, was implemented by giving students journals in which to record the number of words they had learned that day, the words they found to be difficult, and the method they used to remember the words. The self-evaluation process was introduced after use of the other strategies and testing of vocabulary knowledge.

Cognitive Group. Students assigned to the cognitive group received instruction in grouping and imagery that was identical to that given the metacognitive group. What differentiated this group's approach to vocabulary learning was the absence of the metacognitive self-evaluation.

Control Group. The control group received no strategy instruction but instead were told to learn the words in whatever way they normally did. The time they were given to study the words equaled the time the other groups spent in grouping and imaging. The control group was also tested immediately after their study period.

Listening Instruction. The listening task that students were requested to perform was to remember information presented in a five-minute videotape on an academic subject such as history or geography. The videotapes were specifically designed for the project to simulate a lecture experience the students might encounter in school. There were four videotapes presented on different days that covered the following topics: the River Thames, uses of pigs, the life of Houdini, and bilingual education. A short listening comprehension test following each lecture contained items designed to assess Bloom's knowledge, comprehension, and analysis levels.

Videotapes were presented sequentially in order of judged difficulty of the content based on a pilot test. In addition to the training videotapes and their corresponding tests, a pretest videotape was presented on Lewis and Clark's journey to the Pacific Coast, and a posttest videotape was presented on Captain Cook's three trips to the South Pacific. The instruction provided to students in each treatment condition is described in the following sections.

Metacognitive Group. The metacognitive group received instruction on one metacognitive strategy, one cognitive strategy, and one social-affective strategy. The metacognitive strategy was selective attention, the cognitive strategy was note-taking, and the social-affective strategy was cooperation. For *selective attention*, students were instructed to listen selectively for key words typically used in lectures to present an overview, a main topic, main points, examples, and a conclusion or summary. For example, a phrase such as "Today I want to tell you about . . ." suggests the speaker is presenting an overview, while "first", "second", etc. indicate that main points are likely to follow. The videotapes had been designed specifically to include these and other markers. Students were instructed on *note-taking* by means of a T-list (Hamp-Lyons, 1983) in which main points are entered on the left side of a page and corresponding examples or details are entered adjacently to the right. Thus, by selectively attending to phrases or words that often preceded important lecture points, students were able to facilitate note-taking. As a final step, students were instructed to use *cooperation* as a strategy to verify the accuracy of their notes, enabling them to fill in gaps in information or clarify areas of confusion by using their peers as a resource.

Cognitive Group. The strategies taught to the cognitive group for the listening activity were note-taking and cooperation. Instruction in these strategies was identical to that received by the metacognitive group. However, they did not receive any information regarding selective attention or markers that often occur in lectures to highlight important information.

Control Group. Students in the control group received no strategy instruction. They were simply told to listen to the videotapes and do whatever they normally did to help them understand and remember a lecture.

Speaking Instruction. In the speaking task, students were asked to present a brief oral report on one of six subjects that had personal or cultural significance. The topics included the following possibilities: My first day in the United States, two differences between people of my country and people in the United States, special traditions in my country, and the most interesting person I have known. Four separate oral presentations were made on four separate days. Report preparation was completed in class to ensure comparable time on task across treatment groups. In presenting the report, students sat in small groups, spoke or read from written notes, and used a tape recorder. The tape recorder was used to obtain pretest and posttest measures on oral proficiency, but was also used in practice sessions so students would become comfortable with speaking while a tape recorder was running. The following sections present a specific description of the instruction provided to students in each treatment.

Metacognitive Group. The metacognitive group received instruction on one metacognitive strategy, functional planning, and one social-affective strategy, cooperation. *Functional planning* involves having the learner analyze the requirements of a communication task, and determine if he or she has the language skills required to fulfill those requirements. During instruction on the use of this strategy, students were led by the teacher through an analysis of the purposes language serves in an oral report. For example, the topic must be introduced, followed by an overview, the main points and details, and finally by a conclusion and summary. Throughout, use of relevant markers was encouraged to highlight important information and transitions. The markers were the same as those discussed under the listening task, such as "first", "The main point is . . .", and "in conclusion". Having familiarity with what needs to be communicated once the main topic had been selected, students then examined their language repertoires to determine whether they possessed the language required for the communication, and proceeded to learn new language as required for the task. Functional planning is similar to procedures described by Stevick (1984). For the *cooperation* strategy, students practiced presenting their reports with a small group of other students. The other students were responsible for providing corrective feedback on volume, pace, organization, and comprehensibility. Using the group's advice after one practice session, the students then recorded the report.

Cognitive Group. This group received instruction using cooperation as a strategy to improve their report. They were not offered any other strategies in conjunction with the speaking activity.

Control Group. The control group received no strategy instruction but was given the list of topic possibilities and told to prepare an oral report on the topic of their choice in whatever manner they normally prepared for such an activity. This group also tape recorded their report in the presence of a small group of students during practice sessions, but was not instructed to provide systematic feedback to their peers.

Results

Posttest Analyses. Results of the posttest analyses are shown at the top of Table 2. A simple analysis of covariance was used to contrast differences among metacognitive, cognitive, and control groups on each of three posttest variables: the vocabulary, listening, and speaking posttests. In each analysis, the covariate was the pretest for the corresponding outcome variable. Values shown in the table are the group adjusted means and standard deviations, the P-value, or the probability that the obtained F-value was significant, and the R^2, a measure of association between the treatment and the outcomes.

For the vocabulary test, the results of training were not statistically significant, shown by the P-value of .349. The mean score for the control group was slightly higher than the mean for the treatment groups. Thus, students with strategy training were somewhat less efficient in their learning than students using their

TABLE 2. *The Effect of Learning Strategy Training on Selected Language Skills Controlling for Pretest Score*

Variable	Metacognitive (n = 27) Adj Mn	SD	Cognitive (n = 26) Adj Mn	SD	Control (n = 22) Adj Mn	SD	P-value	R^2
Posttests								
Vocabulary	22.66	4.76	21.41	4.23	23.21	4.90	.349	.17
Listening	8.25	2.12	8.18	2.00	7.30	2.31	.162	.30
Speaking	3.60	.88	3.04	.80	2.88	.73	.008	.20
Daily Tests on Listening								
Listening 1	6.03	1.29	5.91	1.45	5.46	1.47	.096	.26
Listening 2	6.45	1.48	6.54	1.22	5.45	1.50	.004	.36
Listening 3	6.27	2.33	6.95	1.61	5.17	2.31	.043	.29
Listening 4	5.25	1.32	5.10	1.68	5.09	1.57	.626	.10

customary strategies. Analyses of daily vocabulary tests did not show any significant differences between the treatment groups.

Students in the treatment groups were observed to have difficulty in implementing the vocabulary strategies, especially Asian students. Asian students were noted to persist in using rote repetitive strategies, whereas Hispanics in the treatment group more readily adopted the strategies presented in training. *Post hoc* analyses of the posttests revealed that Asian students in the treatment group performed more poorly than those in the control group, whereas Hispanics in the treatment group performed better than those in the control group. These effects served to cancel each other out in the overall analysis of variance.

There are at least two possible explanations for the failure of Asian students in the treatment groups to perform better than those in the control group. The first concerns the persistence of familiar strategies. Other investigators have tried unsuccessfully to train students to use strategies that compete with more familiar techniques (Brown *et al.*, 1983). Adopting new strategies may be especially difficult when students know they will be tested within only a few minutes. One other explanation for these results is that the key to enhancing memory for vocabulary, as Levin (in press) suggests, may be exclusively in one-to-one interactive verbal/imagery associations rather than in grouping and imagery. Grouping and imagery used together as a combined strategy may be sufficiently difficult for most persons that only individuals with high imagery can make use of the unified strategy, suggesting differences in cognitive styles. The difficulty of using the combined grouping/imagery strategy might make it advisable to present the training individually, as has been discussed with other associational strategies (Hall, Wilson and Patterson, 1981; Levin *et al.*, 1979; Pressley *et al.*, 1982).

Analyses of posttest scores on listening approached but failed to reach significance, although the scores fell in the predicted direction. Analyses of the daily tests on listening are presented in the lower portion of Table 2. To understand these results, it is important to know that Listening Tests 1 and 2 had 8 items, and Listening Tests 3 and 4 had 9 items. In contrast, there were 13 items on the posttest. The approximate difficulty level of the daily tests can be seen from inspection of the mean scores for the control group, bearing in mind the differences in numbers of items on which these scores are based. Significant effects were obtained on Listening Test 2 beyond the .01 level, and on Listening Test 3 beyond the .05 level. The results for Listening Test 1 approached but did not reach significance. In each case, the treatment groups were superior to the control group, although for Test 2 and 3 the levels for the metacognitive and cognitive group were reversed from the predicted direction. The important point was that the treatment groups outperformed the control group significantly on two out of four daily tests.

One possible reason for not finding significant differences between the two treatment groups and the controls on the first listening test is that the treatment groups needed time to gain familiarity with the strategies. There are at least two possible explanations for the failure to find predicted differences between the two treatment groups and the controls on the fourth listening test and on the posttest. One is that the cues were faded too quickly across successive days of training so that students failed to use the strategies that had proven successful earlier. Process analyses of daily work sheets confirmed that students had difficulty applying the strategies on later tests. A second possibility is that there was an interaction between strategy effectiveness and the difficulty of the task. As noted earlier, the videotapes and daily tests were sequenced in order of increasing difficulty leading up to the posttest, although Listening Test 4 and videotape 4 were judged even more difficult than the posttest. One additional factor contributing to the difficulty of the task was that study time was limited to five minutes. All of this suggests that there may be reasonable limits to the effectiveness of learning strategies training. Strategies may fail to improve performance when the material becomes exceedingly difficult, the cues for strategy use faded too quickly, and the time to study limited.

Posttest analyses for the speaking test were significant in the predicted direction beyond the .01 level. The adjusted mean scores shown can be converted into a 1–5 FSI-type scale to reveal that the metacognitive students scored on the average close to the 2+ level, whereas the control group scores were just below the 2 level. This amount of difference represents a substantial increment in language skills over the control group. The principal differences between a 2 level and a 2+ level on the scoring system used were that a 2+ person had more organization, as suggested by clear subordination and sequencing of parts of the report, and greater comprehensibility.

Discussion

This study focused on determining whether or not learning strategies training influences performance on a variety of language learning tasks required in academic settings. The training was presented in natural classroom instruction rather than as individual laboratory training, which provides exposure to only a single task and strategy. The range of tasks specifically included more complicated language activities to determine whether learning strategies training would be effective with more complex skills such as listening and speaking. The distinction between metacognitive and cognitive strategies was introduced as a means of identifying the effects of including highly generalizable strategies (metacognitive) vs. strategies that were more specific to individual tasks (cognitive).

The effectiveness of learning strategy training for vocabulary learning was never in question owing to the sizeable number of prior studies showing significant results using associational learning strategies such as the keyword method. One issue addressed in this study was whether the associational strategy could be simplified by grouping items on a vocabulary list, thereby reducing the number of images that were required to link the new word with its definition. A second issue was whether this instruction would work with small groups of students, compared to the more commonly presented individual instruction in a laboratory setting. The combined grouping and imagery strategy proved difficult to implement and had to be modified throughout the study. Students trained to use grouping and imagery, with or without self-evaluation, had lower scores than those in a control group using its customary strategies in learning. Informal observations indicated that Asian students, who were highly efficient rote learners of vocabulary lists, were negatively affected by the introduction of grouping and imagery. Hispanic students in the metacognitive group performed consistently better than the cognitive or control groups. The findings with Hispanics in particular should be further explored. We believe that more detailed observation of expert learners is warranted before additional efforts are made to train students to use this approach. Training outcomes may be easier to demonstrate individually before moving to group presentations, where the training effects may be more difficult to control given the variation in individual differences between students.

In the listening skills task, there were indications that the difficulty of the task and the explicitness of directions to perform the strategies may both be important determinants of subsequent performance. Students presented with a task that is too difficult may find little assistance in using learning strategies either because the initial communication is too complicated or the information is so unfamiliar that learning and retention do not occur. Transfer of strategies to new tasks may be extremely sensitive, requiring continued prompts and structured directions until the strategies become autonomous.

Skills in speaking a second language were clearly improved through learning strategies training relative to a control group. Students were extremely adept in learning and applying strategies and, in the process, gained in judged organization and comprehensibility. Informal impressions from training were that the effectiveness of strategy training could have been further enhanced with more structured directions to peers on providing feedback to the student making an oral presentation. The tendency of students to avoid offending another student by being critical, which initially was a problem, was averted by focusing the peer comments on formal portions of the oral presentation and by making the speaker responsible for ensuring that feedback was obtained.

In sum, for two highly important academic language skills, listening and speaking, learning strategies were shown to be effective in enhancing initial learning. Clear direction is provided to teachers interested in helping students to become more effective learners. Teachers should be confident that there exist a number of strategies which can be embedded into their existing curricula, that can be taught to students with only modest extra effort, and that can improve the overall class performance. This means that teachers need not feel that their role is limited to simply providing comprehensible input but can include a variety of learning strategies which can be paired with specific types of language tasks. Future research should be directed to refining the strategy training approaches, identifying effects associated with individual strategies, and determining procedures for strengthening the impact of the strategies on student outcomes.

Follow-up Activities

Discussing the Issues

1. One of the assumptions underlying learner strategy research is that less effective learners can be trained in the use of strategies.
   (a) Does this mean that more effective learners need not receive strategy training?
   (b) Should learners using a limited repertoire of less powerful strategies, such as the Asian students who used rote memorization strategies, be introduced to new strategies?
2. O'Malley's explanation of the results of the training suggests factors that should be taken into account in attempts to develop intervention procedures to refine or modify the strategies learners use. What are they? Can you suggest others?

Applying the Ideas

3. O'Malley does not specify exactly how students were trained to use the cognitive, metacognitive, and social-affective strategies that were the focus of his study.

(a) Prepare some activities or procedures which would help students learn to use these strategies. Try them out in the classroom.

(b) List the problems you encounter in implementing them. How could your activities and procedures be refined so as to avoid these problems?

4. L2 learners need to use a second language for varying purposes, e.g. attend a business conference, travel, work, attend college.

(a) Choose two students you have worked with. List some of the purposes for which they needed to learn a second language.

(b) Make a list of language skills they would need to acquire to communicate adequately in each situation.

(c) Referring to the various strategies outlined in the preceding chapters, determine which cluster of strategies would facilitate the acquisition of which skills.

(d) Using procedures developed by O'Malley as a guide devise a study which would test some of your assumptions about efficient strategy combinations.

Chapter 11

The Learner as Manager: Managing Learning or Managing to Learn?

HENRI HOLEC

What is a "good" learner? A number of studies have been set up in the recent past to uncover at least part of the answer to this question (see references in Chapter 1 and 2). In these studies the ways learners go about learning a second language have been investigated from a number of different angles: the learner as a social being, responding to social constraints whether positive or negative; the learner as a psychological being, whose behavior is influenced by affective as well as intellectual motives; the learning process as a process of integration of linguistic and/or pragmatic knowledge and/or know-how; the learning process as the operation of various learning strategies.

In our study, at the University of Nancy's Centre de Recherches et d'Application Pédagogiques en Langues (CRAPEL), it is the learner as *learner* that has been taken as the major focus of investigation. For we feel that slowly-emerging part of the picture is of crucial importance to our overall and long-standing interest in the development of learner autonomy and its counterpart, self-direction of learning. It is this study, currently under way,[1] that will serve as a basis for the contribution this article will, hopefully, make to the understanding of the term "a good learner". The discussion will aim at clarifying the notion by providing a rationale for the description of the learner as learner. Examples taken from the analysis of a small number of case studies will be used to illustrate our major points.

Learning as "Studying" and "Acquiring"

As a preliminary step in the discussion, what is meant by "learning" should be made clear. The following statements made by learners as well as teachers clearly show that "learning" is not as unambiguous a word as would appear:

(1) "learning a language is hard work"
(2) "for a Frenchman, learning Italian is easier than learning Japanese"
(3) "spelling is one of the major difficulties when learning French"

In (1) "learning" refers to physical and mental activities, to the study tasks one has to fulfil to become competent in another language. In (2) "learning" refers to the process of integration of the language, to acquisition. Because Italian and French are both Latin languages, their structure and taxis are supposed to be more easily understood, remembered and put to use by a Frenchman than a Japanese. In other words, what goes on in a learner's "black box" is somehow thought to be facilitated by the proximity of the two languages. In (3), "learning" probably has both the meanings of (1) and (2): the activities the learner of French has to engage in (copying out words, following directions . . .) and the integration of the knowledge involved.

In other words, "learning" is sometimes equivalent to "studying", sometimes to "acquiring" and sometimes it refers to both these components in what may be taken as a single process. After all, "studying" and "acquiring" are very closely linked. In "real life", one studies to acquire and it is the wish to acquire that leads to engaging in study.[2] Moreover, both terms can refer to the same individual learner.

For the purposes of research, however, it should be made clear whether what is being investigated is the "good learner" as a "good studier" or as a "good acquirer". In our case, it is the "good studier" that is under consideration, and it is learning as studying that is focused on. Our perspective, then, is first of all, one in which language learning refers to the active involvement of an individual in a variety of activities the outcome of which is expected to be the acquisition of the knowledge and know-how which confer competence in the target language. It is a process distinct from, though related to, the process of acquisition. Secondly, we view the learner as an individual who engages in such a process.

Learning as a Management Process

In order to be able to determine whether or not learners are "good", it is necessary to know what they must do, i.e. to look more closely at what "active involvement" in learning entails. In fact, the learning process may be considered as a management process, i.e. as the making of the whole range of decisions necessary to plan and carry out a learning program.

The first of these decisions is choosing objectives. Described in terms of whatever theory of language and whatever metalanguage one prefers to use, what are the acquisition outcomes aimed at, i.e. what vocabulary items? grammatical notions or structures? communicative functions? discourse mode? language skills?

Then, there is the choice of content or materials that will be used to reach the objectives chosen. What is going to be the flesh and bones of the studying activities? Should the materials deal with a particular topic? provide information related to a particular linguistic and/or cultural issue? Should materials be chosen among existing materials or specially devised?

Methods and techniques also have to be decided upon. These decisions are usually taken concurrently with decisions about materials since means and ways are closely interdependent. Will the learning activities be by systematic drills? cloze tests, practicing with a partner, learning lists of words by heart? listening to tape recordings? transcribing them? For how long? how often? when? where?

These decisions all add up to a learning program, a tool to be made use of to develop competence. The various activities that make up this program are put into practice by the individual who wishes to draw from them the acquisition benefits they have been built to gather.

Then, outcomes also have to be assessed. According to the results, decisions are made as to the degree of appropriateness of the chosen objectives, materials, methods and techniques. The degree of faithfulness with which these decisions have been implemented must also be assessed. How much of what was intended to be acquired has, in fact, been acquired? And, if it has not, what are the causes of failure? Is what has been acquired what was aimed at? and if not, why not? Finally, this information is fed back into the whole process and serves as a basis for planning the next stage.

It is this series of decisions and their inter-related planning that constitutes the management of learning referred to earlier. Learning cannot be carried out haphazardly. It requires both preliminary planning and ongoing monitoring to be successful. This is what makes it a process and not just a program, i.e. a collection of language drills, exercises or problem-solving activities.

Role of the Learner

The question can now be raised as to what the role of the learner should be in this process. Traditionally, a majority of teachers and learners alike have tended to think that the learner's responsibility should be limited to being the beneficiary, so to speak, of the process, its active manager being the teacher. This is a social and philosophical choice, and one which is debatable on social and philosophical grounds.[3] But from another standpoint, one to which we fully adhere, it can also be maintained that learners should have the choice between taking full responsibility for the process or simply submitting to it. They should be free to decide whether they want to self-direct their learning or to let others direct it for them. However, to exercise this responsibility, learners must be in a position to do so. The choice would not be real if one of the alternatives were precluded because of the learner's inability to take it up. From this point of view, good learners are learners who are capable of assuming the role of manager of their learning. They know how to make all the decisions involved. In other words, they know how to learn.[4]

Purpose of the Study

Are our learners good learners in the sense just described? If not, how can we, as teachers, help them to learn and to become better learners? These are among the basic questions we are currently engaged in investigating at the CRAPEL. It is these same questions which have prompted us to set up a teaching/learning system in which learners are given the opportunity to self-direct their learning with the help of a counsellor if they choose to do so.

Learners who elect this way of learning do not attend classes or work with a teacher in the traditional sense of the word. Rather they work with a teacher who functions as counsellor in the context of individual non-directive interviews. In the course of these interviews any aspect of self-direction whatever may be discussed: objectives are decided upon; techniques are suggested and demonstrated; and materials provided. Learners make statements about the studying activities they have practiced and what learning difficulties they have met with since their last meeting with the counsellor. They also make decisions concerning the activities they will carry out before their next meeting.[5]

Such a system constitutes a good observatory for watching learners grappling with the implementing of the decision-making process we have been referring to. It is the set-up from which are drawn the case studies we will describe below to show how some real-life learners (1) manage their learning process and (2) how they change as learners over time.

Procedures

The learners to be reported on were randomly chosen from among the group of adult learners who were studying English at the CRAPEL in the teaching/learning scheme described above. Over a period of three months their interviews with the counsellor were tape recorded (5 each in total). Recordings of these learner/counsellor interviews have been transcribed and are, at present, being content-analyzed. The general observations made below and the illustrations provided are taken from this corpus. though they cannot tell what the learners have really done or will really do, they do provide reliable information on the different ways in which they manage their learning.

General Observations

The part of the management process that seems to be the main concern of the learners, at least initially, is *the selection of materials*. As working with materials is what learning almost exclusively means in traditional teaching/learning systems, there is nothing surprising about that. Initially, the majority of learners select materials according to two criteria:

(1) *level*: (difficult/easy)
Helper: "There's an interview of Woody Allen, if you're interested?
Learner: "He speaks very badly, doesn't he? . . . I've been told he swallows his words . . ."
(2) *content*:
Learner: (after listening to an extract of a didactic unit on "How to invite") "No, I don't like that: it doesn't suit me, it's too 'scolaire'. They repeat the same thing over and over . . ."

On the other hand, materials are seldom selected according to the use that is going to be made of them. One learner, for example, decided, "I'll take two cassettes with exercises and two cassettes with texts." But he didn't specify either the type of exercise or the type of text he wanted. Nor did he give any reason for his choice. Even the quantity mentioned is specified only to ascertain whether he is not asking for too much.

Again, materials are very rarely selected according to a specific learning objective. It is only after the helper has pointed out one or several times that materials should be means to reach an end that learners usually start taking objectives into account. Thus, a learner who had previously used a sample of materials geared to asking for information said: "Is there anything available in which . . . documents on how to express happiness, disappointment, and things like?"

Basically, then, materials are usually considered as embodiments of whole learning programs (objectives, content and techniques) and chosen per se.

The management of *methods and techniques* (choice of place and time of study and of studying activities) is usually taken up in three stages. During the first stage, which does not last very long, learners simply wait for the helper to tell them how to proceed. They ask questions like "what do you suggest I should do?" On getting answers like "And you, what do you think?", they quite readily volunteer their own suggestions, based on their previous learning experience.

Learner: "I'll do some written work regularly; it helps to remember, when one writes things out".
Learner: "I prefer texts with questions; when there are questions to answer, one can check whether one has understood the text".
Learner: "I do oral practice when I'm at home, in the evening; written exercises I keep for when I travel . . . in my hotel room".

Then, in a third stage, which usually begins after they have been asked by the helper once or twice to assess the way they are doing their studying, learners start questioning their methods and techniques. They begin to select from among the familiar and the unfamiliar, techniques that suit them best. They begin to abandon their earlier idea that there is only one way of learning properly:

Learner: "I'm not going to use a transcription any more. I'm only too prone to 'cheat'. It's better to listen to the difficult bits five or six times".

Initially, most learners do not make decisions about methods and techniques. This is not because they do not know of any methods or techniques but because they do not know they are open to choice. Once they realize that they can be chosen, their management skills in this area increase rapidly, quantitatively if not qualitatively.

It is the part of the management process bearing on the *definition of objectives* with which learners seem to have most difficulty, and this for two main reasons. First of all, they seem to be utterly unaware of the fact that objectives are not acts of God to submit to but that they can, and in fact, must be chosen. Even when they have been told this, they still seem to have the greatest difficulty transferring this knowledge to practice. Next, in their timid attempts at defining their learning objectives, they more often than not confuse learning objectives (what they want to learn) with post-learning aims (why they want to learn). In other words they confuse objectives with needs.

As a result, in response to the counsellors' questions about objectives (e.g. "what do you want this cassette for?" or "what is it you want to learn?"), learners very often give such information as:

". . . I have mainly production difficulties, oral production difficulties; I'm a little inhibited, a little . . . I find it difficult to utter . . .
"I have a problem with congresses; they're in English, in American, and I can't understand the questions . . ."
"I want to understand conversations, whatever topic crops up".

Moreover, when learners do answers in terms of objectives, they do so in very general and vague terms.

"I want to learn English, oral English . . ."
"I'd like first to get back 'the hang of it'; then after a while, I'll see if I can do something more specific . . ."

In short, in dealing with the management of objectives, our learners not only start from scratch (almost), but they also have great difficulty working against the grain of their previous learning experience.

Finally, as regards *evaluation*, it is important to keep the two following points in mind. Evaluation includes both the assessment of language acquisition (comparing entry-level with present state of knowledge) and assessment of the learning program (passing judgment on learning decisions made). The management of evaluation involves both passing these two types of judgment and using the results yielded as a basis for keeping or modifying the learning program.

Assessment of *entry-level* is something learners regularly do, usually on the basis of their performance when using learning materials. In fact, it is with reference to their own level that they judge the level of difficulty of learning materials. And although they often start by underestimating their level as did the learner who maintained "I'm a beginner", when he had studied English at school a few years back, they very soon become quite accurate in their judgments and are able to discriminate between a general level and particular restricted insufficiencies.

"I had no real difficulty understanding this text; it's just the proper nouns I regularly miss."

On the other hand, they very seldom assess *progress*. First of all, this is because they are not "psychologically ready" to do this (they live in a learning world where only an external "expert" can decide whether something has been acquired or not). Secondly, they would not know how to proceed anyway. They have never been asked to do this before. Finally, as was mentioned earlier, they simply do not have precise enough learning objectives to use as a basis for their assessment. It is a rare exception for a counsellor to hear a learner say ". . . What encourages me a lot is that I've noticed I'm doing better and better . . .". Rather learners either do not answer questions relative to their progress (e.g. "I don't know; it's difficult to tell . . .") or answer in terms of work done, time and energy spent (e.g. "I've worked regularly five hours a week and last week I was on holiday, and I managed to work about 15 hours. So I think I've moved forward quite a lot.").

As a result, they, then, either have no relevant information to feed back into the learning program and so carry on without change. Or, they make decisions that are necessarily limited to quantity of study-decisions which are based on more or less "moral" criteria (a puritan will always decide he does not work hard enough).

If progress is not properly assessed at the outset, *learning programs*, on the contrary, are regularly overhauled (with the restrictions mentioned below):

assessment of materials
"Some of the materials I chose last time are not suitable, don't interest me; they're full of . . . phrases, colloquial phrases . . . everyday things, situations like 'in a taxi', or exchanges about the menu at a restaurant; they're not the sort of things I'm interested in . . ."

assessment of techniques
"I've listened to the recording and I've tried to translate it into French. But, first, this takes too much time, I don't think it's very efficient. Then, as a result, I concentrate too much on individual words and sentences, and I forget the general idea. In fact, I've now stopped doing this . . ."

That learners assess their learning program is induced by the overall system they are engaged in. The purpose of the interviews between counsellors and learners is to monitor learning programs. Therefore, this is their basic and recurrent topic of conversation. But, obviously, the assessment the learner carries out can only deal with those parts of the program that he has made decisions about in the first place, i.e. the choice of materials and techniques. Once objectives start to be defined, though, learners also judge decisions made in this area:

> "I think I'll drop economics for the time being. I'll take this objective up again later. The main thing for me is first to improve my general knowledge of English . . ."

Information thus gathered is fed back into the learning program immediately and naturally as that is why the assessment was carried out. Of course, in the first stages, some learners sometimes hesitate to make the changes, not being too certain whether they are really allowed to do so.

Comments

Learners' Learning Management Skills

The results yielded so far by our analysis of recorded interviews between counsellors and learners give clear indications of how learners engaged in our particular learning system manage their learning and how they change over time.

On the whole, these learners regularly manage the choices of materials, methods and techniques, and to some extent, the evaluation tasks that form part of the learning process. Definition of objectives and evaluation of progress are initially disregarded. Moreover, even the management they do take on in these two areas remains rather crude, as the criteria that they make use of lack precision and are limited in number.

Management also includes, as was stated, taking into account in the decision-making the interrelations that hold between the different areas of the process. Objectives have to be defined in relation to post-learning aims (the so-called "needs" of the learner). Materials have to be geared to objectives and compatible with selected techniques. Techniques should be adapted to objectives and compatible with materials. Evaluation of progress must be referred to objectives, and evaluation of the learning program must be made with reference to decisions made about objectives, materials and techniques.

How do our learners cope with these interrelationships? There seem to be three different cases, corresponding to three stages learners usually go through:

(1) *learners disregard objectives*: in such a case, they obviously cannot assess their progress and the relevance of their objectives to their needs; materials are chosen per se and appropriateness of techniques to objectives is left unheeded

(2) *learners begin to think about objectives*: the objectives they define are unclear; objectives are confused with needs; no great change occurs in the way they manage interrelations within the process

(3) *learners aim their learning at precise objectives*: interrelations are taken into

account, with possibly a slight delay as regards the link between materials or techniques and objectives.

Learners' Representations of the Learning Process

In the initial stages of their management of the learning process, learners appear to be guided by the following main representations. The first is that a "learning program" is equivalent to "learning materials". As has already been stated, for the majority of learners, selecting materials means selecting objectives, resources and techniques. This, consequently, renders unnecessary, or even precludes, a separate choice for each of these components. The second is that "learning" and "acquiring" are one and the same thing. For most of our learners, not only does "learning" mean both "studying" and "acquiring" (the word "apprendre" in French is no less ambiguous than the English word "learn"), but the conflation of these two notions prevents them, apparently, from exploiting the relationship that holds between them. Learning they carry out for learning's sake, and it always comes as a surprise to them when they discover that the hard work they have put into studying activities has not led to increased competence in the situations where that competence is needed. However, foremost among the representations that learners more or less easily and quickly question (de-conditioning process) and alter (reconstruction process) are those concerning their roles and the functions of teachers and teaching materials.

In changing their representations of their role in the learning process, learners gradually replace the belief that they are "consumers" of language courses, of textbooks and exercises, of teacher hours with the belief that they can be "producers" of their own learning program and that this is their right. What "production" means can range from simply choosing the whole or part of an existing program on the basis of *their own criteria* to defining and implementing a part or the whole of a program specifically designed to meet their individual requirements. That such a change can occur is not particularly surprising. After all, learners have at one time or another in their lives been "free-lance" learners of other skills or in other fields of knowledge where they have been "producers" of their learning programs. (In fact, pointing this out to them will put them into a state of "suspension of disbelief" that allows them to question their beliefs.)

In fact, once they have experienced self-direction, even though their experience may remain limited (either because it is direction of a restricted part of the program or because it is co-operative, i.e. helper-learner direction) they overcome their initial disbelief regarding their ability to direct the process. Experiences that may "trigger" this change may be the discovery by learners that they, too, can have ideas about learning activities, exercises and that these ideas are just as good as those of a teacher. Or, it may be the discovery that going through one's own individual learning program is more satisfying and efficient than attending a general course which involves taking part in irrelevant if not entirely useless (with regard to one's needs) learning activities. And when the process of change has been started, it usually "snowballs" to other areas of the learning process. Learners widen their field as "producers of a language program" to other areas in which they feel they have a say. The commonly observed order is from techniques to materials, to objectives and, finally, to evaluation.[6]

This change in the representation of a learner's role entails a concomitant change in their representations of the functions attributed to teachers and teaching materials. From an omniscient "causer" of learning, teachers become, in the learner's mind, experienced language and language-learning resource persons whose function it is to facilitate the learning process. It is their role to give advice, provide explanations, help find suitable materials, suggest procedures, pass on information coming from other learners. Teachers are no longer seen as someone to listen to, to obey, as a pilot to trust blindly. Rather, they are viewed as someone who can help find answers to questions one asks oneself, who can lighten some of the tasks learning involves and, generally, who serves as an informed interlocuter available when needed. When teachers are perceived in this way, the "teaching" that they provide, though it may very well take the form of "lessons" or "classes", is no longer received by the learner as an indivisible learning whole, but as a series of methodological proposals that it is the learner's responsibility to test for efficiency, to adapt to his own case if necessary, to select from or to add to.

In the same way, the role of materials, whether didactic, (specifically designed for language teaching/learning purposes) or authentic (not produced for such purposes) also changes. They are assigned the status of potential learning resources to be selected, adapted, or developed into learning "aids" suited to one's objectives and to one's preferred methods and techniques. Again, as a result of the new role they attribute to themselves, learners become producers. Textbooks, sets of exercises, language games, recordings, films, are all considered as raw material to which they must allot both a purpose and specifications for use.

Gradually, then, learners alter their whole representation of the learning process until finally they view it as a process which involves their active responsibility (learning no longer means "being taught"). It is a responsibility which is exercised with a purpose — language acquisition. "Learning" no longer means "acquiring".

As has been suggested earlier, learners' entering assumptions are a direct reflection upon the teaching/learning system in which they have had previous language learning experience. In "traditional" systems, the function of teaching is to provide learning. Thus, the learner's learning program becomes the teacher's teaching program and who else other than the teacher is allowed to manage it? The teacher (or the institution that does not make any difference to the learner) makes decisions concerning objectives, materials and techniques and the teacher evaluates. Learners do not. Nor do they even ask questions about these decisions, not necessarily because they are not allowed to do so (although that would be questioning the teacher's role), but because they have faith in the "expert" whose job it is to see to these matters. The end result is that they do not get much chance to learn. Instead they internalize the idea that learning means "being taught" doing what a teacher or teaching materials tell you to do.

Are Our Learners Good Learners?

Without going further into first causes, it has to be said that, initially, when they come to us, our learners are not particularly "good" learners. They may be good in the sense that they are hard-working, willing and docile, but they are not very good at managing their learning process. This does not mean that they are necessarily bad acquirers, or even that this prevents them from acquiring. A good learner can be a bad acquirer, and vice versa, and submitting to good teaching may, and often does, lead to satisfactory acquisition (submitting to bad teaching as well, unjustly enough!). What it does mean, though, is that they have limited chances of acquiring a language *without being taught*, which is a disadvantage, a learning handicap. If for one reason or another, teaching fails them (they may not have enough time to attend classes, or enough money, or there may not be any suitable teaching available), they will have a hard time satisfying their acquisition needs. An added disadvantage for learners of this type is that the teaching they eventually get will almost of necessity be group teaching, not individual teaching. This, in turn, will almost certainly mean that what they learn will only match approximately what they need to learn. If it turns out that there is a real gap between what they need and what they get, there will be a corresponding reduction in efficiency.

Under these circumstances, two courses of action are open to us. Either we take the pessimistic view and decide that this inability of learners to manage their learning is inevitable and that nothing can be done about it. In this case, we will have to keep on providing the learning crutches learners need. Or, just as we assume learners can acquire a language they do not know, we acknowledge the fact that learners can acquire the management ability they lack and decide that it is also part of our responsibility to help them become better managers.

It is this second option that we have chosen to implement at the CRAPEL and it did not take very long to get ample empirical evidence that learners are quite capable of improving their management ability even though their rate and degree of improvement remained variable, as was only to be expected. They can acquire the knowledge and the know-how they lack to fulfil satisfactorily the "producer's" tasks they want to assume.[7] In fact, what they need to know is precisely the knowledge on which teachers in "traditional" structures base their decisions, i.e. What is a language? How can a language be described? How is it used? What operations are involved in reading, writing, listening, speaking? Where can one find learning materials? How are criteria of evaluation derived from statements of objectives? This may look like a formidable task, especially to teachers. But it must be born in mind that learners do not have to master this knowledge as academic examination subjects. All they need is a working knowledge, couched in terms most useful to them.

It must also be remembered that they can acquire this knowledge "on the job" as they tackle the learning management problems they are confronted with, getting answers when questions arise. Similarly, the required skills (setting up objectives, analysing and choosing materials, evaluating a performance . . .) are usually acquired by practice — trial and error being in that case the best learning procedure. On the whole, learners do manage to improve their technical competence as learners, a change which usually keeps pace with the development of their representations.

Therefore, our earlier observation that, initially, our learners appear to be rather bad learners, should not be mistakenly interpreted as meaning that, as teachers, we have drawn the short straw. Our learners can and will achieve better learning competence provided the right conditions are created for them to start thinking about the learning process in different terms. And once the ball is set rolling, it will keep rolling and will even gain momentum if the learning environment made available to them takes into account their improvement in competence. That this constitutes a teaching challenge is undeniable, for we, as teachers, are, then, faced with problems unheard of in the training we have received. We, too, will have to change our representations of what teaching and being a teacher means. But can we afford to go on forgetting that better learning requires better learners?

Food for Thought

The general observations and comments that we have made are based on a particular experience, concerning particular learners in a particular socio-cultural setting. We do not make any claims about other learners in other settings. However, we hope they will reassure or encourage teachers and researchers working along new or similar lines. In fact, that is exactly what their presentation, here, was intended to do. If that were to happen, there are a number of questions which would be worth investigating by those teachers/researchers. The following are some which have been raised in our own action research and which might serve as starting points.

1. *How good are other learners at managing their learning?*

Different learners will most certainly present different profiles according to their age, level of education, socio-cultural, ethnic and linguistic background, previous learning experience. What will their profiles be like?

2. *How do free-lance language learners learn?*

Finding out how these learners cope with different learning management problems and what their beliefs are might yield interesting and useful hints for would-be good learners.

3. *Do all types of learners acquire learning competence the same way?*

A better understanding of the way learning competence is acquired will be gained by comparing learners. What learning management skills do they acquire? in what order? at what rate? . . . This is what we intend to do with our learners. The same could be done with other groups.

4. *What are the "brakes" and "accelerators" in the process of learning competence acquisition?*

Just as a start, it might prove very helpful to check whether the findings related to the part played by personality and social factors in second language acquisition are relevant here.

5. *What different forms can helping learners learn to learn take?*

Learning systems that respond to the needs of various types of learners and institutional frameworks need to be devised. At the CRAPEL, we proceed differently in the three types of learning systems we operate: evening class courses, self-directed group learning and self-directed learning with support systems. What is feasible and efficient in other frameworks and especially with other learners learning other languages? (In our case, the languages involved are English and French.)

6. *Once learners have more or less acquired the ability to manage their learning process, what can teaching/learning institutions do to help nurture self-directed learning?*

This question deals with the role of language learning resource centers. What resources should be provided? Should they include the latest information about language, language acquisition and learning methodology? If they should (as we think), how can this information be made available in the center?

7. *How do learners who have learned to learn use their ability in later studies?*

It would be particularly interesting to know how such learners carry out their learning of another language or of an altogether different subject matter or skill. Do they transfer their ability directly or not? Do they add to their competence? And if they do, what, why and how do they add to it?

Conclusion

These general questions, among a number of others that will most certainly have come to our readers' minds, point to some of the more conspicuous areas in which our knowledge remains severely limited. Obviously, what we know at present does not amount to much when compared to what we still have to discover. To a large extent, this is because teachers have not, so far, expended much time or energy on research in second language learning as opposed to second language acquisition. However, recently, more and more teachers are becoming interested in topics such as learner autonomy, self-directed learning, language learning resource centers, learning to learn, learner strategies, that is, they are becoming more interested in the learner *qua* learner. This may very well put us in a position to help learners follow Montaigne's educational principle that "A good head is better than a full head" ("Mieux vaut tête bien faite que tête bien pleine") — four centuries late, admittedly, but better late than never!

Notes

1. A full report of this study, started in the Fall of 1984, will be published by the CRAPEL in the Fall of 1986. It is being carried out by a team of part-time research workers comprising D. Abe, M. J. Gremmo, H. Moulden, P. Riley, C. Trompette and the writer.
2. But it should not be forgotten that some people acquire a lot without studying much while others study a lot without acquiring much.
3. See Wenden (Chapter 1) for a summary of the main arguments.
4. Obviously, it is only logical to think that if he knows how to learn, the learner will self-direct. But there is no necessary causal relation between the two. An autonomous learner, one who knows how to learn, may decide to self-direct only part of his learning, or even, at times, not to self-direct at all, just as someone who knows how to drive a car may sometimes prefer to be driven.
5. For more details about this structure, see Abe and Gremmo, 1981.
6. Beliefs about evaluation die hard, mainly, it appears because of a confusion between social norms of evaluation and individual norms (the former requiring an outside judge to handle, the latter implying no such requirement) and between optional and compulsory external evaluation. As a result, learners believe that only one form of evaluation is valid, i.e. external evaluation carried out by an "objective" judge.
7. For more details about other matters related to learning to learn, see the chapter entitled "Autonomous learning schemes: principles and organizations" in Riley, 1985.

Follow-up Activities

Making Links

1. For Holec a good learner is a successful manager of the learning process.
  (a) What, specifically, does this mean? Is it similar to the view of the successful learner described in Abraham and Vann's research? in Rubin (Chapter 2).
  (b) What is your definition of a good learner? Compare and contrast it with Holec's view.
2. In the ERIC/CLL Bulletin (May, 1978), Omaggio summarizes what we have learned about successful language learners. She says good language learners:
— have insight into their own language learning styles
— take an active approach to the learning task
— will take risks
— are good guessers
— attend to form as well as content
— develop the target language into a separate reference system
— have a tolerant and outgoing approach to the target language.
  (a) Compare this view with Holec's.
  (b) How does it differ from your definition? Abraham and Vann's?
3. Krashen and Terrell (1983: 26–27) claim that adults have two distinct ways of developing competence in a language. The first is via language acquisition and the second is by language learning. Read their discussion and compare their views with Holec's analysis of learning.
4. Wenden (Chapter 1) refers to the literature in adult learning to outline two approaches to promoting autonomy. Analyze the changes in the learners Holec described to determine how autonomy is fostered at the CRAPEL.

Applying the Ideas

4. The approach utilized to promote learner autonomy at the CRAPEL is relatively non-interventionist. The language institute at the University of Nancy offers a self-directed system as one of three alternatives students can choose from. Once enrolled in the self-directed program, students work with a counselor and have access to a learning resource centre. Counselors work with students in a non-directive way — asking questions, helping clarify, making suggestions. They do not make any decisions for them — regarding either their learning program or the activities and techniques they choose to learn. Nor do the counselors evaluate the students' learning attempts or their achieved linguistic competence.
  (a) How does this approach differ from the approach described in O'Malley's paper?
  (b) Which of the approaches, i.e. O'Malley's or Holec's, would you prefer to implement? Why?
  (c) What other ways could you use to help students learn how to learn? Consider materials, activities, institutional arrangements, programs.
5. Find three students who need tutoring. Perhaps they cannot attend a formal class, or, perhaps, they need extra help. Using the interview approach described in Holec's paper, try to help them learn how to learn on their own.
  (a) Refer to a methodology book on non-directive interviewing for guidance in this method of working with learners.
  (b) Tape your interview sessions and use the categories described in Holec's paper to analyze them.
  (c) Note how they change over time — what learning skills or strategies do they learn to use? change? in what order? how do their "representations" or assumptions about the language learning process and their role in it change?
  (d) What personality and/or social factors appear to inhibit or facilitate them as they attempt to learn how to learn? Are they similar to those factors cited in the second language acquisition research as influencing the process of language learning? (cf Chapter 1 for an overview of some of this research).
  (e) Compare the students and try to explain similarities and differences.
6. Assume that you have been funded to develop a learning resource center for adult second language learners.
  (a) Make a list of the decisions you would have to make in planning such a center, e.g. where to locate it — in a university? as a separate institution? materials? activities? content and purpose? . . .
  (b) Using your list as a guide, outline your development plan.
  (c) Draw a floor sketch of the facilities and set up a tentative budget for one year.

Chapter 12

Incorporating Learner Training in the Classroom[1]

ANITA L. WENDEN

In *Toward a Theory of Instruction*, Bruner outlines the ultimate goal of instruction as follows:

> ". . . Finally, it is necessary to reiterate one general point already made in passing. Instruction is a provisional state that has as its object to make the learner or problem solver self-sufficient . . . Otherwise the result of instruction is to create a form of mastery that is contingent upon the perpetual presence of a teacher . . ." (1966:53)

In emphasizing that the product of successful instruction be a self-sufficient problem solver (learner), Bruner implies that teachers do not focus exclusively on the content of learning but also that attention be given to the process. For to be self-sufficient, learners must know how to learn. This is not a new idea and the long list of handbooks for language learners who need to or choose to learn a second language on their own attests to an acknowledgement in the field of second language learning and teaching of the importance of learner training.[2] Still, to my knowledge, learner training remains a secondary concern in many second language classes — one which is focused on incidentally, if at all. This lack of emphasis on what most would agree is a very important set of skills may be due in part to the scant empirical validation of its feasibility and effectiveness in second language learning. It may also be due to the lack of guidelines to direct a more systematic approach in devising materials and activities for its implementation. This paper addresses the second reason. First, it will outline a set of criteria that may be used to guide curriculum development in the area of learner training. Then, four projects will be described to illustrate how these criteria have been applied in second language settings with various student groups.

Criteria for Learner Training Activities

Analysis of selected literature in intervention research in non ESL settings (cf Brown *et al.*, 1983) suggests that the following be taken into account in the development and implementation of activities and materials for learner training: (1) explicitness of purpose (2) content (3) evaluation. A fourth consideration, which emerges from a consideration of learner training projects in ESL settings, is the integration of learner training with language training.

Explicitness of purpose, i.e. should students be informed of the value and purposes of the training or not? In their review of intervention studies in developmental research, Brown *et al.* (1983) distinguish approaches to learner training on the basis of explicitness of purpose. Blind training leaves the trainees in the dark about the importance of the activities they are being induced to use. In such studies, learners are instructed/induced to perform particular strategies but not helped to understand their significance. They are told what to do and led to do it without being informed as to why they should act in a certain way. They are not told that a

159

particular strategy will help performance or when it is appropriate to use it — i.e. that it belongs to a certain class of situations or goals. The emphasis in such instances is on learning *something* rather than on learning to learn. This approach is exemplified in many ESL texts in listening comprehension. As I have written elsewhere (Wenden, 1986b), the tasks set in these books, e.g. pre-listening activities such as explaining key words, providing an advance organizer, and the different kinds of comprehension questions, are, in effect, strategies that students could utilize on their own in other contexts. However, the procedures described in the texts do not provide students opportunities to reflect on that fact and to determine their effectiveness and applicability. Studies referred to in the Brown review have shown that blind training results in improved performance of the task to which it is tied. However, ordinarily, students do not continue to use the strategy. Nor can they identify similar situations in which it can be used. That is, there is no maintenance nor transfer.

On the other hand, informed training tells students that a strategy can be helpful and why. Students are not only instructed in the use of the strategy but in the need for it and its anticipated effects. Together with the rationale for learning it, they are given feedback about their performance so that they can estimate the effectiveness of the training. Informed training places emphasis on learning to learn. Such training has been proven to be more effective. Students use the learned strategy more frequently and more effectively. (cf Brown *et al.*, 1983).

Content of training, i.e. is it sufficient to provide training in the use of specific learning skills, or should training be provided in the more general learning skills? Training in specific learning skills refers to training in the use of cognitive strategies or routines that are tied to a particular learning tasks such as remembering a new word, or decoding the meaning of an unfamiliar word. Specific skills or cognitive strategies are quite focused in their use. General learning skills refer to strategies that can be used to regulate learning, i.e. plan, monitor and evaluate the range of cognitive strategies used to learn. General learning skills also include awareness raising about the nature of learning. These skills have a wider application than the cognitive strategies. They are referred to as metacognitive strategies. In the case of blind training, students are taught to use cognitive strategies. There is no metacognitive supplement. In the case of informed training, students are taught the specific strategy and they are made aware of the importance of what they are doing, i.e. they are led to focus on the nature of learning. There is a limited metacognitive supplement. In self-control training, a third approach described by Brown *et al.* in their review, subjects are trained to use a specific strategy and, then, to monitor their performance to determine whether the use of the strategy is effective or not. In this case, the metacognitive supplement consists of general skills necessary to regulate learning.

In dealing with the question of whether to teach specific skills (i.e. cognitive strategies) or general skills (i.e. metacognitive strategies), Brown *et al.* point to the distinct functions of each type of skill. When applied appropriately and executed properly, specific skills or cognitive strategies are very powerful. Once assessed, problem solution should follow, as when a language learner uses a rehearsal strategy to remember a particular word. The more general skills or metacognitive strategies, on the other hand, can be applied to almost any problem-solving situation. However, without the complement of an appropriate cognitive strategy, they will not lead to learning. In other words, it is of limited use to train language learners to monitor their progress in listening if they do not have a repertoire of cognitive strategies necessary to deal with the difficulties they may perceive themselves to have. On the other hand, language learners who do not reflect on their learning to monitor their progress and evaluate the outcome of their learning endeavors will not likely be induced to draw upon their repertoire of strategies — however varied it may be — or become aware of the need for such strategies. Brown concludes that what is taught should be determined by the needs of the learner and further cites research (cf Brown and Palinscar, 1982) that indicates the superiority of a package that includes both specific (or cognitive) skills and general (or metacognitive) skills.

Integration, i.e. to what extent and how should learner training be a part of language training tasks? Of course, the training in learning will always be tied to a language learning experience, and so, integration is a matter of degree. In some cases, it may be focused on the whole of a language learning experience (e.g. project 3 to follow). In others, the learner training tasks can focus on a particular language skill, such as reading or developing oral skills (e.g. project 1 and 2 to follow). The more specific the language training objective the learner training focuses on the more integrated it will be.

Where and when the learning skill or strategy is actually applied or practiced also determines the extent to which learner training is integrated with language training. If the learner training is incorporated into a language training sequence, then practice sessions will be teacher directed and take place as part of the activities devised with a particular language training objective in mind. Thus, as I have suggested above, a class in listening comprehension would include activities that have students reflect about, practice, and evaluate the use of listening strategies. (Also see project 1 and 2.) Alternatively, a special time can be set aside for introducing students to concepts related to *learning* a language and for demonstrating related skills or strategies. However, students would be expected to apply or use the skills on their own in situations where they deemed it appropriate to do so. In such a case, a teacher would simply introduce students to the notion of "strategy", give them a list of listening strategies, perhaps demonstrate how some of them can be applied. Class time would not be set aside for applying or practicing the skill. In other words, the application of the learning skills would be separate from the initial training period and directed by the students who would apply them to language training objectives of their choosing. (Also see project 3.) Of the two alternatives, the first, which actually incorporates the learner training, including its application or practice, into a particular set of language training activities would be more integrated than the second.

Of course, it is generally acknowledged that learning in context is more effective than learning that is not clearly tied to the purposes it intends to serve. The former enables the learner to perceive the relevance of the task, enhances comprehension, and facilitates retention. Seen from this perspective, for learners who do not immediately appreciate the relevance of learner training, the more integrated the learner training, the more effective it should be. On the other hand, such an approach does not encourage the learner to be autonomous in the use of these skills, for learner training, like language training, becomes a teacher directed activity. Nor does it take into account the time-space constraints that language classes organized in traditional ways place on adult learners. In other words, adult learners cannot afford to set aside the time required to take language classes, or the hours and place of available courses are not compatible with their work schedules. In other instances, their language objectives cannot be met adequately in available courses. In such cases, a course that focuses exclusively on helping students develop the skills necessary to learn the language on their own would appear to be the more appropriate, although less integrated, alternative.

Evaluation, i.e. how is the outcome of learner training measured? The kinds of changes in learner behavior looked for in the intervention studies analyzed include (1) task improvement (2) maintenance, and (3) transfer. In the case of task improvement, this means determining whether learners perform their language tasks with greater facility and accuracy as a result of the training. For second language learners this could mean understanding better, making fewer grammar errors, remembering more vocabulary. The second consideration has to do with durability of behavior. Will learners continue to use this strategy and for how long? If one were to set a similar task a day, week, or even a month after the training, would learners spontaneously use the strategy? use it with prompting? The third consideration, transfer, considers the learners' ability to generalize the use of the strategy to similar classes of tasks within different contexts. For example, would second language learners be able to determine that a rehearsal strategy used to remember vocabulary can also be used to remember specific facts in a science class?

Experience with the implementation of learner training in second language settings suggests that learners' attitude toward learner training also be taken into account in the evaluation of such activities? In other words, to what extent does it influence the effectiveness of learner training?

Learner Training in Second Language Settings

1. *High-schools (Western New York).* Hosenfeld *et al.* (1981) describe a curricular sequence for teaching reading strategies used in Western New York in four different foreign language classrooms with high school students talking French. The sequence consists of seven steps. (1) Teach students to think aloud while reading. (2) Identify students' reading strategies. (3) Help students to understand the concept of "strategy" and to recognize that some strategies are successful, some unsuccessful, and others only "seemingly" successful. (4) Help students to identify strategies that they use to decode native language texts containing unknown words. (5) Help students to identify strategies that they CAN use to decode foreign language texts containing unknown words. (6) Provide instruction/practice/integration for specific reading strategies. (7) Identify students' reading strategies and compare them to the strategies students used before instruction.

This is an example of informed training. Students are helped to understand the concept of "strategy" and led to reflect on the varying usefulness of different strategies (cf step 3). It is an approach which combines training in specific skills with training in general skills. Students are trained in the use of cognitive strategies necessary to better comprehend written texts. They are made aware of the strategies they already use (step 4) — a form of metacognitive training. As indicated in step 6, opportunity was provided to practice the strategies. One assumes strategy practice took place during their reading classes, i.e. strategy practice was closely integrated with reading practice. There is also an evaluation component built into the sequence (step 7). However, since it is not specified exactly when the comparison in strategy use is made, it is not clear whether evaluation will yield strong information on strategy maintenance or simply indicate whether new strategies were learned.

2. *Language institute (England)*. In Holec (1981) Ferris describes five types of activities used for training second language learners of English in self-assessment of their oral communication skills in a Eurocentre language training institute in England. The specific objectives of the training were to provide students with opportunities (1) to discover and learn to use assessment criteria, and (2) to realize what progress they had made in developing their oral skills. One typical activity had students act out and record a simple transaction such as introducing oneself. The language content necessary had already been taught and pre-recording practice necessary to memorize the transaction also provided. After the recording, the teacher provided instruction in the criteria used to assess spoken language, i.e. fluency, intonation, and pronunciation. This included practice in identifying this criteria. Students were, then, given a sheet with these focal points and asked to re-record their interaction and compare the two recordings by referring to the criteria. They organized their notes under the following headings (1) what they said and (2) how they said it. They were encouraged to re-record the transaction if they were not satisfied with the change in their performance. Similar procedures were followed with oral homework. A variation included in some activities consisted in having students assess one another's oral performance and/or having their teacher go through their audiotape with them to point out what they had done well and which points they needed to improve.

While the actual training was not preceded by an explanation of rationale, students were requested to evaluate the usefulness of the training activities, i.e. did it help them learn better? how? why? This would enable them to perceive its relevance. In this sense, then, the training may be considered informed. As indicated by the objectives and activities, the training focused on metacognitive or general learning skills. Students learned to assess their speaking skills and to monitor their progress. The provision of instruction to students in the criteria necessary to assess their oral skills would also refine their metalinguistic awareness. Training, in this situation, may be considered closely integrated. The training activities focused on oral communication skills and were included by the teacher as a part of the actual language training activities devised to practice these skills.

Evaluation of the project was done informally. According to the teachers, students who received the self-assessment training were able to use the criteria to make reliable judgments. Moreover, students who participated in the self-assessment training "enjoyed the activities" and felt a sense of achievement when they perceived progress had been made.

3. *American Language Program (New York City)*. The materials developed by Wenden were first used in the summer of 1982 at Columbia University's language

institute (American Language Program) with two groups of very advanced students of various cultural backgrounds. The students were registered for a seven-week intensive program in English, i.e. 16 class hours and four lab hours. Some of them were taking the course without any specific purpose in mind — they simply wanted to improve their English. Others were planning to enroll in academic courses in a university in the fall. At the beginning of the course, students were told that two of the class hours set aside to develop fluency in discussion would focus on the topic of language learning.

The general objective of the project was to refine and expand student awareness of various aspects of their language learning experience such as the difficulties they encountered, the strategies they utilized to deal with them, and their views on the nature of language and language learning. Materials consisted of mini-lectures and readings adapted from writings about language learning, research findings on learner strategies and student accounts of their learning. Training tasks included (1) comprehension exercises (2) class discussions based on the reading or listening passages (3) out of class practice tasks (4) focused diary writing. The purpose of the tasks was to help students become aware of these aspects of language learning — their views or understandings of them together with alternate ways of viewing them.

The materials take into account the importance of informed training. The first of the modules is intended to help students realize the purpose and significance of the activities involved in the modules that follow as do the discussions that follow the various reading and listening passages in subsequent modules. As the objectives state, the training focuses on the development and refinement of metacognitive awareness, i.e. the students are provided with the concepts necessary to be able to focus more precisely on various aspects of their language learning. They are also led to consider learning skills related to these concepts. In the Columbia project, the training did not focus on specific language objectives that were a part of the curriculum. Of course, the tasks that constituted the modules provided students with opportunities to develop fluency in the aural/oral skills, but this was a secondary effect. Moreover, it (the training) was intended to render more efficient student use of language learning opportunities outside the classroom, so students were expected to apply or practice the skills on their own. In other words, this first use of the materials demonstrates training that is less integrated than the training in the preceding two projects.

At the end of the session a questionnaire was administered to evaluate its effectiveness and student attitudes toward learner training. Of the 23 students who participated, seven indicated that they had changed their approach somewhat and five that they had learned something they did not know. Results were even less positive as regards attitude. Less than 50% of the respondents agreed that the tasks that constituted the training had been useful. However, when asked why, only five of the students gave reasons related to learner training although their answers to a previous question regarding the purpose of the class evidenced a clear understanding of its objectives. Learner training was not considered relevant in its own right. These responses underlined the point already made by one of the participating classes. These students were so resistant to the learner training that after the first three weeks it was discontinued except with a small group of seven students who came after class as much for the opportunity to practice English in a small group setting as to improve their competence in learning. As for the class that continued to participate, they were generally cooperative but there was something almost mechanical about their participation.

These reactions suggested that the materials be more integrated in their approach. Therefore they were revised so that the concept and related set of skills highlighted by each module focus on a particular language learning task or objective, and continued use of the revised materials has proven to be more successful in involving the students.

4. *An engineering college (France)*. This project (Moulden, 1978–80) was undertaken in an engineering college in France. The 32 students who participated were enrolled in engineering courses and in ESL courses. This was their second or third year in the college. They were at an intermediate level of proficiency in English. Learner training was initiated as a result of a decision to autonomize two of the three and one half hours dedicated to oral expression. In other words, during this time students would not be in a classroom with a teacher. Rather, they would work on objectives and materials of their choice when, where and how they pleased.

Training materials consisted of two 20-page booklets given to the students two weeks prior to the initiation of this semi-autonomous system. The first booklet, *Learning English on your own*, described the advantages of planning one's learning autonomously. It outlined procedures for assessing linguistic needs, planning work programs, and monitoring achievement. Strategies students could practice to improve their listening, reading and speaking skills were also listed. The second booklet, *Objectives in English*, served as an instrument for self-assessment. It contained a list of the English skills engineers should have in listening, reading and oral expression. Students were free to add any objectives they wanted to work on not included in this list. Next to each objective was a column where students were invited to rate themselves. Space was also left for marking priorities and any progress made. Students were expected to study the contents of the booklets and bring any questions they needed to clarify to a meeting arranged specifically for that purpose. The other main training activity consisted of weekly interviews (twenty minutes in length) with the teacher to help students plan and assess their progress and to deal with particular linguistic problems they could not resolve on their own.

This project may also be considered an example of informed training. In describing the advantages of planning one's learning autonomously, the first booklet would indicate the purpose or relevance of acquiring learning skills. The training objectives listed in the second booklet included both cognitive strategies (or specific skills) and those metacognitive strategies (or general skills) necessary to plan, monitor, and evaluate learning. The training in this project focused specifically on helping students improve their listening, speaking, or reading skills. In this sense it was more closely integrated with the language training than the previous project (3). However, instruction by the teacher was minimal and separate from the actual language training. Learners were given a booklet outlining procedures and strategies they could use to help themselves learn; opportunities to seek guidance from a teacher in the application of these strategies and procedures were provided. But, they were expected to apply and practice them on their own. From this perspective, then, the learner training is not as closely tied to the language training — it is less integrated. A questionnaire was administered at the end of the semester to evaluate the project. However, it attempted to elicit student attitudes toward learning autonomously not toward the learner training.

Conclusion

The criteria that have been described and illustrated can be summarized in terms of the following tentative guidelines for teachers and administrators who wish to provide students with more systematic training in learning how to learn:

(1) Inform students of the value and significance of the strategies you train them to use — *tell* them about it and have them *experience* their value.

(2) Provide training in both cognitive and metacognitive strategies. Moreover, training in metacognition should include both awareness raising or reflection on the nature of learning *and* training in the skills necessary to plan, monitor and evaluate learning activities.

(3) To determine how to integrate learner training with language training, take into account the following factors:

range and specificity — should a general orientation of all concepts and skills be provided or should the training focus on skills tied to specific language training objectives?
autonomy of application — should opportunities be provided within the training sequence for the actual practice or application of the skills or should learners assume the responsibility to direct this aspect of the training autonomously outside the classroom?
learners' needs — how much time can learners set aside for formal language training? how compatible is a particular language training course with learners' linguistic needs? to what extent do they appreciate the relevance of learner training?

(4) In evaluating learner training it is important to consider the following:

learner attitudes — has learners' appreciation of learner training changed?
skill acquisition — has the learning skill been learned?
task improvement — does the skill facilitate performance of the language task?
durability — does the skill continue to be utilized?
transfer — is the skill utilized in similar contexts?

These tentative guidelines illustrate the application in four ESL settings of insights gleaned from general research in learner training. Teachers who agree with Bruner that making problem solvers self-sufficient is a primary goal of their second language teaching may find them helpful in charting their course into this relatively new field of endeavor in second language teaching and learning. However, they are also encouraged to analyze and evaluate their own activities against these guidelines to modify and expand them and so, to add their own insights into the presently sparse body of information on how classroom activities can enhance and refine the learning skills of learners.

Notes

1. This article has also appeared in *System* 14 (3) 1986.
2. See, for example, Sweet, 1899, Cummings, 1916, Crawford, 1930, Cornelius, 1955, Nida, 1957, Politzer, 1965, Kraft and Kraft, 1966, Hall, 1966, Moulton, 1966, Pei, 1966, Pimsleur, 1980, Rubin and Thompson, 1982 and Cohen and Hosenfeld, forthcoming.
3. Brown *et al.* (1983) define intervention studies as "research that has involved some attempt to elevate the performance of learners". (p. 141) One of its purposes is to develop and evaluate cognitive theory with the belief that "if we understand the cognitive processes and learning mechanism involved in some domain and something about developmental differences, we should be in a strong position to teach someone to perform more effectively". (p. 141).

Follow-up Activities

Making Links

1. According to Bruner, the goal of instruction is an autonomous learner. Still, Wenden suggests that this is not an objective that is systematically implemented in most L2 classrooms. Determine the accuracy of this view by assessing
   (a) the objectives of popular teaching methodologies
   (b) past and present trends in curriculum development
   (c) your classroom practice.
2. What will be the effect on classroom practice of placing more emphasis on making learner's autonomous?

Applying the Ideas

3. Wenden has developed a set of five criteria for guiding the development of learner training activities.
   (a) Use the guidelines to analyze the approach to training illustrated by O'Malley and Holec.
   (b) Review textbooks that purport to teach reading or listening strategies and evaluate their approach to strategy training.
   (c) In "Classroom implementation of cognitive strategy instruction", Petersen and Swing (cf Pressley and Levin, 1983 in Ch.1) suggest guidelines for implementing strategy training. Compare them with Wenden's and amplify her framework.
4. Review some of the handbooks or manuals written to guide independent L2 study referred to by Wenden in note 2 (e.g. Rubin and Thompson's *How to be a more successful language learner*, Pimsleur's *How to learn a foreign language*, Nida's *Learning a foreign language*.)
   (a) Compare the guidelines offered in these handbooks with (i) the research findings presented in Part 2; (ii) objectives of the learner training projects described in Part 3.
   (b) Use the information provided in the handbooks and this volume to develop a learner training curriculum.
   (c) Use the same information to outline the main topics you would include in a handbook or set of materials to orient a group of ESL students to autonomous learning.
5. In a previous question (Chapter 7), you were asked to interview an unsuccessful language learner. Using the information you have obtained, develop a series of training interventions that you will use over an extended period of time to try to modify the learner's approach to L2 learning. You may refer to the procedures and guidelines described in Chapters 10–12.

Implement your plan and keep a log noting the following aspects of the experience:
  (a) the learner's progress and/or lack of it
  (b) criteria you develop for measuring progress
  (c) difficulties encountered by the learner and their causes
  (d) how you help him deal with these difficulties.
At the end of the period evaluate your training model and make necessary revisions. Compare your model with the model of another teacher.

Bibliography

Abe, D. and Gremmo, M. J. 1981. *Mélanges Pédagogiques CRAPEL*. Université de Nancy II.

Anderson, R. C. and Kulhavy, R. W. 1972. Imagery and prose learning. *Journal of Educational Research*, **63**, 242–243.

_____ and Pichert, R. W. 1978. Recall of previously unrecallable information following a shift in perspective. *Journal of Verbal Learning and Verbal Behavior*, **17**, 1–12.

Asher, J. J. 1965. The strategy of the total physical response: An application to learning Russian. *International Review of Applied Linguistics*, **3**, 291–300.

_____ 1966. The learning strategy of the total physical response: A review. *Modern Language Journal*, **50**, 79–84.

_____ and Price, B. S. 1967. The learning strategy of the total physical response: Some age differences. *Child Development*, **38**, 1219–1227.

_____ 1969. The total physical response approach to second language learning. *Modern Language Journal*, **53**, 3–17.

_____ 1972. Implications of psychological research for second language learning. In Dale, L., Lange and C. J. James (eds.), *Foreign Language Education: A Reappraisal* (*Britannica Review of Foreign Language Education*, Vol. 4) Skokie, Ill.: National Textbook Co., pp. 157–186.

_____, Kusudo, J. and de la Torre, R. 1974. Learning a second language through commands: The second field test. *Modern Language Journal*, **58**, 24–32.

Atkinson, R. C. 1975. Mnemotechnics in second-language learning. *American Psychologist*, **30**, 821–828.

_____ and Raugh, M. R. 1975. An application of the mnemonic keyword method to the acquisition of Russian vocabulary. *Journal of Experimental Psychology: Human Learning and Memory*, **104**, 126–133.

Bailey, K. M. and Ochsner, R. 1983. A methodological review of the diary studies: Windmill tilting or social science? In K. M. Bailey, M. H. Long and S. Peck (eds.), *Second Language Acquisition Studies*. Rowley, Mass.: Newbury House, pp. 188–198.

Bakan, D. 1954. A reconsideration of the problem of introspection. *Psychological Bulletin*, **51**, 105–118.

Bartlett, F. C. 1932. *Remembering: A Study in Experimental and Social Psychology*. Cambridge: Cambridge University Press.

Bellezza, F. S. 1981. Mnemonic devices: Classification, characteristics, and criteria. *Review of Educational Research*, **51**, 247–275.

_____ 1983. The spatial arrangement mnemonic. *Journal of Educational Research*, **75**, 830–837.

Bernhardt, E. B. 1984. Toward an information processing perspective in foreign language reading. *Modern Language Journal*, **68**, 322–331.

Bialystok, E. 1978. A theoretical model of second language learning. *Language Learning*, **28**, 69–83.

_____ 1979. The role of conscious strategies in second language proficiency. *Canadian Modern Language Review*, **35**, 372–394. Also see *Modern Language Journal*, 1981, **65**, 24–35.

_____ 1983. Some factors in the selection and implementation of communication strategies. In C. Faerch & G. Kasper (eds.), *Strategies in Interlanguage Communication*. London: Longman.

_____ In press. Inferencing: testing the 'hypothesis-testing' hypothesis. In H. W. Seliger and M. Long (eds.), *Classroom Oriented Research in Language Learning*. Rowley, Mass.: Newbury House.

_____ and Fröhlich, M. 1977. Aspects of second language learning in classroom settings. *Working Papers on Bilingualism*, **13**, 1–26.

Bloom, K. and Schuell, J. 1981. Effects of massed and distributed practice on the learning and retention of second language vocabulary. *Journal of Educational Research*, **74**, 245–248.

Bousfield, W. A. 1953. The occurrence of clustering in the recall of randomly arranged associates. *Journal of General Psychology*, **49**, 229–240.

Bower, G. H. 1973. How to . . . uh . . . remember. *Psychology Today*, **7**, 63–70.

_____ 1978. Experiments on story comprehension and recall. *Discourse Processes*, **11**, 177–220.

_____ and Clark, M. C. 1969. Narrative stories and mediators for serial learning. *Psychonomic Science*, **14**, 181–182.

Bransford, J. D. and Johnson, M. K. 1973. Consideration of some problems of comprehension. In W. G. Chase (ed.), *Viewing Information Processing*. New York: Academic Press.

Brodkey, D. and Shore, H. 1976. Student personality and success in an English language program. *Language Learning*, **26**, 153–167.

Brookfield, S. 1985. Self-directed learning: A critical review of research. In S. Brookfield (ed.), *Self-Directed Learning: from Theory to Practice*. San Francisco: Jossey-Bass Inc.

Brooks, L. W., Dansereau, D. F., Spurlin, J. E. and Holley, C. D. 1983. Effects of headings on text processing. *Journal of Educational Psychology*, **75**, 292–302.

Brown, A. L. and Palinscar, A. S. 1982. Inducing strategic learning from texts by means of informed self-control training. *Topics in Learning and Learning Disabilities*, **2**, 1–17. Special issue on metacognition and learning disabilities.

——————, Bransford, J. D., Ferrara, R. and Campione, J. C. 1983. Learning remembering, and understanding. In J. H. Flavell and E. M. Markham (eds.), *Carmichael's Manual of Child Psychology*, Vol. 1. New York: Wiley.

—————— and Baker, L. 1984. Metacognitive skills and reading. In P. D. Pearson, *Handbook of Reading Research*. New York: Longman.

Bruner, J. 1966. *Toward A Theory of Instruction*. Cambridge, Mass.: Harvard University Press.

Bugelsky, B. R., Kidd, E. and Segmen, E. 1968. Image as a mediator in one-trial paired-associate learning. *Journal of Experimental Psychology*, **76**, 69–73.

Burtoff, M. 1983. Organizational patterns of expository prose: A comparative study of native Arabic, Japanese and English speakers. Paper presented at the 17th Annual TESOL Convention, Toronto, Canada.

Cardelle, M. and Corno, L. 1981. Effects on second language learning of variations in written feedback on homework assignments. *TESOL Quarterly*, **15**, 251–261.

Carrell, P. L. 1983. Three components of background knowledge in reading comprehension. *Language Learning*, **33**, 183–205.

—————— 1984. Evidence of a formal schema in second language comprehension. *Language Learning*, **34**, 87–112.

Carroll, J. B. 1972. Defining language comprehension: Some speculations. In J. B. Carroll and R. O. Freedle (eds.), *Language Comprehension and the Acquisition of Knowledge*. New York: Wiley & Sons, pp. 1–29.

—————— 1973. Implications of aptitude test research and psycholinguistic theory for foreign language teaching. *International Journal of Psycholinguistics*, **2**, 5–14.

—————— 1981. Twenty-five years of research on foreign language aptitude. In K. C. Diller (ed.), *Individual Differences and Universals in Language Learning Aptitude*. Rowley, Mass.: Newbury House.

Carton, A. 1966. *The Method of Inference in Foreign Language Study*. The Research Foundation of the City of New York.

—————— 1971. Inferencing: a process in using and learning language. In P. Pimsleur and T. Quinn (eds.), *The Psychology of Second Language Learning*. Cambridge: Cambridge University Press.

Cavalcanti, M. 1982. Using the unorthodox, unreasonable verbal protocol technique: Quality data in foreign language reading research. In S. Dingwall, S. Mann, and F. Katamba (eds.), *Methods and Problems in Doing Applied Linguistic Research*. Lancaster: Dept. of Linguistics and Modern English Language, University of Lancaster, pp. 72–85.

Chamot, A. U. 1984. Identification of ESL learning strategies. Paper presented at the 18th Annual TESOL Convention. Houston, Texas, 1984.

Chamot, A. U. and O'Malley, J. M. 1984. Using learning strategies to develop skills in English as a second language. *FOCUS*, September 1984, National Clearinghouse for Bilingual Education, p. 1.

Chené, A. 1983. The concept of autonomy in adult education: A philosophical discussion. *Adult Education Quarterly*, **34**, 38–7.

Chipman, S., Segel, J. and Glaser, R. (eds.) In press. *Cognitive Skills and Instruction*. Hillsdale, N.J.: Lawrence Erlbaum Associates.

Clarke, M. A. 1979. Reading in Spanish and English: Evidence from adult ESL students. *Language Learning*, **29**, 121–150.

Cofer, C. N., Bruce, D. R. and Reicher, G. M. 1966. Clustering in free recall as a function of certain methodological variations. *Journal of Experimental Psychology*, **71**, 858–866.

Cohen, A. 1981. Introspection about Second Language Learning. Paper presented at the AILA Congress, Lund, Sweden. Also in *Studia Anglica Posnaniensia*, **15**, 149–156 (1983).

—————— 1983. Reformulating ESL compositions: A potential source of feedback. *TESOL Newsletter*, **17**, 1, 4–5.

—————— 1984. The use of verbal and imagery mnemonics in second language learning. Paper presented at the TESOL Convention, Houston, Texas.

—————— and Robbins, M. 1976. Toward assessing interlanguage performance: The relationship between selected errors, learners' characteristics, and learners' explanation. *Language Learning*, **26**, 45–66.

—————— and Aphek, E. 1980. Retention of second-language vocabulary over time: investigating the role of mnemonic associations. *System*, **8**, 221–235.

—————— and Aphek, E. 1981. Easifying second language learning. *Studies in Second Language Acquisition*, **3**, 221–236.

_____ and Hosenfeld, C. 1981. Some uses of mentalistic data in second language research. *Language Learning*, **31**, 285–313.

Connor, U. 1984. Recall of text: Differences between first and second language readers. *TESOL Quarterly*, **18**, 239–256.

Corbett, A. T. 1977. Retrieval dynamics for rote and visual image mnemonics. *Journal of Verbal Learning and Verbal Behavior*, **16**, 233–246.

Corder, S. P. 1983. Studies in communication. In C. Faerch and G. Kasper (eds.), *Strategies in Interlanguage Communication*. London: Longman.

Cornelius, E. T. Jr. 1955. *How to Learn a Foreign Language*. New York: Thomas Crowell Company.

Craik, F. I. M. and Tulving, E. 1975. Depth of processing and the retention of words in episodic memory. *Journal of Experimental Psychology*, **104**, 268–294.

Crawford, C. and Leitzell, E. M. 1930. *Learning a New Language*. Los Angeles: University of Southern California.

Cumming, A. In press. Teachers' procedures for responding to the writing of students of English as a second language. In M. Maguire and A. Pare (eds.), *Patterns of Development*. Montreal: Canadian Council of Teachers of English.

Cummings, T. F. 1916. *How to Learn a Language*. New York, N.Y.

Curran, C. 1976. *Counseling-Learning in Second Languages*. Apple River, Illinois 61001: Apple River Press.

d'Anglejan, A. and Renaud, C. 1985. Learner characteristics and second language acquisition: A multivariate study of adult immigrants and some thoughts on methodology. *Language Learning*, **35**, 1–19.

Dansereau, D. F., Long, G. L., McDonald, B. A., Atkinson, T. R., Ellis, A. M., Collins, K., Williams, S. and Evans, S. H. 1975. *Effective Learning Strategy Training Program: Development and Assessment*. (AFHRL-TR-41) Brooks Air Force Base, Texas.

_____ 1985. Learning strategy research. In J. Segal, S. Chipman, and R. Glaser (eds.), *Thinking and Learning Skills: Relating Learning to Basic Research*, Vol. 1. Hillsdale, N.J. Erlbaum.

Day, J. C. and Bellezza, F. S. 1983. The relation between visual imagery mediators and recall. *Memory and Cognition*, **11**, 251–257.

Decker, W. H. and Wheatley, P. C. 1982. Spatial grouping, imagery and free recall. *Perceptual and Motor Skills*, **55**, 45–46.

Delaney, H. D. 1978. Interaction of individual differences with visual and verbal elaboration instructions. *Journal of Educational Psychology*, **70**, 306–318.

Delin, P. S. 1969. Learning and retention of English words with successive approximations to a complex mnemonic instruction. *Psychonomic Science*, **17**, 87–88.

Denis, M. 1982. Imaging while reading text: a story of individual differences. *Memory and Cognition*, **10**, 540–545.

Desrochers, A. 1980. *Effects of Imagery Mnemonic on Acquisition and Retention of French Article-Noun Pairs*. Unpublished doctoral dissertation. University of Western Ontario.

Dickel, M. J. and Slack, S. 1983. Imagery vividness and memory for verbal material. *Journal of Mental Imagery*, **7**, 121–125.

DiVesta, F. J. and Sunshine, P. M. 1974. The retrieval of abstract and concrete materials as functions of imagery, mediation and mnemonic aids. *Memory and Cognition*, **2**, 340–344.

Dubitsky, T. M. and Harris, R. F. 1983. Memory for radio mystery presented as a story or drama. *Perceptual and Motor Skills*, **57**, 311–318.

Eamon, D. B. 1978–79. Selection and recall of topical information in prose by better and poorer readers. *Reading Research Quarterly*, **14**, 244–257.

Emig, J. 1971. *The Composing Processes of Twelfth Graders*. National Council of Teachers of English, Research Report No. 13. Urbana, Illinois: National Council of Teachers of English.

Ericsson, K. A. and Simon, H. A. 1980. Verbal reports as data. *Psychological Review*, **87**, 215–251.

Faerch, C. & Kasper, G. (eds.) 1983a. *Strategies in Interlanguage Communication*. London: Longman.

_____ 1983b. Plans and strategies in foreign language communication. In C. Faerch and G. Kasper (eds.), *Strategies in Interlanguage Communication*. London: Longman.

_____ 1983c. On identifying communication strategies in interlanguage production. In C. Faerch and G. Kasper (eds.), *Strategies in Interlanguage Communication*. London: Longman.

Fanselow, J. F. 1977. Beyond RASHOMON — conceptualizing and describing the teaching act. *TESOL Quarterly*, **11**, 17–39.

_____ 1983. "Could I ask you a couple of questions?" Episode 4 in *Breaking Rules: Alternatives in Language Teaching*. New York: Longman.

Fillmore, Lily Wong 1983. The language learner as an individual: implications of research on individual differences for the ESL teacher. In *On TESOL 82: Pacific Perspectives on Language Learning and Teaching*. Mark A. Clarke and Jean Handscombe (eds.). Washington, D.C.: TESOL, pp. 157–173.

Flahive, D. E. 1980. Separating the g factor from reading comprehension. In J. W. Oller, Jr. and K.

Perkins (eds.), *Research in Language Testing*, Rowley, Mass.: Newbury House, pp. 34–46.

Flavell, J. H. 1979. Metacognition and cognitive monitoring: a new area of cognitive-developmental inquiry. *American Psychologist*, **34**, 906–911.

Freebody, F. and Anderson, R. C. 1983. Effects of vocabulary difficulty, text cohesion and schema availability on reading comprehension. *Journal of Verbal Learning and Verbal Behavior*, **18**, 277–294.

Gardner, R. C. and Lambert, W. E. 1972. *Attitudes and Motivation in Second Language Learning*. Rowley, Mass.: Newbury House.

_____, Smythe, P. C. and Clement, R. 1979. Intensive second language study in a bicultural milieu: an investigation of attitudes, motivation, and language proficiency. *Language Learning*, **33**, 305–320.

_____, Lalonde, R. N. and Marcroft, R. 1985. The role of attitudes and motivation in second language learning: correlational and experimental considerations. *Language Learning*, **35**, 207–228.

Gattegno, G. 1974. *Teaching Foreign Languages in Schools: The Silent Way*. New York: Educational Solutions, 1972. Expanded edition.

Genesee, F. 1976. The role of intelligence in second language learning. *Language Learning*, **26**, 267–280.

Geva, E. 1983. Facilitating reading comprehension through flowcharting. *Reading Research Quarterly*, **18**, 384–405.

Godden, D. R. and Baddeley, A. D. 1975. Context-dependent memory in two natural environments: on land and underwater. *British Journal of Psychology*, **66**, 325–332.

Gorman, T. P. 1979. The teaching of composition. In M. Celce-Murcia and L. McIntosh (eds.), *Teaching English as A Second or Foreign Language*. Rowley, Mass.: Newbury House, pp. 189–202.

Groninger, K. D. 1971. Mnemonic imagery and forgetting. *Psychonomic Science*, **23**, 161–163.

Guiora, A., Beit-Hallahmi, B., Brannon, R. C., Dull, C. Y. and Scovel, T. 1972. The effects of experimentally induced stages on ego states on pronunciation ability in a second language: an exploratory study. *Comprehensive Psychiatry*, **13**, 421–428.

_____, Poluzny, M., Beit-Hallahmi, B., Catford, J. C., Cooley, R. E. and Dull, C. Y. 1975. Language and person: studies in language behavior. *Language Learning*, **25**, 43–61.

Haberlandt, K. and Bingham, G. 1984. The effect of input direction on the processing of script statements. *Journal of Verbal Learning and Verbal Behavior*, **23**, 162–177.

Hall, R. Jr. 1973. *New Ways to Learn a Foreign Language*. Ithaca, N.Y.: Spoken Language Services.

Hall, J. W., Wilson, K. P. and Patterson, R. J. 1981. Mnemotechnics: Some limitations of the mnemonic keyword method for the study of foreign language vocabulary. *Journal of Educational Psychology*, **73**, 345–357.

Hamp-Lyons, L. 1983. Survey of materials for teaching advanced listening and note-taking. *TESOL Quarterly*, **17**, 109–122.

Hansen, L. 1984. Field dependence-independence and language testing: evidence from six Pacific island cultures. *TESOL Quarterly*, **18**, 311–324.

Hayes, J. R. and Flower, L. 1983. Uncovering cognitive processes in writing. In P. Mosenthal *et al.* (eds.), *Research in Writing: Principles and Methods*. N.Y.: Longman.

Hayes, M. F. and Daiker, D. A. 1984. Using protocol analysis in evaluating responses to student writing. *Freshmen English News*, **13**, 1–5.

Hendrickson, J. M. 1980. The treatment of error in written work. *Modern Language Journal*, **64**, 216–221.

Henning, G. H. 1974. Remembering foreign language vocabulary: Acoustic and semantic parameters. *Language Learning*, **23**, 185–196.

Higbee, K. L. 1979. Recent research on visual mnemonics: Historical roots and educational fruits. *Review of Educational Research*, **49**, 611–629.

Hinds, J. 1982. Contrastive Rhetoric: Japanese and English. Paper presented at the 16th Annual TESOL Convention, Honolulu, Hawaii.

_____ 1983. Retention of Information Using a Japanese Style of Presentation. Paper presented at the 17th Annual TESOL Convention Toronto, Canada.

Holec, H. 1980. Learner training: meeting needs in self-directed learning. In H. B. Altman and C. V. James (eds.), *Foreign Language Teaching: Meeting Individual Needs*. Oxford: Pergamon Press.

_____ 1981. *Autonomy and Foreign Language Learning*. Prepared for the Council of Europe. Oxford: Pergamon Press.

Horwitz, E. 1982. The relationship between conceptual level and communicative competence in French. *Studies in Second Language Acquisition*, **5**, 65–73.

Horwitz, E. K. 1983. Beliefs about language learning inventory, unpublished instrument. The University of Texas at Austin.

Horwitz, E. K. 1985. Using student beliefs about language learning and teaching in the foreign language methods course, *Foreign Language Annals*, September 1985.

Hosenfeld, C. 1977. A preliminary investigation of the reading strategies of successful and non-successful language learners. *System*, **5**, 110–123.

——————— 1978. Students' mini-theories of second language learning. *Association Bulletin*, **29**, 2.

——————— 1979a. Cindy: A learner in today's foreign language classroom. In W. Born (ed.), *The Foreign Language Learner in Today's Classroom Environment*. Montpelier, Vermont: Northeast Conference on the Teaching of Foreign Languages.

——————— 1979b. A learning-teaching view of second language instruction. *Foreign Language Annals*, **12**, 51–54.

———————, Arnold, V., Kirchofer, J., Laciura, J. and Wilson, L. 1981. Second language reading: a curricular sequence for teaching reading strategies. *Foreign Language Annals*, **4**, 415–422.

Houle, C. O. 1961. *The Inquiring Mind*. Madison, Wisconsin: University of Michigan Press.

Huang, X. H. 1984. An investigation of learning strategies in oral communication that Chinese EFL learners in China employ. Master's thesis. Chinese University of Hong Kong (available: ERIC).

Hudson, T. 1982. The effects of induced schemata on the "short circuit" in L2 reading: Nondecoding factors in L2 reading performance. *Language Learning*, **32**, 1–31.

Hunt, M. 1982. *The Universe Within: A New Science Explores the Human Mind*. New York: Simon & Schuster.

Jones, D. M. 1979. Stress and memory. In M. Gruneberg and P. E. Morris (eds.), *Applied Problems in Memory*. London: Academic Press.

Jones, S. 1982. *Attention to Rhetorical Information While Composing in a Second Language*. Ottawa: Carleton University.

Johnson, N. S. and Mandler, J. M. 1980. A tale of two structures: underlying and surface forms in stories. *Poetics*, **9**, 51–86.

Johnson, P. 1981. Effects on reading comprehension of language complexity and cultural background of text. *TESOL Quarterly*, **15**, 169–181.

——————— 1982. Effects on reading comprehension of building background knowledge. *TESOL Quarterly*, **16**, 503–516.

Johnson-Laird, P. N. and Wason, P. C. (eds.) 1977. *Thinking: Readings in Cognitive Science*. New York: Cambridge University Press.

Johnstone, J. W. and Rivera, R. 1965. *Volunteers for Learning: A Study of the Educational Pursuits of American Adults*. Chicago: Aldine Publishing Co.

Kagan, J. Rosman, B. L., Day, D., Albert, J. and Phillips, W. 1964. Information processing in the child: Significance of analytic and reflective attitudes. *Psychological Monographs: General and Applied*, **78** (1), # 578.

Karmiloff-Smith, A. and Inhelder, B. 1974/75. "If You Want to Get Ahead Get a Theory" *Cognition*, **3**, 195–212.

Kerlinger, F. N. 1973. *Foundations of Behavioral Research*, 2nd Edition. New York: Holt, Rinehart & Winston Inc.

Kintsch, W. M. and Van Dijk, T. A. 1978. Toward a model of text comprehension and production. *Psychological Review*, **85**, 363–394.

——————— and Young, S. R. 1984. Selective recall of decision-relevant information from texts. *Memory and Cognition*, **12**, 112–117.

Knowles, M. 1975. *Self-Directed Learning: A Guide for Learners and Teachers*. Chicago: Association Press.

——————— 1976. *The Modern Practice of Adult Education*. New York: Association Press.

Kraft, C. H. and Kraft, M. E. 1966. *Where Do I Go from Here? A Handbook for Continuing Language Study in the Field*. United States Peace Corps.

Krashen, S. 1976. Formal and informal linguistic environments in language acquisition and language learning. *TESOL Quarterly*, **10**, 157–168.

——————— 1982. *Principles and Practice in Second Language Acquisition*. Oxford: Pergamon.

Kreizman, R. 1984. Student feedback regarding teacher comments on Hebrew native language compositions. Seminar paper, School of Education Hebrew University (in Hebrew).

Kulhavy, R. W. and Swenson, I. 1975. Imagery, instructions and the comprehension of text. *British Journal of Educational Psychology*, **67**, 663–667.

Kopstein, F. F. and Roshal, S. M. 1954. Learning foreign vocabulary from pictures vs. words. *American Psychologist*, **9**, 407–408.

Lambert, L. 1984. How Adults Learn: An Interview Study of Leading Researchers Policy Makers and Student Developers. Paper presented at the annual meeting of the American Educational Research Association. ED 244 929.

Larson, C. and Dansereau, D. G. 1983. Cooperative Learning: The Role of Individual Differences. Paper presented at the annual meeting of the American Educational Research Association, Montreal.

Larson, K. 1981. A study of student test-taking strategies and difficulties. Course paper, ESL Section, Department of English, University of California, Los Angeles.

Laufer, B. and Sim, D. D. 1985. Taking the easy way out — nonuse and misuse of clues in EFL reading. *English Teaching Forum.*

Lefebvre-Pinard, M. 1983. Understanding and auto-control of cognitive functions: implications for the relationship between cognition and behavior. *International Journal of Behavioral Development*, **6**, 15–35.

Levin, J. R. In press. Educational applications of mnemonic pictures. In A. A. Sheikt (ed.), *Imagery and the Educational Process*. Farmingdale, N.Y.: Baywood.

—————— and Divine-Hawkins, P. 1974. Visual imagery as a prose-learning process. *Journal of Reading Behavior*, **6**, 23–30.

——————, Pressley, M., McCormick, C. B., Miller, G. E. and Shriberg, L. K. 1979. Assessing the classroom potential of the keyword method. *Journal of Educational Psychology*, **71**, 583–594.

—————— 1981. The mnemonic 80's: Keywords in the classroom. *Educational Psychologist*, **16**, 65–82.

Lewis, M. M. 1948. Fundamental skills in the learning of a second language. *English Language Teaching Journal*, **1**, 169–173.

Lieberman, D. A. 1979. Behaviorism and the mind: A (limited) call or a return to introspection. *American Psychologist*, **34**, 319–333.

Luftig, R. L. 1983. Abstractive memory, the central-incidental hypothesis, and the use of structural importance in text: control processes or structural factors? *Reading Research Quarterly*, **19**, 28–37.

McDaniel, M. A. 1984. The role of elaborative and schema processes in story memory. *Memory and Cognition*, **12**, 46–51.

McDonald, B. A., Dansereau, D., Garland, J. C., Holley, C. D. and Collins, K. W. 1979. Pair Learning and Transfer of Text Processing Skills. Paper presented at the Annual Meeting of the American Educational Research Association, San Francisco, 1979.

McLaughlin, B. 1978. The monitor model: Some methodological considerations. *Language Learning*, **28**, 309–332.

McLaughlin, B., Rossman, T. and Mcleod, B. 1983. Second language learning: an information-processing perspective. *Language Learning*, **33**, 135–158.

Mandler, G. 1967. Organization and memory. In K. W. Spence and J. T. Spence (eds.), *The Psychology of Learning and Motivation: Advances in Research and Theory*, Volume 1. New York: Academic Press.

Mandler, J. M. 1978. A code in the node: The use of story schema in retrieval. *Discourse Processes*, **1**, 111–151.

—————— and Johnson, N. S. 1977. Remembrance of things parsed: Story structure and recall. *Cognitive Psychology*, **9**, 111–151.

Mann, S. 1982. Verbal reports as data: A focus on retrospection. In S. Dingwall, S. Mann, and F. Katamba (eds.), *Methods and Problems in Doing Applied Linguistic Research*. Lancaster: Dept. of Linguistics and Modern English Language, University of Lancaster, pp. 87–104.

Marzano, R. J. and Arthur, S. 1977. Teacher comments on student essays: It doesn't matter what you say. University of Colorado at Denver. ERIC ED 147 864.

Mason, J. (ed.) 1984. *Self-directed Learning and Self-access in Australia. From Practice to Theory* Conference Proceedings of the National Conference of Adult Migrant Education Program, Melbourne. Council of Adult Education. Melbourne, Australia.

S. Messick and Associates 1978. *Individuality in Learning*. San Francisco: Jossey Bass.

Meyer, B. J. F. 1975. Identification of the structure of prose and its implications for the study of reading and memory. *Journal of Reading Behavior*, **7**, 7–47.

——————, Brandt, D. M. and Bluth, G. 1980. Use of top-level structure in a text: Key for reading comprehension of ninth-grade students. *Reading Research Quarterly*, **16**, 72–103.

—————— and Freedle, R. O. 1984. Effects of discourse type on recall. *American Educational Research Journal*, **21**, 121–143.

Mezirow, J. 1985. A critical theory of self-directed learning. In S. Brookfield (ed.), *Self-Directed Learning: from Theory to Practice*. San Francisco: Jossey-Bass.

Morrison, D. M. and Low, G. 1983. Monitoring and the second language learner. In J. C. Richards and R. W. Schmidt (eds.), *Language and Communication*. London: Longman.

Moulden, H. 1978. Extending self-directed learning in an engineering college. Mélanges Pédagogiques, CRAPEL 81-102.

—————— 1980. Extending self-directed learning in an engineering college. Experiment 2. Mélanges Pédagogiques, CRAPEL 83-116.

Moulton, W. G. 1966. *A Linguistic Guide to Language Learning*. New York: Modern Language Association of America.

Naiman, N., Fröhlich, M., Stern, H. H. and Todesco, A. 1978. *The Good Language Learner*. Toronto, Ontario: Ontario Institute for Studies in Education.

Nida, E. 1957. *Learning a Foreign Language: A Handbook Prepared Especially for Missionaries*. Published by Friendship Press for the National Council of Churches in the USA.

Nisbett, R. E. and Wilson, T. D. 1977. Telling more than we can know: Verbal report on mental processes. *Psychological Review*, **84**, 231–259.

Oller, J. W. Jr. 1981. Language as intelligence? *Language Learning*, **31**, 465–592.

_____ and Richards, J. 1973. *Focus on the Learner: Pragmatic Perspectives for the Language Teacher*. Rowley, Mass.: Newbury House.

_____, Baca, L. and Vigil, A. 1977. Attitudes and attained proficiency in ESL: a sociolinguistic study of Mexican Americans in the South-west. *TESOL Quarterly*, **11**, 173–184.

Omaggio, A. C. 1978. Successful language learners: what do we know about them? *ERIC/CLL News Bulletin*, May 1978, pp. 2–3.

O'Malley, J. M., Russo, R. P., Chamot, A. U., Stewner-Manzanares, G. and Kupper, G. 1983. *A Study of Learning Strategies for Acquiring Skills in Speaking and Understanding English as a Second Language: Uses of Learning Strategies for Different Language Activities by Students at Different Language Proficiency Levels*. Rosslyn, Va: InterAmerica Research Associates.

_____, Russo, R. P. and Chamot, A. U. 1983. *A Review of the Literature on Learning Strategies in the Acquisition of English as a Second Language: The Potential for Research Applications*. Rosslyn, Va: InterAmerica Research Associates.

_____, Chamot, A. U., Stewner-Manzanares, G., Kupper, L. and Russo, R. P. 1983. *Learning Strategies Utilized in Developing Listening and Speaking Skills in English as a Second Language*. Rosslyn, Va: InterAmerica Research Associates.

_____, Chamot, A. U., Stewner-Manzanares, G., Kupper, L. and Russo, R. P. 1985. Learning strategies used by beginning and intermediate ESL students. *Language Learning*, **35**, 21–46.

_____, Chamot, A. U., Stewner-Manzanares, G., Russo, R. P. and Kupper, L. 1985. Learning strategy applications with students of English as a second language. *TESOL Quarterly*, **19** (3).

O'Neill, H. F. Jr. (ed.) 1978. *Learning Strategies*. New York: Academic Press.

Ott, C. E., Blake, R. S. and Butler, D. C. 1976. Implications of mental elaboration for the acquisition of foreign language vocabulary. *International Review of Applied Linguistics*, **14**, 37–48.

Paivio, A. 1971. *Imagery and Verbal Processes*. New York: Holt, Rinehart, and Winston.

_____ and Desrochers, A. 1979. Effects of an imagery mnemonic on second language recall and comprehension. *Canadian Journal of Psychology*, **33**, 17–28.

_____ 1981. Mnemonic techniques in second language learning. *Journal of Educational Psychology*, **73**, 780–795.

Pei, M. 1966. *How To Learn Languages and What Languages to Learn*. New York: Harper and Row.

Penland, P. 1978. *Self-Planned Learning in America*. Paper presented at the Adult Education Research Conference. San Antonio. ED 152 987.

Perl, S. 1979. The composing processes of unskilled college writers. *Research in the Teaching of English*, **13**, 317–336.

Piaget, J. 1976. *The Grasp of Consciousness: Action and Concept in the Young Child*. Cambridge, Mass.: Harvard University Press.

Pica, T. 1982. Variations on a theme: An interactional approach to ESL writing. Philadelphia: Graduate School of Education, University of Pennsylvania.

Pichert, J. W. and Anderson, R. C. 1977. Taking a different perspective on a story. *Journal of Educational Psychology*, **69**, 309–315.

Pimsleur, P. 1980. *How to Learn A Foreign Language*. Boston, Mass: Heinle and Heinle Publishers, Inc.

Politzer, R. 1965. *Foreign Language Learning: A Linguistic Introduction*. New Jersey: Prentice Hall, Inc.

Politzer, R. L. and McGroarty, M. 1985. An exploratory study of learning behaviors and their relationships to gains in linguistic and communicative competence. *TESOL Quarterly*, **19**, 103–123.

Pressley, M. 1977. Children's use of the keyword method to learn simple Spanish vocabulary words. *Journal of Educational Psychology*, **69**, 465–472.

Pressley, M., Levin, J. R., Hall, J. W., Miller, G. E. and Berry, J. K. 1980. The keyword method and foreign word acquisition. *Journal of Experimental Psychology: Human Learning and Memory*, **6**, 163–173.

_____, Levin, J. R., Nakamura, G. V., Hope, D. J., Bisbo, J. G. and Toye, A. R. 1980. The keyword method of foreign vocabulary learning: An investigation of its generalizability. *Journal of Applied Psychology*, **65**, 635–642.

_____, Levin, J. R., Kuiper, N. A., Bryant, S. L. and Michener, S. 1981. Mnemonic versus nonmnemonic vocabulary-learning strategies: Putting "depth" to rest. Working Paper No 312.

Madison, WI: Wisconsin Research and Development Center for Individualized Schooling University of Wisconsin.

——————, Levin, J. R. and Miller, G. E. 1981. How does the keyword method affect vocabulary comprehension and usage? *Reading Research Quarterly*, **16**, 213–226.

——————, Levin, J. R. and Delaney, J. D. 1982. The mnemonic keyword method. *Review of Educational Research*, **52**, 61–91.

——————, Levin, J. R., Digdon, N., Bryant, S. L., McGivern, J. E. and Ray, K. 1982. Re-examining the "limitations" of the mnemonic keyword method. Working Paper No. 329. Madison WI: Wisconsin Center for Educational Research, University of Wisconsin.

—————— and Levin, J. R. 1983. Developmental constraints associated with children's use of the keyword method of foreign language vocabulary learning. *Journal of Experimental Child Psychology*, **75**, 866–891.

—————— and Levin, J. R. 1983. *Cognitive Strategy Research: Educational Applications*. New York: Springer-Verlag.

——————, Levin, J. R. and Ghatala, E. S. 1984. Memory strategy monitoring in adults and children. *Journal of Verbal Learning and Verbal Behavior*, **23**, 270–288.

Radford, J. 1974. Reflections on introspection. *American Psychologist*, **29**, 245–250.

Raimes, A. 1983. *Techniques in Teaching Writing*. New York: Oxford.

—————— 1985. *An Investigation of How ESL Students Write*. N.Y.: Department of English, Hunter College C.U.N.Y.

Rassias, J. 1968. *A Philosophy of Language Instruction*. Hanover, New Hampshire: Dartmouth College.

—————— 1972. Why we must change. *ADFL Bulletin*.

Raugh, M. R., Schupach, R. D. and Atkinson, R. C. 1977. Teaching a large Russian vocabulary by the mnemonic keyword method. *Instructional Science*, **6**, 199–221.

Raven, J. C., Court, J. H. and Raven, J. 1983. *Manual for Raven's Standard Progressive Matrices and Vocabulary Scales:* Section 3. London: H. K. Lewis and Co.

Reid, J. 1985. Learning style preferences of non-native speakers of English. Intensive English Program, Colorado State University.

Reisberg, D., Rappaport, I. and O'Shaughnessy, M. 1984. Limits of working memory: The digit digit-span. *Journal of Experimental Psychology*, **10**, 203–221.

Richards, J. R. 1975. Simplification: a strategy in the adult acquisition of a foreign language: an example from Indonesian-Malay. *Language Learning*, **25**, 115–126.

Riley, P. 1980. Mud and stars: personal constructs, sensitization and learning. *Mélanges Pédagogiques*, CRAPEL.

—————— (ed.) 1985. *Discourse and Learning*. New York: Longman.

Rubin, J. 1975. What the good language learner can teach us. *TESOL Quarterly*, **9**, 41–51.

—————— 1981. The study of cognitive processes in second language learning. *Applied Linguistics*, **2**, 117–131.

—————— and Henze, R. 1981. The foreign language requirement: a suggestion to enhance its educational role in teacher training. *TESOL Newsletter*, **15**, 17, 19, 24.

Rubin, J. and Thompson, I. 1982. *How to be a More Successful Language Learner*. Boston, Mass.: Heinle & Heinle Publishers, Inc.

Rumelhart, D. E. 1975. Notes on a schema for stories. In D. B. Bobrow and A. M. Collins (eds.), *Representation and Understanding. Studies in Cognitive Science*. New York: Academic Press, pp. 211–236.

—————— 1977. Understanding and summarizing brief stories. In D. Laberge and S. J. Samuels (eds.), *Basic Processes in Reading: Comprehension and Perception*. Hillsdale, N.J.: Erlbaum.

—————— 1980. Schemata: the building blocks of cognition. In R. J. Spiro, B. C. Bruce and W. F. Brewer (eds.), *Theoretical Issues in Reading Comprehension*. Hillsdale, N.J.: Erlbaum.

Savicevic, D. 1968. Training adult educationists in Yugoslavia. *Convergence*, **1**, 69.

Satz, E. and Dunnenworth-Nolan, R. 1981. Does motoric imagery facilitate memory for sentences? A selective interference test. *Journal of Verbal Learning and Verbal Behavior*, **20**, 322–332.

Saville-Troike, M. 1984. What really matters in second language learning for academic achievement? *TESOL Quarterly*, **18**, 199–219.

Schumann, F. M. and Schumann, J. H. 1977. Diary of a language learner: An introspective study of second language learning. In H. D. Brown *et al.* (eds.), *On TESOL 77. Teaching and Learning English as a Second Language*. Washington, D.C.: TESOL, pp. 241–249.

Schumann, J. H. 1976. Social distance as a factor in second language acquisition. *Language Learning*, **25**, 135–143.

—————— 1978. The acculturation model for second-language acquisition. In R. C. Gingras (ed.), *Second Language Acquisition and Foreign Language Teaching*, Arlington, Va: Center for Applied Linguistics.

Seliger, H. W. 1983a. The language learner as linguist: Of metaphors and realities. *Applied Linguistics*, **4**, 179–191.

—————— 1983b. Processing universals in second language acquisition. In F. Eckman (ed.), *Universals of Second Language Acquisition*. Rowley, Mass.: Newbury House.

Semke, H. D. 1984. Effects of the red pen. *Foreign Language Annals*, **17**, 195–202.

Serrano, N. S. 1984. Patterns of reading in L1 and L2. In D. M. Singleton and D. G. Little (eds.), *Language Learning in Formal and Informal Contexts*. Dublin: Irish Association for Applied Linguistics, pp. 165–176.

Singer, H. and Donlan, D. 1982. Active comprehension: Problem-solving schema with question generation for comprehension of complex short stories. *Reading Research Quarterly*, **17**, 166–185.

Skinner, B. F. 1938. *The Behavior of Organisms: an Experimental Analysis*. New York: Appleton-Century-Crofts, Inc.

Slavin, R. E. 1983. *Cooperative Learning*. New York: Longman.

Smith, M. S. 1981. Consciousness-raising and the second language learner. *Applied Linguistics*, **11** (2).

Sommers, N. 1982. Responding to student writing. *College Composition and Communication*, **33**, 148–156.

Stanfield, C. and Hansen, J. 1983. Field dependence-independence as a variable in second language cloze test performance. *TESOL Quarterly*, **17**, 29–38.

Steffenson, M. S., Joag-dev, C. and Anderson, R. C. 1979. A cross-cultural perspective on reading comprehension. *Reading Research Quarterly*, **15**, 10–29.

Steinberg, R. J., Conway, B. E., Ketron, B. L., Bernstein, M. 1980. People's conceptions of intelligence. Technical Report #28. Department of Psychology, Yale University. ED 198 148.

Steingal, S. K. and Glock, M. D. 1979. Imagery and the recall of connected discourse. *Reading Research Quarterly*, **15**, 66–83.

Stern, H. H. 1975. What can we learn from the good language learner? *Canadian Modern Language Review*, **31**, 304–318.

Stevens, K. C. 1982. Can we improve reading by teaching background information? *Journal of Reading*, **25**, 326–329.

Stevick, E. 1976. *Memory Meaning and Method: Some Psychological Perspectives on Language Learning*. Rowley, Mass.: Newbury House.

—————— 1981. Learning a foreign language: The natural ways. In M. Hines and W. Rutherford (eds.), *On TESOL 81*. Washington, D.C.: TESOL, pp. 1–10.

—————— 1984. Curriculum development at the Foreign Service Institute. In T. H. Higgs (ed.), *Teaching for Proficiency, the Organizing Principle*. Lincolnwood, Ill: National Textbook Company.

Strong, M. 1983. Social styles and the second language acquisition of Spanish-speaking kindergarteners. *TESOL Quarterly*, **17**, 241–258.

Sweet, H. 1899. *The Practical Study of Languages: A Guide for Teachers and Learners*. New York: Holt, Rinehart and Winston.

Tarone, E. 1977. Conscious communication strategies in interlanguage. In H. D. Brown *et al.* (eds.), *On TESOL 1977*. Washington, D.C.: TESOL.

—————— 1981. Decoding a Primary Language: the Crucial Role of Strategic Competence. Paper presented at the conference on Interpretive Strategies in Language Learning. University of Lancaster.

—————— 1983. Some thoughts on the notion of 'communication strategy'. In C. Faerch and G. Kasper (eds.), *Strategies in Interlanguage Communication*. London: Longman.

——————, Cohen, A. D. and Dumas, G. 1983. A closer look at some interlanguage terminology: A framework for communication strategies. In C. Faerch and G. Kasper (eds.), *Strategies in Interlanguage Communication*. New York: Longman.

Taylor, B. M. and Beach, R. W. 1984. The effects of text structure instruction on middle-grade students' comprehension and production of expository text. *Reading Research Quarterly*, **19**, 134–146.

Taylor, B. P. 1975. The use of overgeneralization and transfer learning strategies by elementary and intermediate students of ESL. *Language Learning*, **25**, 73–107.

Teitlebaum, H., Edwards, A. and Hudson, A. 1975. Ethnic attitudes and the acquisition of Spanish as a second language. *Language Learning*, **25**, 255–266.

Tetroe, J. and Jones, S. 1982. *Transfer of Planning Skills in Second Language Writing*. Ottawa: Linguistics Department, Carleton University.

Thorndyke, P. W. 1977. Cognitive structures in comprehension and memory of narrative discourse. *Cognitive Psychology*, **9**, 77–110.

Tough, A. 1971. *The Adult's Learning Projects*. Ontario: OISE.

Trepanier, M. L. 1982. How do I remember? Young children's understanding of the memory process. Paper presented at the annual meeting of the National Association for the Education of Young Children. ED 226 831.

Tulving, E. 1968. Theoretical issues in free-recall. In T. Dixon and D. Horton (eds.), *Verbal Behavior and General Verbal Theory*. Englewood Cliffs, N.J.: Prentice-Hall.

_____ and Thompson, D. M. 1973. Encoding specificity and retrieval processes in episodic memory. *Psychological Review*, **80**, 352–373.

Walker, C. H. and Yekovich, F. R. 1984. Script-based inferences: effects of text and knowledge variables on recognition memory. *Journal of Verbal Learning and Verbal Behavior*, **23**, 357–370.

Webber, N. E. 1978. Pictures and words as stimuli in learning foreign language responses. *The Journal of Psychology*, **98**, 57–63.

Weinstein, C. E. 1978. Elaboration skills as a learning strategy. In H. F. O'Neill, Jr. (ed.), *Learning Strategies*. New York: Academic Press.

_____ and Mayer, R. E. 1985. The teaching of learning strategies. In M. C. Wittrock (ed.), *Handbook of Research on Teaching*, 3rd ed. New York: Macmillan.

Wenden, A. 1982. *The Processes of Self-Directed Learning: A Study of Adult Language Learners*. Unpublished doctoral dissertation, Teachers College, Columbia University.

_____ 1986a. What do L2 learners know about their language learning? A second look at retrospective accounts. *Applied Linguistics*, **7**, 186–201.

_____ 1986b. Helping L2 learners think about learning. *English Language Teaching Journal*, **40**, 3–12.

Wesche, M. B. 1975. *The Good Adult Language Learner: A Study of Learning Strategies and Personality Factors in an Intensive Course*. Unpublished doctoral dissertation, University of Toronto.

_____ 1979. Learning behaviors of successful adult students on intensive language training. *Canadian Modern Language Journal*, **35**, 415–427.

_____, Edwards, H. and Wells, W. 1982. Foreign language aptitude and intelligence. *Applied Psycholinguistics*, **3**, 127–140.

Whaley, J. F. 1981. Readers' expectations for story structure. *Reading Research Quarterly*, **7**, 90–114.

White, P. 1980. Limitations on verbal report of internal events. *Psychological Review*, **87**, 105–112.

Wilhite, S. 1983. Prepassage questions: The influence of structural importance. *Journal of Educational Psychology*, **75**, 234–244.

Wingfield, A. and Byrnes, D. L. 1981. *The Psychology of Human Memory*. New York: Academic Press.

Winitz, H. (ed.) 1981. *Native Language and Foreign Language Acquisition*. New York: New York Academy of Sciences.

Witkin, H. A., Oltman, E. R. and Karp, S. A. 1971. *A Manual for the Embedded Test*. Palo Alto, California: Consulting Psychologists Press.

Wittrock, M. C. 1983. Writing and the teaching of reading. *Language Arts*, **60**, 600–606.

Wong-Fillmore, L. 1976. *The Second Time Around*. Unpublished doctoral dissertation, Stanford University.

_____ 1983. The language learner as an individual: implications of research on individual differences for the ESL teacher. In Mark A. Clarke and Jean Handscombe (eds.) *On TESOL 82: Pacific perspectives on language learning and teaching*. Washington, D.C.: TESOL.

Wundt, W. 1904. *Principles of Physiological Psychology*, 5th edition translated by E. B. Titchener. New York: Macmillan. Originally published as *Grundzüge der physiologischen Psychologie*. Leipzig: Engelmann, 1874.

_____ 1897. *Outlines of Psychology*. transl. by C. H. Judd. Leipzig: Engelmann.

Yates, F. 1966. *The Art of Memory*. London: Routledge and Kegan Paul.

Zamel, V. 1985. Responding to student writing. *TESOL Quarterly*, **19**, 79–101.

Index

n after entry refers to note in text.

academic competence, 71
active learning, 17–18, 107
advance organization, 76
advance organizers, 77–79, 160
advance preparation, 77–79
affective variables, 19, 111, 113
ambiguity, 19, 20
analytic approach, 15
associations, 22, 28, 46, 141
   (*see also* mnemonics)
attention models, 39*n*
auditory representation, 78, 80
   (*see also* mnemonics)
aural/oral skills, 112, 161, 163, 164
avoidance strategies, 26

BALLI (Beliefs About Language Learning
   Inventory), 120–26
   difficulties of language learning, 123
   foreign language aptitude, 122
   learning and communication strategies,
   124
   motivations, 125
   nature of language learning, 123
background factors, 86, 87, 95–96, 97
   (*see also* psychological variables, social
   factors)
behaviorist theories, 4–5

CRAPEL (Centre de Recherche et
   d'Application Pédagogiques en
   Langues, University of Nancy), 145–154
Chomsky, Noam, 5
circumlocution, 20, 21, 32
clarification, 23, 76–79, 82, 87, 88
cognates, 16, 26
cognitive abilities, 3
cognitive behavior, 15, 22
cognitive knowledge, 23
cognitive processes, 4–5, 36–38
cognitive science, 4, 5
cognitive strategies, 18, 23, 72, 76–79,
   86–94, 109, 136, 142
cognitive tasks, 37
communication strategies, 20, 21, 25–27,
   86–94, 109
   oral, 96, 163
   (*see also* speaking)
contextualization, 77–79, 82
conversational strategies, 21, 26, 27, 82, 94

cooperation, 76–79, 136, 138, 139, 140
correctness of grammar, 87, 94
creative faculty, 18
critical faculty, 18–19
cultural aspects of learning, 3, 19, 97, 119
curriculum development, 9

deductive reasoning, 24, 88, 98
deduction, 77–79
delayed production, 76–79
diary writing, 16, 35, 81
directed attention, 77–79
directed physical response, 77–79

educational background, 95–96, 97
elaboration, 77–79, 80
empathy, 19

feedback, 82, 143, 151
   errors by students, 106
   errors by teachers, 57
   experiment with, 59–67
   lack of processing by students, 57, 59
   misinterpretation by students, 58
   student processing, 57–67
   teaching, 41
   weaknesses of, 57
field dependence, 3, 86, 87, 96, 126
field independence, 3, 86, 87, 95, 126
functional planning, 136, 139

GEFT (Group Embedded Figures Test), 87
grammar, 94
grouping, 46, 77–79, 80, 136, 137, 138, 141
guessing, 21, 23, 36, 89

imagery, 77–79, 137, 138, 141
impulsivity, 93, 96
inferencing, 18, 19–20, 21, 23, 24, 28, 35,
   77–79, 87–94
information processing model, 6
intelligence, 3
internalization, 17–18
introspection, 4
intuitive approach, 15

keyword method, 44, 77–79, 134, 160
   (*see also* mnemonics)

language acquisition
   processes, 32
   theories, 5